PENGUIN
ARKANA

The Second Ring of Power

Carlos Castaneda was a graduate student in
anthropology at the University of California,
Los Angeles, gathering information on various
medicinal herbs used by the Indians in Sonora,
Mexico, when he met the old Yaqui Indian, don
Juan.

His first book, *The Teachings of Don Juan*, was
the story of the first five years these two men
spent together as master and pupil. This was followed by the other volumes in the series, *A
Separate Reality*, *Journey to Ixtlan*, *Tales of
Power* and *The Eagle's Gift* which are all published by Arkana.

Carlos Castaneda

The Second
Ring of Power

ARKANA
PENGUIN BOOKS

ARKANA

Published by the Penguin Group
Penguin Books Ltd, 27 Wrights Lane, London W8 5TZ, England
Penguin Books USA Inc., 375 Hudson Street, New York, New York 10014, USA
Penguin Books Australia Ltd, Ringwood, Victoria, Australia
Penguin Books Canada Ltd, 10 Alcorn Avenue, Toronto, Ontario, Canada M4V 3B2
Penguin Books (NZ) Ltd, 182–190 Wairau Road, Auckland 10, New Zealand

Penguin Books Ltd, Registered Offices: Harmondsworth, Middlesex, England

First published in the USA 1977
First published in Great Britain by
Hodder & Stoughton 1978
Published in Penguin Books 1979
Published by Arkana 1990
10 9 8 7 6 5 4 3

Printed in England by Clays Ltd, St Ives plc
Set in Monotype Plantin

Contents

Preface

A flat, barren mountaintop on the western slopes of the Sierra Madre in central Mexico was the setting for my final meeting with don Juan and don Genaro and their other two apprentices, Pablito and Nestor. The solemnity and the scope of what took place there left no doubt in my mind that our apprenticeships had come to their concluding moment, and that I was indeed seeing don Juan and don Genaro for the last time. Towards the end we all said good-bye to one another, and then Pablito and I jumped together from the top of the mountain into our abyss.

Prior to that jump don Juan had presented a fundamental principle for all that was going to happen to me. According to him, upon jumping into the abyss I was going to become pure perception and move back and forth between the two inherent realms of all creation, the tonal and the nagual.

In my jump my perception went through seventeen elastic bounces between the tonal and the nagual. In my moves into the nagual I perceived my body disintegrating. I could not think or feel in the coherent, unifying sense that I ordinarily do, but I somehow thought and felt. In my moves into the tonal I burst into unity. I was whole. My perception had coherence. I had visions of order. Their compelling force was so intense, their vividness so real and their complexity so vast that I have not been capable of explaining them to my satisfaction. To say that they were visions, vivid dreams or even hallucinations does not say anything to clarify their nature.

After having examined and analysed in a most thorough and careful manner my feelings, perceptions and interpretations of that jump into the abyss, I had come to the point where I could not rationally believe that it had actually happened. And yet another part of me held on steadfast to the feeling that it did happen, that I did jump.

Don Juan and don Genaro are no longer available and their absence has created in me a most pressing need, the need to make headway in the midst of apparently insoluble contradictions.

I went back to Mexico to see Pablito and Nestor to seek their help in resolving my conflicts. But what I encountered on my trip cannot be described in any other way except as a final assault on my reason, a concentrated attack designed by don Juan himself. His apprentices, under his absentee direction, in a most methodical and precise fashion demolished in a few days the last bastion of my reason. In those few days they revealed to me one of the two practical aspects of their sorcery, the art of dreaming, which is the core of the present work.

The art of stalking, the other practical aspect of their sorcery and also the crowning stone of don Juan's and don Genaro's teachings, was presented to me during subsequent visits and was by far the most complex facet of their being in the world as sorcerers.

1 THE TRANSFORMATION OF DOÑA SOLEDAD

I had a sudden premonition that Pablito and Nestor were not home. My certainty was so profound that I stopped my car. I was at the place where the asphalt came to an abrupt end, and I wanted to reconsider whether or not to continue that day the long and difficult drive on the steep, coarse gravel road to their hometown in the mountains of central Mexico.

I rolled down the window of my car. It was rather windy and cold. I got out to stretch my legs. The tension of driving for hours had stiffened my back and neck. I walked to the edge of the paved road. The ground was wet from an early shower. Rain was still falling heavily on the slopes of the mountains to the south, a short distance from where I was. But right in front of me, towards the east and also towards the north, the sky was clear. At certain points on the winding road I had been able to see the bluish peaks of the sierras shining in the sunlight a great distance away.

After a moment's deliberation I decided to turn back and go to the city because I had had a most peculiar feeling that I was going to find don Juan in the market. After all, I had always done just that, found him in the marketplace, since the beginning of my association with him. As a rule, if I did not find him in Sonora I would drive to central Mexico and go to the market of that particular city, and sooner or later don Juan would show up. The longest I had ever waited for him was two days. I was so habituated to meeting him in that manner that I had the most absolute certainty that I would find him again, as always.

I waited in the market all afternoon. I walked up and down

the aisles pretending to be looking for something to buy. Then I waited around the park. At dusk I knew that he was not coming. I had then the clear sensation that he had been there but had left. I sat down on a park bench where I used to sit with him and tried to analyse my feelings. Upon arriving in the city I was elated with the sure knowledge that don Juan was there in the streets. What I felt was more than the memory of having found him there countless times before; my body knew that he was looking for me. But then, as I sat on the bench I had another kind of strange certainty. I knew that he was not there any more. He had left and I had missed him.

After a while I discarded my speculations. I thought that I was beginning to be affected by the place. I was starting to get irrational; that had always happened to me in the past after a few days in that area.

I went to my hotel room to rest for a few hours and then I went out again to roam the streets. I did not have the same expectation of finding don Juan that I had had in the afternoon. I gave up. I went back to my hotel in order to get a good night's sleep.

Before I headed for the mountains in the morning, I drove up and down the main streets in my car, but somehow I knew that I was wasting my time. Don Juan was not there.

It took me all morning to drive to the little town where Pablito and Nestor lived. I arrived around noon. Don Juan had taught me never to drive directly into the town so as not to arouse the curiosity of onlookers. Every time I had been there I had always, driven off the road, just before reaching the town, on to a flat field where youngsters usually played soccer. The dirt was well packed all the way to a walking trail which was wide enough for a car and which passed by Pablito's and Nestor's houses in the foothills south of town. As soon as I got to the edge of the field I found that the walking trail had been turned into a gravel road.

I deliberated whether to go to Nestor's house or Pablito's. The feeling that they were not there still persisted. I opted to go to Pablito's; I reasoned that Nestor lived alone, while

Pablito lived with his mother and his four sisters. If he was not there the women could help me find him. As I got closer to his house I noticed that the path leading from the road up to the house had been widened. It looked as if the ground was hard, and since there was enough space for my car, I drove almost to the front door. A new porch with a tile roof had been added to the adobe house. There were no dogs barking but I saw an enormous one sitting calmly behind a fenced area, alertly observing me. A flock of chickens that had been feeding in front of the house scattered around, cackling. I turned the motor off and stretched my arms over my head. My body was stiff.

The house seemed deserted. The thought crossed my mind that perhaps Pablito and his family had moved away and someone else was living there. Suddenly the front door opened with a bang and Pablito's mother stepped out as if someone had pushed her. She stared at me absentmindedly for an instant. As I got out of my car she seemed to recognize me. A graceful shiver ran through her body and she ran towards me. I thought that she must have been napping and that the noise of the car had woken her, and when she came out to see what was going on she did not know at first who I was. The incongruous sight of the old woman running towards me made me smile. When she got closer I had a moment of doubt. Somehow she moved so nimbly that she did not seem like Pablito's mother at all.

'My goodness what a surprise!' she exclaimed.

'Doña Soledad?' I asked, incredulously.

'Don't you recognize me?' she replied, laughing.

I made some stupid comments about her surprising agility.

'Why do you always see me as a helpless old woman?' she asked, looking at me with an air of mock challenge.

She bluntly accused me of having nicknamed her 'Mrs Pyramid'. I remembered that I had once said to Nestor that her shape reminded me of a pyramid. She had a very broad and massive behind and a small pointed head. The long dresses that she usually wore added to the effect.

'Look at me,' she said. 'Do I still look like a pyramid?'

She was smiling but her eyes made me feel uncomfortable. I attempted to defend myself by making a joke but she cut me off and coaxed me to admit that I was responsible for the nickname. I assured her that I had never intended it as such and that anyway, at that moment she was so lean that her shape was the farthest thing from a pyramid.

'What's happened to you, doña Soledad?' I asked. 'You're transformed.'

'You said it,' she replied briskly, 'I've been transformed!'

I meant it figuratively. However, upon closer examination I had to admit that there was no room for a metaphor. She was truly a changed person. I suddenly had a dry, metallic taste in my mouth. I was afraid.

She placed her fists on her hips and stood with her legs slightly apart, facing me. She was wearing a light green gathered skirt and a whitish blouse. Her skirt was shorter than those she used to wear. I could not see her hair: she had it tied with a thick band, a turban-like piece of cloth. She was barefoot and she rhythmically tapped her big feet on the ground as she smiled with the candour of a young girl. I had never seen anyone exude as much strength as she did. I noticed a strange gleam in her eyes, a disturbing gleam but not a frightening one. I thought that perhaps I had never really examined her appearance carefully. Among other things I felt guilty for having glossed over many people during my years with don Juan. The force of his personality had rendered everyone else pale and unimportant.

I told her that I had never imagined that she could have such a stupendous vitality, that my carelessness was to blame for not really knowing her, and that no doubt I would have to meet everyone else all over again.

She came closer to me. She smiled and put her right hand on the back of my left arm, grabbing it gently.

'That's for sure,' she whispered in my ear.

Her smile froze and her eyes became glazed. She was so close to me that I felt her breasts rubbing my left shoulder. My discomfort increased as I tried to convince myself that there was no reason for alarm. I repeated to myself over and over that I really had never known Pablito's mother, and that in spite of her odd behaviour she was probably being her normal self. But some frightened part of me knew that those were only bracing thoughts with no substance at all, because no matter how much I may have glossed over her person, not only did I remember her very well but I had known her very well. She represented to me the archetype of a mother; I thought her to be in her late fifties or even older. Her weak muscles moved her bulky weight with extreme difficulty. Her hair had a lot of grey in it. She was, as I remembered her, a sad, sombre woman with kind, handsome features, a dedicated, suffering mother, always in the kitchen, always tired. I also remembered her to be a very gentle and unselfish woman, and a very timid one, timid to the point of being thoroughly subservient to anyone who happened to be around. That was the picture I had of her, reinforced throughout years of casual contact. That day something was terribly different. The woman I was confronting did not at all fit the image I had of Pablito's mother, and yet she was the same person, leaner and stronger, looking twenty years younger, than the last time I had seen her. I felt a shiver in my body.

She moved a couple of steps in front of me and faced me.

'Let me look at you,' she said. 'The Nagual told us that you're a devil.'

I remembered then that all of them, Pablito, his mother, his sisters and Nestor, had always seemed unwilling to voice don Juan's name and called him 'the Nagual', a usage which I myself adopted when talking with them.

She daringly put her hands on my shoulders, something she had never done before. My body tensed. I really did not know what to say. There was a long pause that allowed me to take stock of myself. Her appearance and behaviour had frightened me to the point that I had forgotten to ask about Pablito and Nestor.

'Tell me, where is Pablito?' I asked her with a sudden wave of apprehension.

'Oh, he's gone to the mountains,' she responded in a noncommittal tone and moved away from me.

'And where is Nestor?'

She rolled her eyes as if to show her indifference.

'They are together in the mountains,' she said in the same tone.

I felt genuinely relieved and told her that I had known without the shadow of a doubt that they were all right.

She glanced at me and smiled. A wave of happiness and ebullience came upon me and I embraced her. She boldly returned the embrace and held me; that act was so outlandish that it took my breath away. Her body was rigid. I sensed an extraordinary strength in her. My heart began to pound. I gently tried to push her away as I asked her if Nestor was still seeing don Genaro and don Juan. During our farewell meeting don Juan had expressed doubts that Nestor was ready to finish his apprenticeship.

'Genaro has left forever,' she said letting go of me.

She fretted nervously with the edge of her blouse.

'How about don Juan?'

'The Nagual is gone too,' she said, puckering her lips.

'Where did they go?'

'You mean you don't know?'

I told her that both of them had said good-bye to me two years before, and that all I knew was that they were leaving at that time. I had not really dared to speculate where they had gone. They had never told me their whereabouts in the past, and I had come to accept the fact that if they wanted to disappear from my life all they had to do was to refuse to see me.

'They're not around, that's for sure,' she said, frowning, 'And they won't be coming back, that's also for sure.'

Her voice was extremely unemotional. I began to feel annoyed with her. I wanted to leave.

'But you're here,' she said, changing her frown into a smile. 'You must wait for Pablito and Nestor. They've been dying to see you.'

She held my arm firmly and pulled me away from my car. Compared to the way she had been in the past, her boldness was astounding.

'But first, let me show you my friend,' she said and forcibly led me to the side of the house.

There was a fenced area, like a small corral. A huge male dog was there. The first thing that attracted my attention was his healthy, lustrous, yellowish-brown fur. He did not seem to be a mean dog. He was not chained and the fence was not high enough to hold him. The dog remained impassive as we got closer to him, not even wagging his tail. Doña Soledad pointed to a good-sized cage in the back. A coyote was curled up inside.

'That's my friend,' she said. 'The dog is not. He belongs to my girls.'

The dog looked at me and yawned. I liked him. I had a nonsensical feeling of kinship with him.

'Come, let's go into the house,' she said, pulling me by the arm.

I hesitated. Some part of me was utterly alarmed and wanted to get out of there quickly, and yet another part of me would not have left for the world.

'You're not afraid of me, are you?' she asked in an accusing tone.

'I most certainly am!' I exclaimed.

She giggled, and in a most comforting tone she declared that she was a clumsy, primitive woman who was very awkward with words, and that she hardly knew how to treat people. She looked straight into my eyes and said that don Juan had commissioned her to help me, because he worried about me.

'He told us that you're not serious and go around causing a lot of trouble to innocent people,' she said.

Up to that point her assertions had been coherent to me, but I could not conceive don Juan saying those things about me.

We went inside the house. I wanted to sit down on the bench, where Pablito and I usually sat. She stopped me.

'This is not the place for you and me,' she said. 'Let's go to my room.'

'I'd rather sit here,' I said firmly. 'I know this spot and I feel comfortable on it.'

She clicked her lips in disapproval. She acted like a disappointed child. She contracted her upper lip until it looked like the flat beak of a duck.

'There is something terribly wrong here,' I said. 'I think I am going to leave if you don't tell me what's going on.'

She became very flustered and argued that her trouble was not knowing how to talk to me. I confronted her with her unmistakable transformation and demanded that she tell me what had happened. I had to know how such a change had come about.

'If I tell you, will you stay?' she asked in a child's voice.

'I'll have to.'

'In that case I'll tell you everything. But it has to be in my room.'

I had a moment of panic. I made a supreme effort to calm myself and we walked into her room. She lived in the back, where Pablito had built a bedroom for her. I had once been in the room while it was being built and also after it was finished, just before she moved in. The room looked as empty as I had seen it before, except that there was a bed in the very centre of it and two unobtrusive chests of drawers by the door. The whitewash of the walls had faded into a very soothing yellowish white. The wood of the ceiling had also weathered. Looking at the smooth, clean walls I had the impression they were scrubbed daily with a sponge. The room looked more like a monastic cell, very frugal and ascetic. There were no ornaments of any sort. The windows had thick, removable wood panels reinforced with an iron bar. There were no chairs or anything to sit on.

Doña Soledad took my writing pad away from me, held it to her bosom and then sat down on her bed, which was made up of two thick mattresses with no box springs. She indicated that I should sit down next to her.

'You and I are the same,' she said as she handed me my notebook.

'I beg your pardon?'

'You and I are the same,' she repeated without looking at me.

I could not figure out what she meant. She stared at me, as if waiting for a response.

'Just what is that supposed to mean, doña Soledad?' I asked. My question seemed to baffle her. Obviously she expected me to know what she meant. She laughed at first, but then, when I insisted that I did not understand, she got angry. She sat up straight and accused me of being dishonest with her. Her eyes flared with rage; her mouth contracted in a very ugly gesture of wrath that made her look extremely old.

I honestly was at a loss and felt that no matter what I said it would be wrong. She also seemed to be in the same predicament. Her mouth moved to say something but her lips only quivered. At last she muttered that it was not impeccable to act the way I did at such a serious moment. She turned her back to me.

'Look at me, doña Soledad!' I said forcefully. 'I'm not mystifying you in any sense. You must know something that I know nothing about.'

'You talk too much,' she snapped angrily. 'The Nagual told me never to let you talk. You twist everything.'

She jumped to her feet and stomped on the floor, like a spoiled child. I became aware at that moment that the room had a different floor. I remembered it to be a dirt floor, made from the dark soil of the area. The new floor was reddish pink. I momentarily put off a confrontation with her and walked around the room. I could not imagine how I could have missed noticing the floor when I first entered. It was magnificent. At first I thought that it was red clay that had been laid like cement, when it was soft and moist, but then I saw that there were no cracks in it. Clay would have dried, curled up, cracked, and clumps would have formed. I bent down and gently ran my fingers over it. It was as hard as bricks. The clay had been fired. I became aware then that the floor was made of very large flat slabs of clay put together over a bed of soft clay that served as a matrix. The slabs made a most intricate and fascinating design, but a thoroughly unobtrusive one, unless one paid deliberate attention to it. The skill with which the slabs had been placed in position indicated to me a very well-conceived plan.

I wanted to know how such big slabs had been fired without being warped. I turned around to ask doña Soledad. I quickly desisted. She would not have known what I was talking about. I paced over the floor again. The clay was a bit rough, almost like sandstone. It made a perfect slide-proof surface.

'Did Pablito put down this floor?' I asked.

She did not answer.

'It's a superb piece of work,' I said. 'You should be very proud of him.'

I had no doubt that Pablito had done it. No one else could have had the imagination and the capacity to conceive of it. I figured that he must have made it during the time I had been away. But on second thought I realized that I had never entered doña Soledad's room since it had been built, six or seven years before.

'Pablito! Pablito! Bah!' she exclaimed in an angry, raspy voice. 'What makes you think he's the only one who can make things?'

We exchanged a long, sustained look, and all of a sudden I knew that it was she who had made the floor, and that don Juan had put her up to it.

We stood quietly, looking at each other for some time. I felt it would have been thoroughly superfluous to ask if I was correct.

'I made it myself,' she finally said in a dry tone. 'The Nagual told me how.'

Her statements made me feel euphoric. I practically lifted her up in an embrace. I twirled her around. All I could think to do was to bombard her with questions. I wanted to know how she had made the slabs, what the designs represented, where she got the clay. But she did not share my exhilaration. She remained quiet and impassive, looking at me askance from time to time.

I paced on the floor again. The bed had been placed at the very epicentre of some converging lines. The clay slabs had been cut in sharp angles to create converging motifs that seemed to radiate out from under the bed.

'I have no words to tell you how impressed I am,' I said.

'Words! Who needs words?' she said cuttingly.

I had a flash of insight. My reason had been betraying me. There was only one possible way of explaining her magnificent metamorphosis; don Juan must have made her his apprentice. How else could an old woman like doña Soledad turn into such a weird, powerful being? That should have been obvious to me from the moment I laid eyes on her, but my set of expectations about her had not included that possibility.

I deduced that whatever don Juan had done to her must have taken place during the two years I had not seen her, although two years seemed hardly any time at all for such a superb alteration.

'I think I know now what happened to you,' I said in a casual and cheerful tone. 'Something has cleared up in my mind right now.'

'Oh, is that so?' she said, thoroughly uninterested.

'The Nagual is teaching you to be a sorceress, isn't that true?'

She glared at me defiantly. I felt that I had said the worst possible thing. There was an expression of true contempt on her face. She was not going to tell me anything.

'What a bastard you are!' she exclaimed suddenly, shaking with rage.

I thought that her anger was unjustified. I sat down on one end of the bed while she nervously tapped on the floor with her heel. Then she sat down on the other end, without looking at me.

'What exactly do you want me to do?' I asked in a firm and intimidating tone.

'I told you already!' she said in a yell. 'You and I are the same.'

I asked her to explain her meaning and not to assume for one instant that I knew anything. Those statements angered her even more. She stood up abruptly and dropped her skirt to the ground.

'This is what I mean!' she yelled, caressing her pubic area.

My mouth opened involuntarily. I became aware that I was staring at her like an idiot.

'You and I are one here!' she said.

I was dumbfounded. Doña Soledad, the old Indian woman, mother of my friend Pablito, was actually half-naked a few feet away from me, showing me her genitals. I stared at her, incapable of formulating any thoughts. The only thing I knew was that her body was not the body of an old woman. She had beautifully muscular thighs, dark and hairless. The bone structure of her hips was broad, but there was no fat on them.

She must have noticed my scrutiny and flung herself on the bed.

'You know what to do,' she said, pointing to her pubis. 'We are one here.'

She uncovered her robust breasts.

'Doña Soledad, I implore you!' I exclaimed. 'What's come over you? You're Pablito's mother.'

'No, I'm not!' she snapped. 'I'm no one's mother.'

She sat up and looked at me with fierce eyes.

'I am just like you, a piece of the Nagual,' she said. 'We're made to mix.'

She opened her legs and I jumped away.

'Wait a minute, doña Soledad,' I said. 'Let's talk for a while.'

I had a moment of wild fear, and a sudden crazy thought occurred to me. Would it be possible, I asked myself, that don Juan was hiding somewhere around there laughing his head off?

'Don Juan!' I bellowed.

My yell was so loud and profound that doña Soledad jumped off her bed and covered herself hurriedly with her skirt. I saw her putting it on as I bellowed again.

'Don Juan!'

I ran through the house bellowing don Juan's name until my throat was sore. Doña Soledad, in the meantime, had run outside the house and was standing by my car, looking puzzled at me.

I walked over to her and asked her if don Juan had told her to do all that. She nodded affirmatively. I asked if he was around. She said no.

'Tell me everything,' I said.

She told me that she was merely following don Juan's orders. He had commanded her to change her being into a warrior's in order to help me. She declared that she had been waiting for years to fulfil that promise.

'I'm very strong now,' she said softly. 'Just for you. But you disliked me in my room, didn't you?'

I found myself explaining that I did not dislike her, that what counted were my feelings for Pablito; then I realized that I did not have the vaguest idea of what I was saying.

Doña Soledad seemed to understand my embarrassing position and said that our mishap had to be forgotten.

'You must be famished,' she said vivaciously. 'I'll make you some food.'

'There's a lot that you haven't explained to me,' I said. 'I'll be frank with you, I wouldn't stay here for anything in the world. You frighten me.'

'You are obligated to accept my hospitality, if it is only for a cup of coffee,' she said unruffled. 'Come, let's forget what happened.'

She made a gesture of going into the house. At that moment I heard a deep growl. The dog was standing, looking at us, as if he understood what was being said.

Doña Soledad fixed a most frightening gaze on me. Then she softened it and smiled.

'Don't let my eyes bother you,' she said. 'The truth is that I am old. Lately I've been getting dizzy. I think I need glasses.'

She broke into a laugh and clowned, looking through cupped fingers as if they were glasses.

'An old Indian woman with glasses! That'll be a laugh,' she said giggling.

I made up my mind then to be rude and get out of there, without any explanation. But before I drove away I wanted to leave some things for Pablito and his sisters. I opened the boot of the car to get the gifts I had brought for them. I leaned way into it to reach first for the two packages that were lodged against the wall of the back seat, behind the spare tyre. I got hold of one and was about to grab the other when I felt a soft, furry hand on the nape of my neck. I shrieked involuntarily and hit my head on the open lid. I turned to look. The pressure of the furry hand did not let me turn completely, but I was able to catch a fleeting glimpse of a silvery arm or paw hovering over my neck. I wriggled in panic and pushed myself away from the boot and fell down on my seat with the package still in my hand. My whole body shook, the muscles of my legs contracted and I found myself leaping up and running away.

'I didn't mean to frighten you,' doña Soledad said apologetically, as I watched her from ten feet away.

She showed me the palms of her hands in a gesture of surrender, as if assuring me that what I had felt was not her hand.

'What did you do to me?' I asked, trying to sound calm and detached.

She seemed to be either thoroughly embarrassed or baffled. She muttered something and shook her head as though she could not say it, or did not know what I was talking about.

'Come on, doña Soledad,' I said, coming closer to her, 'don't play tricks on me.'

She seemed about to weep. I wanted to comfort her, but some part of me resisted. After a moment's pause I told her what I had felt and seen.

'That's just terrible!' She said in a shrieking voice.

In a very childlike gesture she covered her face with her right forearm. I thought she was crying. I came over to her and tried to put my arm around her shoulders. I could not bring myself to do it.

'Come now, doña Soledad,' I said, 'let's forget all this and let me give you these packages before I leave.'

I stepped in front of her to face her. I could see her black, shining eyes and part of her face behind her arm. She was not crying. She was smiling.

I jumped back. Her smile terrified me. Both of us stood motionless for a long time. She kept her face covered but I could see her eyes watching me.

As I stood there almost paralysed with fear I felt utterly despondent. I had fallen into a bottomless pit. Doña Soledad was a witch. My body knew it, and yet I could not really believe it. What I wanted to believe was that doña Soledad had gone mad and was being kept in the house instead of an asylum.

I did not dare move or take my eyes away from her. We must have stayed in that position for five or six minutes. She had kept her arm raised and yet motionless. She was standing at the rear of the car, almost leaning against the left bumper. The lid of the boot was still open. I thought of making a dash for the right door. The keys were in the ignition.

I relaxed a bit in order to gain the momentum to run. She seemed to notice my change of position immediately. Her arm moved down, revealing her whole face. Her teeth were clenched. Her eyes were fixed on mine. They looked hard and mean. Suddenly she lurched towards me. She stomped with her right foot, like a fencer, and reached out with clawed hands to grab me by my waist as she let out the most chilling shriek.

My body jumped back out of her reach. I ran for the car, but with inconceivable agility she rolled to my feet and made me trip over her. I fell facedown and she grabbed me by the left foot. I contracted my right leg, and I would have kicked her in the face with the sole of my shoe had she not let go of me and rolled back. I jumped to my feet and tried to open the door of the car. It was locked. I threw myself over the bonnet to reach the other side but somehow doña Soledad got there before I did. I tried to roll back over the bonnet, but midway I felt a sharp pain in my right calf. She had grabbed me by the leg. I could not kick her with my left foot; she had pinned down both of my legs against the bonnet. She pulled me towards her and I fell on top of her. We wrestled on the ground. Her strength was magnificent and her shrieks were terrifying. I could hardly move under the gigantic pressure of her body. It was not a matter of weight but rather tension, and she had it. Suddenly I heard a growl and the enormous dog jumped on her back and shoved her away from me. I stood up. I wanted to get into the car, but the woman and the dog were fighting by the door. The only retreat was to go inside the house. I made it in one or two seconds. I did not turn to look at them but rushed inside and closed the door behind me, securing it

with the iron bar that was behind it. I ran to the back and did
the same with the other door.

From inside I could hear the furious growling of the dog
and the woman's inhuman shrieks. Then suddenly the dog's
barking and growling turned into whining and howling as if
he were in pain, or as if something were frightening him. I felt
a jolt in the pit of my stomach. My ears began to buzz. I realized that I was trapped inside the house. I had a fit of sheer
terror. I was revolted at my stupidity in running into the house.
The woman's attack had confused me so intensely that I had
lost all sense of strategy and had behaved as if I were running
away from an ordinary opponent who could be shut out by
simply closing a door. I heard someone come to the door and
lean against it, trying to force it open. Then there were loud
knocks and banging on it.

'Open the door,' doña Soledad said in a hard voice. 'That
goddamned dog has mauled me.'

I deliberated whether or not to let her in. What came to my
mind was the memory of a confrontation I had had years before with a sorceress, who had, according to don Juan, adopted
his shape in order to fool me and deliver a deadly blow. Obviously doña Soledad was not as I had known her, but I had
reasons to doubt that she was a sorceress. The time element
played a decisive role in my conviction. Pablito, Nestor and
I had been involved with don Juan and don Genaro for years
and we were not sorcerers at all; how could doña Soledad be
one? No matter how much she had changed she could not
improvise something that would take a lifetime to accomplish.

'Why did you attack me?' I asked, speaking loudly so as
to be heard through the thick door.

She answered that the Nagual had told her not to let me go.
I asked her why.

She did not answer; instead she banged on the door furiously
and I banged back even harder. We went on hitting the door
for a few minutes. She stopped and started begging me to
open it. I had a surge of nervous energy. I knew that if I
opened the door I might have a chance to flee. I moved the

iron bar from the door. She staggered in. Her blouse was torn.
The band that held her hair had fallen off and her long hair
was all over her face.

'Look what that son of a bitch dog did to me!' she yelled.
'Look! Look!'

I took a deep breath. She seemed to be somewhat dazed. She
sat down on a bench and began to take off her tattered blouse.
I seized that moment to run out of the house and make a dash
for the car. With a speed that was born only out of fear, I got
inside, shut the door, automatically turned on the motor and
put the car in reverse. I stepped on the gas and turned my head
to look back through the rear window. As I turned I felt a hot
breath on my face; I heard a horrendous growl and saw in a
flash the demoniacal eyes of the dog. He was standing on the
back seat. I saw his horrible teeth almost in my eyes. I ducked
my head. His teeth grabbed my hair. I must have curled my
whole body on the seat, and in doing so I let my foot off the
clutch. The jerk of the car made the beast lose his balance. I
opened the door and scrambled out. The head of the dog
jutted out through the door. I heard his enormous teeth click
as his jaws closed tight, missing my heels by a few inches. The
car began to roll back and I made another dash for the house.
I stopped before I had reached the door.

Doña Soledad was standing there. She had tied her hair up
again. She had thrown a shawl over her shoulders. She stared
at me for a moment and then began to laugh, very softly at
first as if her wounds hurt her, and then loudly. She pointed a
finger at me and held her stomach as she convulsed with
laughter. She bent over and stretched, seemingly to catch her
breath. She was naked above the waist. I could see her breasts,
shaking with the convulsions of her laughter.

I felt that all was lost. I looked back towards the car. It had
come to a stop after rolling four or five feet; the door had
closed again, sealing the dog inside. I could see and hear the
enormous beast biting the back of the front seat and pawing
the windows.

A most peculiar decision faced me at that moment. I did not

know who scared me the most, doña Soledad or the dog. After a moment's thought I decided that the dog was just a stupid beast.

I ran back to the car and climbed up on the roof. The noise enraged the dog. I heard him ripping the upholstery. Lying on the roof I managed to open the driver's door. My idea was to open both doors and then slide from the roof into the car, through one of them, after the dog had gone out the other one. I leaned over to open the right door. I had forgotten that it was locked. At that moment the dog's head came out through the opened door. I had an attack of blind panic at the idea that the dog was going to jump out of the car and on to the roof.

In less than a second I had leaped to the ground and found myself standing at the door of the house.

Doña Soledad was bracing herself in the doorway. Laughter came out of her in spurts that seemed almost painful.

The dog had remained inside the car, still frothing with rage. Apparently he was too large and could not squeeze his bulky frame over the front seat. I went to the car and gently closed the door again. I began to look for a stick long enough to release the safety lock on the right-hand door.

I searched in the area in front of the house. There was not a single piece of wood lying around. Doña Soledad, in the meantime, had gone inside. I assessed my situation. I had no other alternative but to ask her help. With great trepidation, I crossed the threshold, looking in every direction in case she might have been hiding behind the door, waiting for me.

'Doña Soledad!' I yelled out.

'What the hell do you want?' she yelled back from her room.

'Would you please go out and get your dog out of my car?' I said.

'Are you kidding?' she replied. 'That's not my dog. I've told you already, he belongs to my girls.'

'Where are your girls?' I asked.

'They are in the mountains,' she replied.

She came out of her room and faced me.

'Do you want to see what that goddamned dog did to me?'
she asked in a dry tone. 'Look!'

She unwrapped her shawl and showed me her naked back.

I found no visible tooth marks on her back; there were only
a few long, superficial scratches she might have gotten by
rubbing against the hard ground. For all that matter, she could
have scratched herself when she attacked me.

'You have nothing there,' I said.

'Come and look in the light,' she said and went over by the
door.

She insisted that I look carefully for the gashes of the dog's
teeth. I felt stupid. I had a heavy sensation around my eyes,
especially on my brow. I went outside instead. The dog had
not moved and began to bark as soon as I came out the
door.

I cursed myself. There was no one to blame but me. I had
walked into that trap like a fool. I resolved right then to walk
to town. But my wallet, my papers, everything I had was in
my briefcase on the floor of the car, right under the dog's feet.
I had an attack of despair. It was useless to walk to town. I did
not have enough money in my pockets even to buy a cup of
coffee. Besides, I did not know a soul in town. I had no other
alternative but to get the dog out of the car.

'What kind of food does that dog eat?' I yelled from the
door.

'Why don't you try your leg?' doña Soledad yelled back
from her room, and cackled.

I looked for some cooked food in the house. The pots were
empty. There was nothing else for me to do but to confront
her again. My despair had turned into rage. I stormed into her
room ready for a fight to the death. She was lying on her bed,
covered with her shawl.

'Please forgive me for having done all those things to you,'
she said bluntly, looking at the ceiling.

Her boldness stopped my rage.

'You must understand my position,' she went on. 'I couldn't
let you go.'

She laughed softly, and in a clear, calm and very pleasing

voice said that she was guilty of being greedy and clumsy, that she had nearly succeeded in scaring me away with her antics, but that the situation had suddenly changed. She paused and sat up in her bed, covering her breasts with her shawl, then added that a strange confidence had descended into her body. She looked up at the ceiling and moved her arms in a weird, rhythmical flow, like a windmill.

'There is no way for you to leave now,' she said.

She scrutinized me without laughing. My internal rage had subsided but my despair was more acute than ever. I honestly knew that in matters of sheer strength I was no match for her or the dog.

She said that our appointment had been set up years in advance, and that neither of us had enough power to hurry it, or break it.

'Don't knock yourself out trying to leave,' she said. 'That's as useless as my trying to keep you here. Something besides your will will release you from here, and something besides my will will keep you here.'

Somehow her confidence had not only mellowed her, but had given her a great command over words. Her statements were compelling and crystal clear. Don Juan had always said that I was a trusting soul when it came to words. As she talked I found myself thinking that she was not really as threatening as I thought. She no longer projected the feeling of having a chip on her shoulder. My reason was almost at ease but another part of me was not. All the muscles of my body were like tense wires, and yet I had to admit to myself that although she scared me out of my wits I found her most appealing. She watched me.

'I'll show you how useless it is to try to leave,' she said, jumping out of bed. 'I'm going to help you. What do you need?'

She observed me with a gleam in her eyes. Her small white teeth gave her smile a devilish touch. Her chubby face was strangely smooth and fairly free of wrinkles. Two deep lines running from the sides of her nose to the corners of her mouth gave her face the appearance of maturity, but not age. In standing up from the bed she casually let her shawl fall straight down, uncovering her full breasts. She did not bother to cover herself. Instead she swelled up her chest and lifted her breasts.

'Oh, you've noticed, eh?' she said, and rocked her body from side to side as if pleased with herself. 'I always keep my hair tied behind my head. The Nagual told me to do so. The pull makes my face younger.'

I had been sure that she was going to talk about her breasts. Her shift was a surprise to me.

'I don't mean that the pull on my hair is going to make me look younger,' she went on with a charming smile. 'The pull on my hair makes me younger.'

'How is that possible?' I asked.

She answered me with a question. She wanted to know if I had correctly understood don Juan when he said that anything was possible if one wants it with unbending intent. I was after a more precise explanation. I wanted to know what else she did besides tying her hair, in order to look so young. She said that she lay in her bed and emptied herself of any thoughts and feelings and then let the lines of her floor pull her wrinkles away. I pressed her for more details: any feelings, sensations, perceptions that she had experienced while lying on her bed. She insisted that she felt nothing, that she did not know how the lines in her floor worked, and that she only knew not to let her thoughts interfere.

She placed her hands on my chest and shoved me very gently. It seemed to be a gesture to show that she had had enough of my questions. We walked outside, through the back door. I told her that I needed a long stick. She went directly to a pile of firewood, but there were no long sticks. I asked her if she could get me a couple of nails in order to join together two pieces of firewood. We looked unsuccessfully all over the house for nails. As a final resort I had to dislodge the longest stick I could find in the chicken coop that Pablito had built in the back. The stick, although it was a bit flimsy, seemed suited for my purpose.

Doña Soledad had not smiled or joked during our search. She seemed to be utterly absorbed in her task of helping me.

Her concentration was so intense that I had the feeling she was wishing me to succeed.

I walked to my car, armed with the long stick and a shorter one from the pile of firewood. Doña Soledad stood by the front door.

I began to tease the dog with the short stick in my right hand and at the same time I tried to release the safety lock with the long one in my other hand. The dog nearly bit my right hand and made me drop the short stick. The rage and power of the enormous beast were so immense that I nearly lost the long one too. The dog was about to bite it in two when doña Soledad came to my aid; pounding on the back window she drew the dog's attention and he let go of it.

Encouraged by her distracting manoeuvre I dived, headfirst, and slid across the length of the front seat and managed to release the safety lock. I tried to pull back immediately, but the dog charged towards me with all his might and actually thrust his massive shoulders and front paws over the front seat, before I had time to back out. I felt his paws on my shoulder. I cringed. I knew that he was going to maul me. The dog lowered his head to go in for the kill, but instead of biting me he hit the steering wheel. I scurried out and in one move climbed over the bonnet and on to the roof. I had goose pimples all over my body.

I opened the right-hand door. I asked doña Soledad to hand me the long stick and with it I pushed the lever to release the backrest from its straight position. I conceived that if I teased the dog he would ram it forward, allowing himself room to get out of the car. But he did not move. He bit furiously on the stick instead.

At that moment doña Soledad jumped on to the roof and lay next to me. She wanted to help me tease the dog. I told her that she could not stay on the roof because when the dog came out I was going to get in the car and drive away. I thanked her for her help and said that she should go back in the house. She shrugged her shoulders, jumped down and went back to the door. I pushed down the release again and with my cap I teased the dog. I snapped it around his eyes, in front of his muzzle. The dog's fury was beyond anything I had seen but he would not leave the seat. Finally his massive jaws jerked the stick out of my grip. I climbed down to retrieve it from underneath the car. Suddenly I heard doña Soledad screaming.

'Watch out! He's getting out!'

I glanced up at the car. The dog was squeezing himself over the seat. He had gotten his hind paws caught in the steering wheel; except for that, he was almost out.

I dashed to the house and got inside just in time to avoid being run down by that animal. His momentum was so powerful that he rammed against the door.

As she secured the door with its iron bar doña Soledad said in a cackling voice, 'I told you it was useless.'

She cleared her throat and turned to look at me.

'Can you tie the dog with a rope?' I asked.

I was sure that she would give me a meaningless answer, but to my amazement she said that we should try everything, even luring the dog into the house and trapping him there.

Her idea appealed to me. I carefully opened the front door. The dog was no longer there. I ventured out a bit more. There was no sight of him. My hope was that the dog had gone back to his corral. I was going to wait another instant before I made a dash for my car, when I heard a deep growl and saw the massive head of the beast inside my car. He had crawled back on to the front seat.

Doña Soledad was right; it was useless to try. A wave of sadness enveloped me. Somehow I knew my end was near. In a fit of sheer desperation I told doña Soledad that I was going to get a knife from the kitchen and kill the dog, or be killed by him, and I would have done that had it not been that there was not a single metal object in the entire house.

'Didn't the Nagual teach you to accept your fate?' doña Soledad asked as she trailed behind me. 'That one out there is no ordinary dog. That dog has power. He is a warrior. He will do what he has to do. Even kill you.'

I had a moment of uncontrollable frustration and grabbed her by the shoulders and growled. She did not seem surprised or affected by my sudden outburst. She turned her back to me and dropped her shawl to the floor. Her back was very strong and beautiful. I had an irrepressible urge to hit her, but I ran my hand across her shoulders instead. Her skin was soft and smooth. Her arms and shoulders were muscular without being big. She seemed to have a minimal layer of fat that rounded off her muscles and gave her upper body the appearance of smoothness, and yet when I pushed on any part of it with the tips of my fingers I could feel the hardness of unseen muscles below the smooth surface. I did not want to look at her breasts.

She walked to a roofed, open area in the back of the house that served as a kitchen. I followed her. She sat down on a bench and calmly washed her feet in a pail. While she was putting on her sandals, I went with great trepidation into a new outhouse that had been built in the back. She was standing by the door when I came out.

'You like to talk,' she said casually, leading me into her room. 'There is no hurry. Now we can talk forever.'

She picked up my writing pad from the top of her chest of drawers, where she must have placed it herself, and handed it to me with exaggerated care. Then she pulled up her bedspread and folded it neatly and put it on top of the same chest of drawers. I noticed then that the two chests were the colour of the walls, yellowish white, and the bed without the spread was pinkish red, more or less the colour of the floor. The bedspread, on the other hand, was dark brown, like the wood of the ceiling and the wood panels of the windows.

'Let's talk,' she said, sitting comfortably on the bed after taking off her sandals.

She placed her knees against her naked breasts. She looked like a young girl. Her aggressive and commandeering manner had subdued and changed into charm. At that moment she was the antithesis of what she had been earlier. I had to laugh at the way she was urging me to write. She reminded me of don Juan.

'Now we have time,' she said. 'The wind has changed. Didn't you notice it?'

I had. She said that the new direction of the wind was her

own beneficial direction and thus the wind had turned into her helper.

'What do you know about the wind, doña Soledad?' I asked as I calmly sat down on the foot of her bed.

'Only what the Nagual taught me,' she said. 'Each one of us, women that is, has a peculiar direction, a particular wind. Men don't. I am the north wind; when it blows I am different. The Nagual said that a warrior can use her particular wind for whatever she wants. I used it to trim my body and remake it. Look at me! I am the north wind. Feel me when I come through the window.'

There was a strong wind blowing through the window, which was strategically placed to face the north.

'Why do you think men don't have a wind?' I asked.

She thought for a moment and then replied that the Nagual had never mentioned why.

'You wanted to know who made this floor,' she said, wrapping her blanket around her shoulders. 'I made it myself. It took me four years to put it down. Now this floor is like myself.'

As she spoke I noticed that the converging lines in the floor were oriented to originate from the north. The room, however, was not perfectly aligned with the cardinal points; thus her bed was at odd angles with the walls and so were the lines in the clay slabs.

'Why did you make the floor red, doña Soledad?'

'That's my colour. I am red, like red dirt. I got the red clay in the mountains around here. The Nagual told me where to look and he also helped me carry it, and so did everyone else. They all helped me.'

'How did you fire the clay?'

'The Nagual made me dig a pit. We filled it with firewood and then stacked up the clay slabs with flat pieces of rock in between them. I closed the pit with a lid of dirt and wire and set the wood on fire. It burned for days.'

'How did you keep the slabs from warping?'

'I didn't. The wind did that, the north wind that blew while the fire was on. The Nagual showed me how to dig the pit so it would face the north and the north wind. He also made me leave four holes for the north wind to blow into the pit. Then he made me leave one hole in the centre of the lid to let the smoke out. The wind made the wood burn for days; after the pit was cold again I opened it and began to polish and even out the slabs. It took me over a year to make enough slabs to finish my floor.'

'How did you figure out the design?'

'The wind taught me that. When I made my floor the Nagual had already taught me not to resist the wind. He had showed me how to give in to my wind and let it guide me. It took him a long time to do that, years and years. I was a very difficult, silly old woman at first; he told me that himself and he was right. But I learned very fast. Perhaps because I'm old and no longer have anything to lose. In the beginning, what made it even more difficult for me was the fear I had. The mere presence of the Nagual made me stutter and faint. The Nagual had the same effect on everyone else. It was his fate to be so fearsome.'

She stopped talking and stared at me.

'The Nagual is not human,' she said.

'What makes you say that?'

'The Nagual is a devil from who knows what time.'

Her statements chilled me. I felt my heart pounding. She certainly could not have found a better audience. I was intrigued to no end. I begged her to explain what she meant by that.

'His touch changed people,' she said. 'You know that. He changed your body. In your case, you didn't even know that he was doing that. But he got into your old body. He put something in it. He did the same with me. He left something in me and that something took over. Only a devil can do that. Now I am the north wind and I fear nothing, and no one. But before he changed me I was a weak, ugly old woman who would faint at the mere mention of his name. Pablito, of course, was no help to me because he feared the Nagual more than death itself.

'One day the Nagual and Genaro came to the house when I was alone. I heard them by the door, like prowling jaguars. I crossed myself; to me they were two demons, but I came out to see what I could do for them. They were hungry and I gladly fixed food for them. I had some thick bowls made out of gourd and I gave each man a bowl of soup. The Nagual didn't seem to appreciate the food; he didn't want to eat food prepared by such a weak woman and pretended to be clumsy and knocked the bowl off the table with a sweep of his arm. But the bowl, instead of turning over and spilling all over the floor, slid with the force of the Nagual's blow and fell on my foot, without spilling a drop. The bowl actually landed on my foot and stayed there until I bent over and picked it up. I set it up on the table in front of him and told him that even though I was a weak woman and had always feared him, my food had good feelings.

'From that very moment the Nagual changed towards me. The fact that the bowl of soup fell on my foot and didn't spill proved to him that power had pointed me out to him. I didn't know that at the time and I thought that he changed towards me because he felt ashamed of having refused my food. I thought nothing of his change. I still was petrified and couldn't even look him in the eye. But he began to take more and more notice of me. He even brought me gifts: a shawl, a dress, a comb and other things. That made me feel terrible. I was ashamed because I thought that he was a man looking for a woman. The Nagual had young girls, what would he want with an old woman like me? At first I didn't want to wear or even consider looking at his gifts, but Pablito prevailed on me and I began to wear them. I also began to be even more afraid of him and didn't want to be alone with him. I knew that he was a devilish man. I knew what he had done to his woman.'

I felt compelled to interrupt her. I told her that I had never known of a woman in don Juan's life.

'You know who I mean,' she said.

'Believe me, doña Soledad, I don't.'

'Don't give me that. You know that I'm talking about la Gorda.'

The only 'la Gorda' I knew of was Pablito's sister, an enormously fat girl nicknamed Gorda, Fatso. I had had the feeling, although no one ever talked about it, that she was not really doña Soledad's daughter. I did not want to press her for any more information. I suddenly remembered that the fat girl had disappeared from the house and nobody could or dared to tell me what had happened to her.

'One day I was alone in the front of the house,' doña Soledad went on. 'I was combing my hair in the sun with the comb that the Nagual had given me; I didn't realize that he had arrived and was standing behind me. All of a sudden I felt his hands grabbing me by the chin. I heard him say very softly that I shouldn't move because my neck might break. He twisted my head to the left. Not all the way but a bit. I became very frightened and screamed and tried to wriggle out of his grip, but he held my head firmly for a long, long time.

'When he let go of my chin, I fainted. I don't remember what happened then. When I woke up I was lying on the ground, right here where I'm sitting now. The Nagual was gone. I was so ashamed that I didn't want to see anyone, especially la Gorda. For a long time I even thought that the Nagual had never twisted my neck and I had had a nightmare.'

She stopped. I waited for an explanation of what had happened. She seemed distracted, pensive perhaps.

'What exactly happened, doña Soledad?' I asked, incapable of containing myself. 'Did he do something to you?'

'Yes. He twisted my neck in order to change the direction of my eyes,' she said and laughed loudly at my look of surprise.

'I mean, did he . . .?'

'Yes. He changed my direction,' she went on, oblivious to my probes. 'He did that to you and to all the others.'

'That's true. He did that to me. But why do you think he did that?'

'He had to. That is the most important thing to do.'

She was referring to a peculiar act that don Juan had deemed absolutely necessary. I had never talked about it with anyone. In fact, I had almost forgotten about it. At the beginning of my apprenticeship, he once built two small fires in the mountains of northern Mexico. They were perhaps twenty feet apart. He made me stand another twenty feet away from them, holding my body, especially my head, in a most relaxed and natural position. He then made me face one fire, and coming from behind me, he twisted my neck to the left, and aligned my eyes, but not my shoulders, with the other fire. He held my head in that position for hours, until the fire was extinguished. The new direction was the southeast, or rather he had aligned the second fire in a southeasterly direction. I had understood the whole affair as one of don Juan's inscrutable peculiarities, one of his nonsensical rites.

'The Nagual said that all of us throughout our lives develop one direction to look,' she went on. 'That becomes the direction of the eyes of the spirit. Through the years that direction becomes overused, and weak and unpleasant, and since we are bound to that particular direction we become weak and unpleasant ourselves. The day the Nagual twisted my neck and held it until I fainted out of fear, he gave me a new direction.'

'What direction did he give you?'

'Why do you ask that?' she said with unnecessary force. 'Do you think that perhaps the Nagual gave me a different direction?'

'I can tell you the direction that he gave me,' I said.

'Never mind,' she snapped. 'He told me that himself.'

She seemed agitated. She changed position and lay on her stomach. My back hurt from writing. I asked her if I could sit on her floor and use the bed as a table. She stood up and handed me the folded bedspread to use as a cushion.

'What else did the Nagual do to you?' I asked.

'After changing my direction the Nagual really began to talk to me about power,' she said, lying down again. 'He mentioned things in a casual way at first, because he didn't know exactly what to do with me. One day he took me for a short walking trip in the sierras. Then another day he took me on a bus to his homeland in the desert. Little by little I became accustomed to going away with him.'

'Did he ever give you power plants?'

'He gave me Mescalito, once when we were in the desert. But since I was an empty woman Mescalito refused me. I had a horrid encounter with him. It was then that the Nagual knew that he ought to acquaint me with the wind instead. That was, of course, after he got an omen. He had said, over and over that day, that although he was a sorcerer that had learned to *see*, if he didn't get an omen he had no way of knowing which way to go. He had already waited for days for a certain indication about me. But power didn't want to give it. In desperation, I suppose, he introduced me to his guaje, and I saw Mescalito.'

I interrupted her. Her use of the word 'guaje', gourd, was confusing to me. Examined in the context of what she was telling me, the word had no meaning. I thought that perhaps she was speaking metaphorically, or that gourd was a euphemism.

'What is a guaje, doña Soledad?'

There was a look of surprise in her eyes. She paused before answering.

'Mescalito is the Nagual's guaje,' she finally said.

Her answer was even more confusing. I felt mortified by the fact that she really seemed concerned with making sense to me. When I asked her to explain further, she insisted that I knew everything myself. That was don Juan's favourite stratagem to foil my probes. I said to her that don Juan had told me that Mescalito was a deity, or force contained in the peyote buttons. To say that Mescalito was his gourd made absolutely no sense.

'The Nagual can acquaint you with anything through his gourd,' she said after a pause. 'That is the key to his power. Anyone can give you peyote, but only a sorcerer, through his gourd, can acquaint you with Mescalito.'

She stopped talking and fixed her eyes on me. Her look was ferocious.

'Why do you have to make me repeat what you already know?' she asked in an angry tone.

I was completely taken aback by her sudden shift. A moment before she had been almost sweet.

'Never mind my changes of mood,' she said, smiling again. 'I'm the north wind. I'm very impatient. All my life I never dared to speak my mind. Now I fear no one. I say what I feel. To meet with me you have to be strong.'

She slid closer to me on her stomach.

'Well, the Nagual acquainted me with the Mescalito that came out of his gourd,' she went on. 'But he couldn't guess what would happen to me. He expected something like your own meeting or Eligio's meeting with Mescalito. In both cases he was at a loss and let his gourd decide what to do next. In both cases his gourd helped him. With me it was different; Mescalito told him never to bring me around. The Nagual and I left that place in a great hurry. We went north instead of coming home. We took a bus to go to Mexicali, but we got out in the middle of the desert. It was very late. The sun was setting behind the mountains. The Nagual wanted to cross the road and go south on foot. We were waiting for some speeding cars to go by, when suddenly he tapped my shoulder and pointed towards the road ahead of us. I saw a spiral of dust. A gust of wind was raising dust on the side of the road. We watched it move towards us. The Nagual ran across the road and the wind enveloped me. It actually made me spin very gently and then it vanished. That was the omen the Nagual was waiting for. From then on we went to the mountains or the desert for the purpose of seeking the wind. The wind didn't like me at first, because I was my old self. So the Nagual endeavoured to change me. He first made me build this room and this floor. Then he made me wear new clothes and sleep on a mattress instead of a straw mat. He made me wear shoes, and have drawers full of clothes. He forced me to walk hundreds of miles and taught me to be quiet. I learned very fast. He also made me do strange things for no reason at all.

'One day, while we were in the mountains of his homeland, I listened to the wind for the first time. It came directly to my womb. I was lying on top of a flat rock and the wind twirled around me. I had already seen it that day whirling around the bushes, but this time it came over me and stopped. It felt like a bird that had landed on my stomach. The Nagual had made me take off all my clothes; I was stark naked but I was not cold because the wind was warming me up.'

'Were you afraid, doña Soledad?'

'Afraid? I was petrified. The wind was alive; it licked me

from my head to my toes. And then it got inside my whole body. I was like a balloon, and the wind came out of my ears and my mouth and other parts I don't want to mention. I thought I was going to die, and I would've run away had it not been that the Nagual held me to the rock. He spoke to me in my ear and calmed me down. I lay quietly and let the wind do whatever it wanted with me. It was then that it told me what to do.'

'What to do with what?'

'With my life, my things, my room, my feelings. It was not clear at first. I thought it was me thinking. The Nagual said that all of us do that. When we are quiet, though, we realize that it is something else telling us things.'

'Did you hear a voice?'

'No. The wind moves inside the body of a woman. The Nagual says that that is so because women have wombs. Once it's inside the womb the wind simply picks you up and tells you to do things. The more quiet and relaxed the woman is the better the results. You may say that all of a sudden the woman finds herself doing things that she had no idea how to do.

'From that day on the wind came to me all the time. It spoke to me in my womb and told me everything I wanted to know. The Nagual saw from the beginning that I was the north wind. Other winds never spoke to me like that, although I had learned to distinguish them.'

'How many kinds of winds are there?'

'There are four winds, like there are four directions. That's, of course, for sorcerers and for whatever sorcerers do. Four is a power number for them. The first wind is the breeze, the morning. It brings hope and brightness; it is the herald of the day. It comes and goes and gets into everything. Sometimes it is mild and unnoticeable; other times it is nagging and bothersome.

'Another wind is the hard wind, either hot or cold or both. A midday wind. Blasting full of energy but also full of blindness. It breaks through doors and brings down walls. A sorcerer must be terribly strong to tackle the hard wind.

'Then there is the cold wind of the afternoon. Sad and trying. A wind that would never leave you in peace. It will chill you and make you cry. The Nagual said that there is such depth to it, though, that it is more than worthwhile to seek it.

'And at last there is the hot wind. It warms and protects and envelops everything. It is a night wind for sorcerers. Its power goes together with the darkness.

'Those are the four winds. They are also associated with the four directions. The breeze is the east. The cold wind is the west. The hot one is the south. The hard wind is the north.

'The four winds also have personalities. The breeze is gay and sleek and shifty. The cold wind is moody and melancholy and always pensive. The hot wind is happy and abandoned and bouncy. The hard wind is energetic and commandeering and impatient.

'The Nagual told me that the four winds are women. That is why female warriors seek them. Winds and women are alike. That is also the reason why women are better than men. I would say that women learn faster if they cling to their specific wind.'

'How can a woman know what her specific wind is?'

'If the woman quiets down and is not talking to herself, her wind will pick her up, just like that.'

She made a gesture of grabbing.

'Does she have to lie naked?'

'That helps. Especially if she is shy. I was a fat old woman. I had never taken off my clothes in my life. I slept in them and when I took a bath I always had my slip on. For me to show my fat body to the wind was like dying. The Nagual knew that and played it for all it was worth. He knew of the friendship of women and the wind, but he introduced me to Mescalito because he was baffled by me.

'After turning my head that first terrible day, the Nagual found himself with me on his hands. He told me that he had no idea what to do with me. But one thing was for sure, he didn't want a fat old woman snooping around his world. The Nagual said that he felt about me the way he felt about you. Baffled. Both of us shouldn't be here. You're not an Indian and

I'm an old cow. We are both useless if you come right down to it. And look at us. Something must have happened.

'A woman, of course, is much more supple than a man. A woman changes very easily with the power of a sorcerer. Especially with the power of a sorcerer like the Nagual. A male apprentice, according to the Nagual, is extremely difficult. For example, you yourself haven't changed as much as la Gorda, and she started her apprenticeship way after you did. A woman is softer and more gentle, and above all a woman is like a gourd; she receives. But somehow a man commands more power. The Nagual never agreed with that, though. He believed that women are unequalled, tops. He also believed that I felt men were better only because I am an empty woman. He must be right. I have been empty for so long that I can't remember what it feels like to be complete. The Nagual said that if I ever become complete I will change my feelings about it. But if he was right his Gorda would have done as well as Eligio, and as you know, she hasn't.'

I could not follow the flow of her narrative because of her unstated assumption that I knew what she was referring to. In this case I had no idea what Eligio or la Gorda had done.

'In what way was la Gorda different from Eligio?' I asked.

She looked at me for a moment as if measuring something in me. Then she sat up with her knees against her chest.

'The Nagual told me everything,' she said briskly. 'The Nagual had no secrets from me. Eligio was the best; that's why he is not in the world now. He didn't return. In fact he was so good that he didn't have to jump from a precipice when his apprenticeship was over. He was like Genaro; one day while he was working in the field something came to him and took him away. He knew how to let go.'

I felt like asking her if I had really jumped into the abyss. I deliberated for a moment before going ahead with my question. After all I had come to see Pablito and Nestor to clarify that point. Any information I could get on the topic from anyone involved in don Juan's world was indeed a bonus to me.

She laughed at my question, as I had anticipated.

'You mean you don't know what you yourself did?' she asked.

'It's too farfetched to be real,' I said.

'That is the Nagual's world for sure. Not a thing in it is real. He himself told me not to believe anything. But still the male apprentices have to jump. Unless they are truly magnificent, like Eligio.

'The Nagual took us, me and la Gorda, to that mountain and made us look down to the bottom of it. There he showed us the kind of flying Nagual he was. But only la Gorda could follow him. She also wanted to jump into the abyss. The Nagual told her that that was useless. He said female warriors have to do things more painful and more difficult than that. He also told us that the jump was only for the four of you. And that is what happened, the four of you jumped.'

She had said that the four of us had jumped, but I only knew of Pablito and myself having done that. In light of her statements I figured that don Juan and don Genaro must have followed us. That did not seem odd to me; it was rather pleasing and touching.

'What are you talking about?' she asked after I had voiced my thoughts. 'I meant you and the three apprentices of Genaro. You, Pablito and Nestor jumped on the same day.'

'Who is the other apprentice of don Genaro? I know only Pablito and Nestor?'

'You mean that you didn't know that Benigno was Genaro's apprentice?'

'No, I didn't.'

'He was Genaro's oldest apprentice. He jumped before you did and he jumped by himself.'

Benigno was one of five Indian youths I had once found while roaming in the Sonoran Desert with don Juan. They were in search of power objects. Don Juan told me that all of them were apprentices of sorcery. I struck up a peculiar friendship with Benigno in the few times I had seen him after that day. He was from southern Mexico. I liked him very much. For some unknown reason he seemed to delight himself by creating a tantalizing mystery about his personal life. I could never find out who he was or what he did. Every time I talked to him he baffled me with the disarming candour with which he evaded my probes. Once don Juan volunteered some information about Benigno and said that he was very fortunate in having found a teacher and a benefactor. I took don Juan's statements as a casual remark that meant nothing. Doña Soledad had clarified a ten-year-old mystery for me.

'Why do you think don Juan never told me anything about Benigno?'

'Who knows? He must've had a reason. The Nagual never did anything thoughtlessly.'

I had to prop my aching back against her bed before resuming writing.

'Whatever happened to Benigno?'

'He's doing fine. He's perhaps better off than anyone else. You'll see him. He's with Pablito and Nestor. Right now they're inseparable. Genaro's brand is on them. The same thing happened to the girls; they're inseparable because the Nagual's brand is on them.'

I had to interrupt her again and ask her to explain what girls she was talking about.

'My girls,' she said.

'Your daughters? I mean Pablito's sisters?'

'They are not Pablito's sisters. They are the Nagual's apprentices.'

Her disclosure shocked me. Ever since I had met Pablito, years before, I had been led to believe that the four girls who lived in his house were his sisters. Don Juan himself had told me so. I had a sudden relapse of the feeling of despair I had experienced all afternoon. Doña Soledad was not to be trusted; she was engineering something. I was sure that don Juan could not under any conditions have misled me so grossly.

Doña Soledad examined me with overt curiosity.

'The wind just told me that you don't believe what I'm telling you,' she said, and laughed.

'The wind is right,' I said dryly.

'The girls that you've seen over the years are the Nagual's.

They were his apprentices. Now that the Nagual is gone they are the Nagual himself. But they are also my girls. Mine!'

'You mean that you're not Pablito's mother and they are really your daughters?'

'I mean they are mine. The Nagual gave them to me for safekeeping. You are always wrong because you rely on words to explain everything. Since I am Pablito's mother and you heard that they were my girls, you figured out that they must be brother and sisters. The girls are my true babies. Pablito, although he's the child that came out of my womb, is my mortal enemy.'

My reaction to her statements was a mixture of revulsion and anger. I thought that she was not only an aberrated woman, but a dangerous one. Somehow, part of me had known that since the moment I had arrived.

She watched me for a long time. To avoid looking at her I sat down on the bedspread again.

'The Nagual warned me about your weirdness,' she said suddenly, 'but I couldn't understand what he meant. Now I know. He told me to be careful and not to anger you because you're violent. I'm sorry I was not as careful as I should've been. He also said that as long as you can write you could go to hell itself and not even feel it. I haven't bothered you about that. Then he told me that you're suspicious because words entangle you. I haven't bothered you there, either. I've been talking my head off, trying not to entangle you.'

There was a silent accusation in her tone. I felt somehow embarrassed at being annoyed with her.

'What you're telling me is very hard to believe,' I said. 'Either you or don Juan has lied to me terribly.'

'Neither of us has lied. You understand only what you want to. The Nagual said that that is a condition of your emptiness.

'The girls are the Nagual's children, just like you and Eligio are his children. He made six children, four women and two men. Genaro made three men. There are nine altogether. One of them, Eligio, already made it, so now it is up to the eight of you to try.'

'Where did Eligio go?'

'He went to join the Nagual and Genaro.'

'And where did the Nagual and Genaro go?'

'You know where they went. You're just kidding me, aren't you?'

'But that's the point, doña Soledad. I'm not kidding you.'

'Then I will tell you. I can't deny you anything. The Nagual and Genaro went back to the same place they came from, to the other world. When their time was up they simply stepped out into the darkness out there, and since they did not want to come back, the darkness of the night swallowed them up.'

I felt it was useless to probe her any further. I was ready to change the subject, but she spoke first.

'You caught a glimpse of the other world when you jumped,' she went on. 'But maybe the jump has confused you. Too bad. There is nothing that anyone can do about it. It is your fate to be a man. Women are better than men in that sense. They don't have to jump into an abyss. Women have their own ways. They have their own abyss. Women menstruate. The Nagual told me that that was the door for them. During their period they become something else. I know that that was the time when he taught my girls. It was too late for me; I'm too old so I really don't know what that door looks like. But the Nagual insisted that the girls pay attention to everything that happens to them during that time. He would take them during those days into the mountains and stay with them there until they would see the crack between the worlds.

'The Nagual, since he had no qualms or fear about doing anything, pushed them without mercy so they could find out for themselves that there is a crack in women, a crack that they disguise very well. During their period, no matter how well-made the disguise is, it falls away and women are bare. The Nagual pushed my girls until they were half-dead to open that crack. They did it. He made them do it, but it took them years.'

'How did they become apprentices?'

'Lidia was his first apprentice. He found her one morning when he had stopped at a dishevelled hut in the mountains. The Nagual told me that there was no one in sight and yet there

had been omens calling him to that house since early morning.
The breeze had bothered him terribly. He said that he couldn't
even open his eyes every time he tried to walk away from that
area. So when he found the house he knew that something was
there. He looked under a pile of straw and twigs and found a
girl. She was very ill. She could hardly talk, but still she told
him that she didn't need anyone to help her. She was going to
keep .on sleeping there and if she didn't wake up anymore no
one would lose a thing. The Nagual liked her spirit and talked
to her in her language. He told her that he was going to cure
her and take care of her until she was strong again. She refused.
She was an Indian who had known only hardships and pain.
She told the Nagual that she had already taken all the medicine
that her parents had given her and nothing helped.

'The more she talked the more the Nagual understood that
the omen had pointed her out to him in a most peculiar way.
The omen was more like a command.

'The Nagual picked the girl up and put her on his shoulders,
like a child, and brought her to Genaro's place. Genaro made
medicine for her. She couldn't open her eyes anymore. The
lids were stuck together. They were swollen and had a yellowish
crud on them. They were festering. The Nagual tended her
until she was well. He hired me to look after her and cook her
meals. I helped her to get well with my food. She is my first
baby. When she was well, and that took nearly a year, the
Nagual wanted to return her to her parents, but the girl refused
to go and went with him instead.

'A short time after he had found Lidia, while she was still
sick and in my care, the Nagual found you. You were brought
to him by a man he had never seen before in his life. The
Nagual *saw* that the man's death was hovering above his head,
and he found it very odd that the man would point you out to
him at such a time. You made the Nagual laugh and right
away the Nagual set a test for you. He didn't take you, he told
you to come and find him. He has tested you ever since like he
has tested no one else. He said that that was your path.

'For three years he had only two apprentices, Lidia and
you. Then one day while he was visiting his friend Vicente,

a curer from the north, some people brought in a crazy girl, a girl who did nothing else but cry. The people took the Nagual for Vicente and placed the girl in his hands. The Nagual told me that the girl ran to him and clung to him as if she knew him. The Nagual told her parents they had to leave her with him. They were worried about the cost but the Nagual assured them that it would be free. I suppose that the girl was such a pain in the ass to them that they didn't mind getting rid of her.

'The Nagual brought her to me. That was hell! She was truly crazy. That was Josefina. It took the Nagual years to cure her. But even to this day she's crazier than a bat. She was, of course, crazy about the Nagual and there was a terrible fight between Lidia and Josefina. They hated each other. But I liked them both. But the Nagual, when he saw that they couldn't get along, became very firm with them. As you know the Nagual can't get mad at anyone. So he scared them half to death. One day Lidia got mad and left. She had decided to find herself a young husband. On the road she found a tiny chicken. It had just been hatched and was lost in the middle of the road. Lidia picked it up, and since she was in a deserted area with no houses around, she figured that the chicken belonged to no one. She put it inside her blouse, in between her breasts to keep it warm. Lidia told me that she ran and in doing so the little chicken began to move to her side. She tried to bring him back to the front but she couldn't catch him. The chicken ran very fast around her sides and her back, inside her blouse. The chicken's feet tickled her at first and then they drove her crazy. When she realized that she couldn't get him out, she came back to me, screaming out of her mind, and told me to get the damn thing out of her blouse. I undressed her but that was to no avail. There was no chicken at all, and yet she still felt its feet on her skin going around and around.

'The Nagual came over then and told her that only when she let go of her old self would the chicken stop running. Lidia was crazy for three days and three nights. The Nagual told me to tie her up. I fed her and cleaned her and gave her water. On the fourth day she became very peaceful and calm. I untied her and she put on her clothes and when she was dressed again, as she had been the day she ran away, the little chicken came out. She took him in her hand and petted and thanked him and returned him to the place where she had found him. I walked with her part of the way.

'From that time on Lidia never bothered anyone. She accepted her fate. The Nagual is her fate; without him she would have been dead. So what was the point of trying to refuse or mould things which can only be accepted?

'Josefina went off next. She was already afraid of what happened to Lidia but she soon forgot about it. One Sunday afternoon, when she was coming back to the house, a dry leaf got stuck in the threads of her shawl. Her shawl was loosely woven. She tried to pick out the small leaf, but she was afraid of ruining her shawl. So when she came into the house she immediately tried to loosen it, but there was no way, it was stuck. Josefina, in a fit of anger, clutched her shawl and the leaf and crumbled it inside her hand. She figured that small pieces would be easier to pick out. I heard a maddening scream and Josefina fell to the ground. I ran to her and found that she couldn't open her hand. The leaf had cut her hand to shreds as if it were pieces of a razor blade. Lidia and I helped her and nursed her for seven days. Josefina was more stubborn than anyone else. She nearly died. At the end she managed to open her hand, but only after she had in her own mind resolved to drop her old ways. She still gets pains in her body from time to time, especially in her hand, due to the ugly disposition that still returns to her. The Nagual told both of them that they shouldn't count on their victory because it's a lifetime struggle that each of us wages against our old selves.

'Lidia and Josefina never fought again. I don't think they like each other, but they certainly get along. I love those two the most. They have been with me all these years. I know that they love me too.'

'What about the other two girls? Where do they fit?'

'A year later Elena came; she is la Gorda. She was by far in the worst condition you could imagine. She weighed two hundred and twenty pounds. She was a desperate woman. Pablito had given her shelter in his shop. She did laundry and ironing to support herself. The Nagual came one night to get Pablito and found the fat girl working while a circle of moths flew over her head. He said that the moths had made a perfect circle for him to watch. He *saw* that the woman was near the end of her life, yet the moths must have had all the confidence in the world, in order for them to give him such an omen. The Nagual acted fast and took her with him.

'She did fine for a while, but the bad habits that she had learned were too deep and she couldn't give them up. So one day the Nagual sent for the wind to help her. It was a matter of helping her or finishing her off. The wind began to blow on her until it drove her out of the house; she was alone that day and no one saw what was happening. The wind pushed her over hills and into ravines until she fell into a ditch, a hole in the ground like a grave. The wind kept her there for days. When the Nagual finally found her she had managed to stop the wind, but she was too weak to walk.'

'How did the girls manage to stop whatever was acting upon them?'

'Well, in the first place what was acting upon them was the gourd that the Nagual carried tied to his belt.'

'And what is in the gourd?'

'The allies that the Nagual carries with him. He said that the ally is funnelled through his gourd. Don't ask me any more because I know nothing more about the ally. All I can tell you is that the Nagual commands two allies and makes them help him. In the case of my girls the ally backed down when they were ready to change. For them, of course, it was a case of either change or death. But that's the case with all of us, one way or another. And la Gorda changed more than anyone else. She was empty, in fact more empty than I, but she worked her spirit until she became power itself. I don't like her. I'm afraid of her. She knows me. She gets inside me and my feelings and that bothers me. But no one can do anything to her because she never lets her guard down. She doesn't hate me, but she thinks I am an evil woman. She may be right. I think that she knows me too well, and I'm not as impeccable as I want to be; but the Nagual told me not to worry about my feelings towards her. She is like Eligio; the world no longer touches her.'

'What did the Nagual do to her that was so special?'

'He taught her things he never taught anyone else. He never pampered her or anything like that. He trusted her. She knows everything about everybody. The Nagual also told me everything except things about her. Maybe that's why I don't like her. The Nagual told her to be my gaoler. Wherever I go I find her. She knows whatever I do. Right now, for instance, I wouldn't be surprised if she shows up.'

'Do you think she would?'

'I doubt it. Tonight, the wind is with me.'

'What is she supposed to do? Does she have a special task?'

'I've told you enough about her. I'm afraid that if I keep on talking about her she will notice me from wherever she is, and I don't want that to happen.'

'Tell me, then, about the others.'

'Some years after he found la Gorda, the Nagual found Eligio. He told me that he had gone with you to his homeland. Eligio came to see you because he was curious about you. The Nagual didn't notice him. He had known him since he was a kid. But one morning, as the Nagual walked to the house where you were waiting for him, he bumped into Eligio on the road. They walked together for a short distance and then a dried piece of cholla got stuck on the tip of Eligio's left shoe. He tried to kick it loose but its thorns were like nails; they had gone deep into the sole of the shoe. The Nagual said that Eligio pointed up to the sky with his finger and shook his foot and the cholla came off like a bullet and went up into the air. Eligio thought it was a big joke and laughed, but the Nagual knew that he had power, although Eligio himself didn't even suspect it. That is why, with no trouble at all, he became the perfect, impeccable warrior.

'It was my good fortune that I got to know him. The Nagual thought that both of us were alike in one thing. Once we hook on to something we don't let go of it. The good fortune of knowing Eligio was a fortune that I shared with no one else, not even with la Gorda. She met Eligio but didn't really get to know him, just like yourself. The Nagual knew from the beginning that Eligio was exceptional and he isolated him. He knew that you and the girls were on one side of the coin and Eligio was by himself on the other side. The Nagual and Genaro were indeed very fortunate to have found him.

'I first met him when the Nagual brought him over to my house. Eligio didn't get along with my girls. They hated him and feared him too. But he was thoroughly indifferent. The world didn't touch him. The Nagual didn't want you, in particular, to have much to do with Eligio. The Nagual said that you are the kind of sorcerer one should stay away from. He said that your touch doesn't soothe, it spoils instead. He told me that your spirit takes prisoners. He was somehow revolted by you and at the same time he liked you. He said that you were crazier than Josefina when he found you and that you still are.'

It was an unsettling feeling to hear someone else telling me what don Juan thought of me. At first I tried to disregard what doña Soledad was saying, but then I felt utterly stupid and out of place trying to protect my ego.

'He bothered with you,' she went on, 'because he was commanded by power to do so. And he, being the impeccable warrior he was, yielded to his master and gladly did what power told him to do with you.'

There was a pause. I was aching to ask her more about don Juan's feelings about me. I asked her to tell me about her other girl instead.

'A month after he found Eligio, the Nagual found Rosa,' she said. 'Rosa was the last one. Once he found her he knew that his number was complete.'

'How did he find her?'

'He had gone to see Benigno in his homeland. He was approaching the house when Rosa came out from the thick bushes on the side of the road, chasing a pig that had gotten loose and was running away. The pig ran too fast for Rosa. She bumped into the Nagual and couldn't catch up with the pig. She then turned against the Nagual and began to yell at him. He made a gesture to grab her and she was ready to fight him. She insulted him and dared him to lay a hand on her. The Nagual liked her spirit immediately but there was no omen. The Nagual said that he waited a moment before walking away, and then the pig came running back and stood beside him. That was the omen. Rosa put a rope around the pig. The Nagual asked her point-blank if she was happy in her job. She said no. She was a live-in servant. The Nagual asked her if she would go with him and she said that if it was what she thought it was for, the answer was no. The Nagual said it was for work and she wanted to know how much he would pay. He gave her a figure and then she asked what kind of work it was. The Nagual said that it was to work with him in the tobacco fields of Veracruz. She told him then that she had been testing him; if he would have said he wanted her to work as a maid, she would have known that he was a liar, because he looked like someone who had never had a home in his life.

'The Nagual was delighted with her and told her that if she wanted to get out of the trap she was in she should come to Benigno's house before noon. He also told her that he would wait no longer than twelve; if she came she had to be prepared for a difficult life and plenty of work. She asked him how far was the place of the tobacco fields. The Nagual said three days' ride in a bus. Rosa said that if it was that far she would certainly be ready to go as soon as she got the pig back in his pen. And she did just that. She came here and everyone liked her. She was never mean or bothersome; the Nagual didn't have to force her or trick her into anything. She doesn't like me at all, and yet she takes care of me better than anyone else. I trust her, and yet I don't like her at all, and when I leave I will miss her the most. Can you beat that?'

I saw a flicker of sadness in her eyes. I could not sustain my distrust. She wiped her eyes with a casual movement of her hand.

There was a natural break in the conversation at that point. It was getting dark by then and writing was very difficult; besides I had to go to the bathroom. She insisted that I use the outhouse before she did as the Nagual himself would have done.

Afterwards she brought two round tubs the size of a child's bathtub, filled them half-full with warm water and added some green leaves after mashing them thoroughly with her hands. She told me in an authoritative tone to wash myself in one of the tubs while she did the same in the other. The water had an almost perfumed smell. It caused a ticklish sensation. It felt like a mild menthol on my face and arms.

We went back to her room. She put my writing gear, which I had left on her bed, on top of one of her chests of drawers. The windows were open and there was still light. It must have been close to seven.

Doña Soledad lay on her back. She was smiling at me. I thought that she was the picture of warmth. But at the same time and in spite of her smile, her eyes gave out a feeling of ruthlessness and unbending force.

I asked her how long she had been with don Juan as his woman or apprentice. She made fun of my cautiousness in labelling her. Her answer was seven years. She reminded me then that I had not seen her for five. I had been convinced up to that point that I had seen her two years before. I tried to remember the last time, but I could not.

She told me to lie down next to her. I knelt on the bed, by her side. In a very soft voice she asked me if I was afraid. I said no, which was the truth. There in her room, at that moment, I was being confronted by an old response of mine, which had manifested itself countless times, a mixture of curiosity and suicidal indifference.

Almost in a whisper she said that she had to be impeccable with me and tell me that our meeting was crucial for both of us. She said that the Nagual had given her direct and detailed orders of what to do. As she talked I could not help laughing at her tremendous effort to sound like don Juan. I listened to her statements and could predict what she would say next.

Suddenly she sat up. Her face was a few inches from mine. I could see her white teeth shining in the semidarkness of the room. She put her arms around me in an embrace and pulled me on top of her.

My mind was very clear, and yet something was leading me

deeper and deeper into a sort of morass. I was experiencing myself as something I had no conception of. Suddenly I knew that I had, somehow, been feeling her feelings all along. She was the strange one. She had mesmerized me with words. She was a cold, old woman. And her designs were not those of youth and vigour, in spite of her vitality and strength. I knew then that don Juan had not turned her head in the same direction as mine. That thought would have been ridiculous in any other context; nonetheless, at that moment I took it as a true insight. A feeling of alarm swept through my body. I wanted to get out of her bed. But there seemed to be an extraordinary force around me that kept me fixed, incapable of moving away. I was paralysed.

She must have felt my realization. All of a sudden she pulled the band that tied her hair and in one swift movement she wrapped it around my neck. I felt the tension of the band on my skin, but somehow it did not seem real.

Don Juan had always said to me that our great enemy is the fact that we never believe what is happening to us. At the moment doña Soledad was wrapping the cloth like a noose around my throat, I knew what he meant. But even after I had had that intellectual reflection, my body did not react. I remained flaccid, almost indifferent to what seemed to be my death.

I felt the exertion of her arms and shoulders as she tightened the band around my neck. She was choking me with great force and expertise. I began to gasp. Her eyes stared at me with a maddening glare. I knew then that she intended to kill me.

Don Juan had said that when we finally realize what is going on it is usually too late to turn back. He contended that it is always the intellect that fools us, because it receives the message first, but rather than giving it credence and acting on it immediately, it dallies with it instead.

I heard then, or perhaps I felt, a snapping sound at the base of my neck, right behind my windpipe. I knew that she had cracked my neck. My ears buzzed and then they tingled. I experienced an exceptional clarity of hearing. I thought that I must be dying. I loathed my incapacity to do anything to defend myself. I could not even move a muscle to kick her. I was unable to breathe any more. My body shivered, and suddenly I stood up and was free, out of her deadly grip. I looked down on the bed, I seemed to be looking down from the ceiling. I saw my body, motionless and limp on top of hers. I saw horror in her eyes. I wanted her to let go of the noose. I had a fit of wrath for having been so stupid and hit her smack on the forehead with my fist. She shrieked and held her head and then passed out, but before she did I caught a fleeting glimpse of a phantasmagoric scene. I saw doña Soledad being hurled out of the bed by the force of my blow. I saw her running towards the wall and huddling up against it like a frightened child.

The next impression I had was of having a terrible difficulty in breathing. My neck hurt. My throat seemed to have dried up so intensely that I could not swallow. It took me a long time to gather enough strength to get up. I then examined doña Soledad. She was lying unconscious on the bed. She had an enormous red lump on her forehead. I got some water and splashed it on her face, the way don Juan had always done with me. When she regained consciousness I made her walk, holding her by the armpits. She was soaked in perspiration. I applied towels with cold water on her forehead. She threw up, and I was almost sure she had a brain concussion. She was shivering. I tried to pile clothes and blankets over her for warmth but she took off all her clothes and turned her body to face the wind. She asked me to leave her alone and said that if the wind changed direction, it would be a sign that she was going to get well. She held my hand in a sort of brief handshake and told me that it was fate that had pitted us against each other.

'I think one of us was supposed to die tonight,' she said.

'Don't be silly. You're not finished yet,' I said and really meant it.

Something made me feel confident that she was all right. I went outside, picked up a stick and walked to my car. The dog growled. He was still curled up on the seat. I told him to get out. He meekly jumped out. There was something different about him. I saw his enormous shape trotting away in the semidarkness. He went to his corral.

I was free. I sat in the car for a moment to deliberate. No, I was not free. Something was pulling me back into the house. I had unfinished business there. I was no longer afraid of doña Soledad. In fact, an extraordinary indifference had taken possession of me. I felt that she had given me, deliberately or unconsciously, a supremely important lesson. Under the horrendous pressure of her attempt to kill me, I had actually acted upon her from a level that would have been inconceivable under normal circumstances. I had nearly been strangled; something in that confounded room of hers had rendered me helpless and yet I had extricated myself. I could not imagine what had happened. Perhaps it was as don Juan had always maintained, that all of us have an extra potential, something which is there but rarely gets to be used. I had actually hit doña Soledad from a phantom position.

I took my flashlight from the car, went back into the house, lit all the kerosene lanterns I could find and sat down at the table in the front room to write. Working relaxed me.

Towards dawn doña Soledad stumbled out of her room. She could hardly keep her balance. She was completely naked. She became ill and collapsed by the door. I gave her some water and tried to cover her with a blanket. She refused it. I became concerned with the possibility of her losing body heat. She muttered that she had to be naked if she expected the wind to cure her. She made a plaster of mashed leaves, applied it to her forehead and fixed it in place with her turban. She wrapped a blanket around her body and came to the table where I was writing and sat down facing me. Her eyes were red. She looked truly sick.

'There is something I must tell you,' she said in a weak voice. 'The Nagual set me up to wait for you; I had to wait even if it took twenty years. He gave me instructions on how to entice you and steal your power. He knew that sooner or later you had to come to see Pablito and Nestor, so he told me to use that opportunity to bewitch you and take everything you have. The Nagual said that if I lived an impeccable life my power would bring you here when there would be no one else in the house. My power did that. Today you came when everybody was gone. My impeccable life had helped me. All that was left for me to do was to take your power and then kill you.'

'But why would you want to do such a horrible thing?'

'Because I need your power for my own journey. The Nagual had to set it up that way. You had to be the one; after all, I really don't know you. You mean nothing to me. So why shouldn't I take something I need so desperately from someone who doesn't count at all? Those were the Nagual's very words.'

'Why would the Nagual want to hurt me? You yourself said that he worried about me.'

'What I've done to you tonight has nothing to do with what he feels for you or myself. This is only between the two of us. There have been no witnesses to what took place today between the two of us, because both of us are part of the Nagual himself. But you in particular have received and kept something of him that I don't have, something that I need desperately, the special power that he gave you. The Nagual said that he had given something to each of his six children. I can't reach Eligio. I can't take it from my girls, so that leaves you as my prey. I made the power the Nagual gave me grow, and in growing it changed my body. You made your power grow too. I wanted that power from you and for that I had to kill you. The Nagual said that even if you didn't die, you would fall under my spell and become my prisoner for life if I wanted it so. Either way, your power was going to be mine.'

'But how could my death benefit you?'

'Not your death but your power. I did it because I need a boost; without it I will have a hellish time on my journey. I don't have enough guts. That's why I dislike la Gorda. She's young and has plenty of guts. I'm old and have second thoughts and doubts. If you want to know the truth, the real struggle is between Pablito and myself. He is my mortal enemy, not you. The Nagual said that your power could make my journey easier and help me get what I need.'

'How on earth can Pablito be your enemy?'

'When the Nagual changed me, he knew what would eventually happen. First of all, he set me up so my eyes would face the north, and although you and my girls are the same, I am the opposite of you people. I go in a different direction. Pablito, Nestor and Benigno are with you; the direction of their eyes is the same as yours. All of you will go together toward Yucatán.

'Pablito is my enemy not because his eyes were set in the opposite direction, but because he is my son. This is what I had to tell you, even though you don't know what I am talking about. I have to enter into the other world. Where the Nagual is now. Where Genaro and Eligio are now. Even if I have to destroy Pablito to do that.'

'What are you saying, doña Soledad? You're crazy!'

'No, I am not. There is nothing more important for us living beings than to enter into that world. I will tell you that for me that is true. To get to that world I live the way the Nagual taught me. Without the hope of that world I am nothing, nothing. I was a fat old cow. Now that hope gives me a guide, a direction, and even if I can't take your power, I still have my purpose.'

She rested her head on the table, using her arms as a pillow. The force of her statements had numbed me. I had not understood what exactly she had meant, but I could almost empathize with her plea, although it was the strangest thing I had yet heard from her that night. Her purpose was a warrior's purpose, in don Juan's style and terminology. I never knew, however, that one had to destroy people in order to fulfil it.

She lifted up her head and looked at me with half-closed eyelids.

'At the beginning everything worked fine for me today,' she said. 'I was a bit scared when you drove up. I had waited years for that moment. The Nagual told me that you like women. He said you are an easy prey for them, so I played you for a quick finish. I figured that you would go for it. The Nagual had taught me how I should grab you at the moment when you are the weakest. I was leading you to that moment with my body. But you became suspicious. I was too clumsy. I had taken you to my room, as the Nagual told me to do, so the lines of my floor would entrap you and make you helpless.

But you fooled my floor by liking it and by watching its lines intently. It had no power as long as your eyes were on its lines. Your body knew what to do. Then you scared my floor, yelling the way you did. Sudden noises like that are deadly, especially the voice of a sorcerer. The power of my floor died out like a flame. I knew it, but you didn't.

'You were about to leave then so I had to stop you. The Nagual had shown me how to use my hand to grab you. I tried to do that, but my power was low. My floor was scared. Your eyes had numbed its lines. No one else has ever laid eyes on them. So I failed in my attempt to grab your neck. You got out of my grip before I had time to squeeze you. I knew then that you were slipping away and I tried one final attack. I used the key the Nagual said would affect you the most, fright. I frightened you with my shrieks and that gave me enough power to subdue you. I thought I had you, but my stupid dog got excited. He's stupid and knocked me off of you when I had you almost under my spell. As I see it now, perhaps my dog was not so stupid after all. Maybe he noticed your double and charged against it but knocked me over instead.'

'You said he wasn't your dog.'

'I lied. He was my trump card. The Nagual taught me that I should always have a trump card, an unsuspected trick. Somehow, I knew that I might need my dog. When I took you to see my friend, it was really him; the coyote is my girls' friend. I wanted my dog to sniff you. When you ran into the house I had to be rough with him. I pushed him inside your car, making him yell with pain. He's too big and could hardly fit over the seat. I told him right then to maul you to shreds. I knew that if you had been badly bitten by my dog you would have been helpless and I could have finished you off without any trouble. You escaped again, but you couldn't leave the house. I knew then that I had to be patient and wait for the darkness. Then the wind changed direction and I was sure of my success.

'The Nagual had told me that he knew without a doubt that you would like me as a woman. It was a matter of waiting for the right moment. The Nagual said that you would kill your-

self once you realized I had stolen your power. But in case I
failed to steal it, or in case you didn't kill yourself, or in case
I didn't want to keep you alive as my prisoner, I should then
use my headband to choke you to death. He even showed me
the place where I had to throw your carcass: a bottomless pit,
a crack in the mountains, not too far from here, where goats
always disappear. The Nagual never mentioned your awesome
side, though. I've told you that one of us was supposed to die
tonight. I didn't know it was going to be me. The Nagual gave
me the feeling that I would win. How cruel of him not to
tell me everything about you.'

'Think of me, doña Soledad. I knew even less than you did.'

'It's not the same. The Nagual prepared me for years for
this. I knew every detail. You were in my bag. The Nagual
even showed me the leaves I should always keep fresh and
handy to make you numb. I put them in the tub as if they
were for fragrance. You didn't notice that I used another
kind of leaf for my tub. You fell for everything I had prepared
for you. And yet your awesome side won in the end.'

'What do you mean my awesome side?'

'The one that hit me and will kill me tonight. Your horrendous double that came out to finish me. I will never forget
it and if I live, which I doubt, I will never be the same.'

'Did it look like me?'

'It was you, of course, but not as you look now. I can't
really say what it looked like. When I want to think about it
I get dizzy.'

I told her about my fleeting perception that she had left her
body with the impact of my blow. I intended to prod her with
the account. It seemed to me that the reason behind the whole
event had been to force us to draw from sources that are ordinarily barred to us. I had positively given her a dreadful blow;
I had caused profound damage to her body, and yet I could
not have done it myself. I did feel I had hit her with my left
fist, the enormous red lump on her forehead attested to that,
yet I had no swelling in my knuckles or the slightest pain or
discomfort in them. A blow of that magnitude could even
have broken my hand.

Upon hearing my description of how I had seen her huddling against the wall, she became thoroughly desperate. I asked her if she had had any inkling of what I had seen, such as a sensation of leaving her body, or a fleeting perception of the room.

'I know now that I am doomed,' she said. 'Very few survive a touch of the double. If my soul has left already I won't survive. I'll get weaker and weaker until I die.'

Her eyes had a wild glare. She raised herself and seemed to be on the verge of striking me, but she slumped back.

'You've taken my soul,' she said. 'You must have it in your pouch now. Why did you have to tell me, though?'

I swore to her that I had had no intentions of hurting her, that I had acted in whatever form only in self-defence and therefore I bore no malice towards her.

'If you don't have my soul in your pouch, it's even worse,' she said. 'It must be roaming aimlessly around. I will never get it back, then.'

Doña Soledad seemed to be void of energy. Her voice became weaker. I wanted her to go and lie down. She refused to leave the table.

'The Nagual said that if I failed completely I should then give you his message,' she said. 'He told me to tell you that he had replaced your body a long time ago. You are himself now.'

'What did he mean by that?'

'He's a sorcerer. He entered into your old body and replaced its luminosity. Now you shine like the Nagual himself. You're not your father's son any more. You are the Nagual himself.'

Doña Soledad stood up. She was groggy. She appeared to want to say something else but had trouble vocalizing. She walked to her room. I helped her to the door; she did not want me to enter. She dropped the blanket that covered her and lay down on her bed. She asked in a very soft voice if I would go to a hill a short distance away and watch from there to see if the wind was coming. She added in a most casual manner that I should take her dog with me. Somehow her request did not sound right. I said that I would climb up on the roof and look from there. She turned her back to me and said that the least I could do for her was to take her dog to the hill so that he could lure the wind. I became very irritated with her. Her room in the darkness gave out a most eerie feeling. I went into the kitchen and got two lanterns and brought them back with me. At the sight of the light she screamed hysterically. I let out a yell myself but for a different reason. When the light hit the room I saw the floor curled up, like a cocoon, around her bed. My perception was so fleeting that the next instant I could have sworn that the shadow of the wire protective masks of the lanterns had created that ghastly scene. My phantom perception made me furious. I shook her by the shoulders. She wept like a child and promised not to try any more of her tricks. I placed the lanterns on the chest of drawers and she fell asleep instantly.

By midmorning the wind had changed. I felt a strong gust coming through the north window. Around noon doña Soledad came out again. She seemed a bit wobbly. The redness in her eyes had disappeared and the swelling on her forehead had diminished; there was hardly any visible lump.

I felt that it was time for me to leave. I told her that although I had written down the message that she had given me from don Juan, it did not clarify anything.

'You're not your father's son any more. You are now the Nagual himself,' she said.

There was something truly incongruous about me. A few hours before I had been helpless and doña Soledad had actually tried to kill me; but at that moment, when she was speaking to me, I had forgotten the horror of that event. And yet, there was another part of me that could spend days mulling over meaningless confrontations with people concerning my personality or my work. That part seemed to be the real me, the me that I had known all my life. The me, however, who had gone through a bout with death that night, and then forgotten about it, was not real. It was me and yet it was not. In the light of such incongruities don Juan's claims seemed to be less farfetched, but still unacceptable.

Doña Soledad seemed absentminded. She smiled peacefully. 'Oh, they are here!' she said suddenly. 'How fortunate for me. My girls are here. Now they'll take care of me.'

She seemed to have had a turn for the worse. She looked as strong as ever, but her behaviour was more dissociated. My fears mounted. I did not know whether to leave her there or take her to a hospital in the city, several hundred miles away.

All of a sudden she jumped up like a little child and ran out the front door and down the driveway towards the main road. Her dog ran after her. I hurriedly got in my car in order to catch up with her. I had to drive down the path in reverse since there was no space to turn around. As I approached the road I saw through the back window that doña Soledad was surrounded by four young women.

2 THE LITTLE SISTERS

Doña Soledad seemed to be explaining something to the four women who surrounded her. She moved her arms in dramatic gestures and held her head in her hands. It was obvious she was telling them about me. I drove up the driveway to where I had been parked before. I intended to wait for them there. I deliberated whether to remain in the car or to sit casually on the left bumper. I opted to stand by the car door, ready to jump in and drive away if something like the events of the previous day were going to be repeated.

I was very tired. I had not slept a wink for over twenty-four hours. My plan was to disclose to the young women as much as I could about the incident with doña Soledad, so they could take the necessary steps to aid her, and then I would leave. Their presence had brought about a definite change. Everything seemed to be charged with new vigour and energy. I felt the change when I saw doña Soledad surrounded by them.

Doña Soledad's revelation that they were don Juan's apprentices had given them such a tantalizing appeal that I could hardly wait to meet them. I wondered if they were like doña Soledad. She had said that they were like myself and that we were going in the same direction. That could be easily interpreted in a positive sense. I wanted to believe that more than anything else.

Don Juan used to call them 'las hermanitas', the little sisters, a most befitting name at least for the two I had met, Lidia and Rosa, two wispy, pixie-like, charming young women. I figured that they must have been in their early twenties when I had first met them, although Pablito and Nestor always refused to talk about their ages. The other two, Josefina and Elena, were a total mystery to me. I used to hear their names being mentioned from time to time, always in some unfavourable context. I had deduced from passing remarks made by don Juan that they were somehow freakish, one was crazy and the other obese; thus they were kept in isolation. Once I bumped into Josefina as I walked into the house with don Juan. He introduced me to her, but she covered her face and ran away before I had time to greet her. Another time I caught Elena washing clothes. She was enormous. I thought that she must be suffering from a glandular disorder. I said hello to her but she did not turn around. I never saw her face.

After the buildup that doña Soledad had given them with her disclosure, I felt driven to talk with the mysterious 'hermanitas', and at the same time I was almost afraid of them.

I casually looked down the driveway, bracing myself to meet all of them at once. The driveway was deserted. There was no one approaching, and only a minute before they had been no more than thirty yards from the house. I climbed up on the roof of the car to look. There was no one coming, not even the dog. I panicked. I slid down and was about to jump in the car and drive away when I heard someone say, 'Hey, look who's here.'

I quickly turned around to face two girls who had just stepped out of the house. I deduced that all of them must have run ahead of me and entered the house through the back door. I sighed with relief.

The two young girls came towards me. I had to admit to myself that I had never really noticed them before. They were beautiful, dark and extremely lean, but without being skinny. Their long black hair was braided. They wore plain skirts, blue denim jackets and low-heeled, soft-soled brown shoes. They were barelegged and their legs were shapely and muscular. They must have been about five feet three or five feet four inches. They seemed to be very physical; they moved with great prowess. One of them was Lidia, the other was Rosa.

I greeted them, and then in unison they initiated a handshake. They flanked me. They looked healthy and vigorous.

I asked them to help me get the packages out of the boot. As we were carrying them into the house, I heard a deep growl, so deep and near that it seemed more like a lion's roar.

'What was that?' I asked Lidia.

'Don't you know?' she asked with a tone of disbelief.

'It must be the dog,' Rosa said as they ran into the house, practically dragging me with them.

We placed the packages on the table and sat on two benches. Both girls were facing me. I told them that doña Soledad was very ill and that I was about to take her to the hospital in the city, since I did not know what else to do to help her.

As I spoke I realized that I was treading on dangerous ground. I had no way of assessing how much information I should divulge to them about the true nature of my bout with doña Soledad. I began to look for clues. I thought that if I watched carefully, their voices or the expression on their faces would betray how much they knew. But they remained silent and let me do all the talking. I began to doubt that I should volunteer any information at all. In my effort to figure out what to do and not blunder, I ended up talking nonsense. Lidia cut me off. In a dry tone she said that I should not concern myself with doña Soledad's health because they had already taken steps to help her. That statement forced me to ask her if she knew what doña Soledad's trouble was.

'You've taken her soul,' she said accusingly.

My first reaction was to defend myself. I began to talk vehemently but ended up contradicting myself. They stared at me. I was making no sense at all. I tried again to say the same thing in a different way. My fatigue was so intense that I could hardly organize my thoughts. Finally I gave up.

'Where are Pablito and Nestor?' I asked after a long pause.

'They'll be here shortly,' Lidia said briskly.

'Were you with them?' I asked.

'No!' she exclaimed, and stared at me.

'We never go together,' Rosa explained. 'Those bums are different from us.'

Lidia made an imperative gesture with her foot to shut her up. She seemed to be the one who gave the orders. Catching the movement of her feet brought to my awareness a most peculiar facet of my relationship with don Juan. In the countless times that we had roamed together, he had succeeded in teaching me, without really trying, a system of covert communication through some coded movements of the feet. I watched Lidia give Rosa the sign for horrible, a sign given when anything that happens to be in sight of the signers is unpleasant or dangerous. In this case me. I laughed. I remembered that don Juan had given me that sign when I first met don Genaro.

I pretended not to be aware of what was going on in order to find out if I could decode all their signs.

Rosa made the sign that she wanted to step on me. Lidia answered with an imperative sign for no.

According to don Juan, Lidia was very talented. As far as he was concerned she was more sensitive and alert than Pablito and Nestor and myself. I had always been incapable of making friends with her. She was aloof, and very cutting. She had enormous, black, shifty eyes that never looked straight at anyone, high cheekbones and a chiselled nose, which was a bit flat and broad at the bridge. I remembered her having red, sore eyelids and everyone taunting her on account of that. The redness of her eyelids had disappeared but she continued to rub her eyes and blink a great deal. During my years of association with don Juan and don Genaro I had seen Lidia the most, and yet we had probably never exchanged more than a dozen words with each other. Pablito regarded her as a most dangerous being. I always thought she was just extremely shy.

Rosa, on the other hand, was very boisterous. I thought she was the youngest. Her eyes were very frank and shiny. She was never shifty, but very bad-tempered. I had talked with Rosa more than anyone else. She was friendly, very bold and very funny.

'Where are the others?' I asked Rosa. 'Aren't they going to come out?'

'They will be out shortly,' Lidia answered.

I could tell from their expressions that friendliness was not what they had in mind. Judging from their foot messages they were as dangerous as doña Soledad, and yet as I sat there looking at them it occurred to me that they were gorgeously beautiful. I had the warmest feelings for them. In fact, the more they stared into my eyes the more intense that feeling became. At one moment it was sheer passion that I felt for them. They were so alluring that I could have sat there for hours just looking at them, but a sobering thought made me stand up. I was not going to repeat my bungling of the night before. I decided that the best defence was to put my cards on the table. In a firm tone I told them that don Juan had set up some sort of trial for me using doña Soledad, or vice versa. Chances were that he had also set them up in the same fashion, and we were going to be pitted against one another in some sort of battle that could result in injury to some of us. I appealed to their sense of warriorship. If they were the truthful heirs of don Juan, they had to be impeccable with me, reveal their designs and not behave like ordinary, greedy human beings.

I turned to Rosa and asked her the reason for wishing to step on me. She was taken aback for an instant and then she became angry. Her eyes flared with rage; her small mouth contracted.

Lidia, in a very coherent manner, said that I had nothing to fear from them, and that Rosa was angry with me because I had hurt doña Soledad. Her feelings were purely a personal reaction.

I said then that it was time I left. I stood up. Lidia made a gesture to stop me. She seemed scared or deeply concerned. She began to protest, when a noise coming from outside the door distracted me. The two girls jumped to my side. Something heavy was leaning or pushing against the door. I noticed then that the girls had secured it with the heavy iron bar. I had a feeling of disgust. The whole affair was going to be repeated again and I was sick and tired of it all.

The girls glanced at each other, then looked at me and then looked at each other again.

I heard the whining and heavy breathing of a large animal outside the house. It might have been the dog. Exhaustion blinded me at that point. I rushed to the door, removed the heavy iron bar and started to open it. Lidia threw herself against the door and shut it again.

'The Nagual was right,' she said, out of breath. 'You think and think. You're dumber than I thought.'

She pulled me back to the table. I rehearsed, in my mind, the best way to tell them, once and for all, that I had had enough. Rosa sat next to me, touching me; I could feel her leg nervously rubbing against mine. Lidia was standing facing me, looking at me fixedly. Her burning black eyes seemed to be saying something I could not understand.

I began to speak but I did not finish. I had a sudden and most profound awareness. My body was aware of a greenish light, a fluorescence outside the house. I did not see or hear anything. I was simply aware of the light as if I were suddenly falling asleep and my thoughts were turning into images that were superimposed on the world of everyday life. The light was moving at a great speed. I could sense it with my stomach. I followed it, or rather I focused my attention on it for an instant as it moved around. A great clarity of mind ensued from focusing my attention on the light. I knew then that in that house, in the presence of those people, it was wrong and dangerous to behave as an innocent bystander.

'Aren't you afraid?' Rosa asked, pointing to the door.

Her voice disrupted my concentration.

I admitted that whatever was there was scaring me at a very deep level, enough to make me die of fright. I wanted to say more, but right then I had a surge of wrath and I wanted to see and talk with doña Soledad. I did not trust her. I went directly to her room. She was not there. I began to call her, bellowing her name. The house had one more room. I pushed the door open and rushed inside. There was no one in there. My anger increased in the same proportion as my fear.

I went out the back door and walked around to the front. Not even the dog was in sight. I banged on the front door furiously. Lidia opened it. I entered. I yelled at her to tell me where everybody was. She lowered her eyes and did not answer. She wanted to close the door but I would not let her. She quickly walked away and went into the other room.

I sat down again at the table. Rosa had not moved. She seemed to be frozen on the spot.

'We are the same,' she said suddenly. 'The Nagual told us that.'

'Tell me, then, what was prowling around the house?' I asked.

'The ally,' she said.

'Where is it now?'

'It is still here. It won't go. The moment you're weak it'll squash you. But we're not the ones who can tell you anything.'

'Who can tell me, then?'

'La Gorda!' Rosa exclaimed, opening her eyes as wide as she could. 'She's the one. She knows everything.'

Rosa asked me if she could close the door, just to be on the safe side. Without waiting for an answer she inched her way to the door and slammed it shut.

'There is nothing we can do except wait until everyone is here ' she said.

Lidia came back into the room with a package, an object wrapped up in a piece of dark yellow cloth. She seemed very relaxed. I noticed that she had a most commandeering touch. Somehow she imparted her mood to Rosa and myself.

'Do you know what I have here?' she asked me.

I did not have the vaguest idea. She began to unwrap it in a very deliberate manner, taking her time. Then she stopped and looked at me. She seemed to vacillate. She grinned as if she were too shy to show what was in the bundle.

'This package was left by the Nagual for you,' she muttered, 'but I think we'd better wait for la Gorda.'

I insisted that she unwrap it. She gave me a ferocious look and took the package out of the room without saying another word.

I enjoyed Lidia's game. She had performed something quite in line with don Juan's teachings. She had given me a demonstration of how to get the best use out of an average situation.

By bringing the package to me and pretending that she was going to open it, after disclosing that don Juan had left it for me, she had indeed created a mystery that was almost unbearable. She knew that I had to stay if I wanted to find out the contents of that package. I could think of a number of things that might be in that bundle. Perhaps it was the pipe don Juan used when handling psychotropic mushrooms. He had intimated that the pipe would be given to me for safekeeping. Or it might have been his knife, or his leather pouch, or even his sorcery power objects. On the other hand, it might have been merely a ploy on Lidia's part; don Juan was too sophisticated, too abstract to leave me an heirloom.

I told Rosa that I was dead on my feet and weak from hunger. My idea was to drive to the city, rest for a couple of days and then come back to see Pablito and Nestor. I said that by then I might even get to meet the other two girls.

Lidia returned then and Rosa told her of my intention to leave.

'The Nagual gave us orders to attend to you as if you were himself,' Lidia said. 'We are all the Nagual himself, but you are even more so, for some reason that no one understands.'

Both of them talked to me at once and guaranteed in various ways that no one was going to attempt anything against me as doña Soledad had. Both of them had such a fierce look of honesty in their eyes that my body was overwhelmed. I trusted them.

'You must stay until la Gorda comes back,' Lidia said.

'The Nagual said that you should sleep in his bed,' Rosa added.

I began to pace the floor in the throes of a weird dilemma. On the one hand, I wanted to stay and rest; I felt physically at ease and happy in their presence, something I had not felt the day before with doña Soledad. My reasonable side, on the other hand, had not relaxed at all. At that level, I was as frightened as I had been all along. I had had moments of blind despair and had taken bold actions, but after the momentum of those actions had ceased, I had felt as vulnerable as ever.

I engaged in some soul-searching analysis as I paced the

room almost frantically. The two girls remained quiet, looking at me anxiously. Then all of a sudden the riddle was solved; I knew that something in me was just pretending to be afraid. I had become accustomed to reacting that way in don Juan's presence. Throughout the years of our association I had relied heavily on him to furnish me with convenient pacifiers for my fright. My dependency on him had given me solace and security. But it was no longer tenable. Don Juan was gone. His apprentices did not have his patience, or his sophistication, or his sheer command. With them my need to seek solace was plain stupidity.

The girls led me to the other room. The window faced the southeast, and so did the bed, which was a thick mat, like a mattress. A two-foot-long, bulky piece of maguey stalk had been carved so that the porous tissue served as a pillow, or a neckrest. In the middle part of it there was a gentle dip. The surface of the maguey was very smooth. It appeared to have been hand rubbed. I tried the bed and the pillow. The comfort and bodily satisfaction I experienced were unusual. Lying on don Juan's bed I felt secure and fulfilled. An unequalled peace swept through my body. I had had a similar feeling once before when don Juan had made a bed for me on top of a hill in the desert in northern Mexico. I fell asleep.

I woke up in the early evening. Lidia and Rosa were nearly on top of me, sound asleep. I stayed motionless for one or two seconds, then both of them woke up at once.

Lidia yawned and said that they had had to sleep next to me in order to protect me and make me rest. I was famished. Lidia sent Rosa to the kitchen to make us some food. In the meantime she lit all the lanterns in the house. When the food was ready we sat down at the table. I felt as if I had known them or been with them all my life. We ate in silence.

When Rosa was clearing the table I asked Lidia if all of them slept in the Nagual's bed; it was the only other bed in the house besides doña Soledad's. Lidia said, in a matter-of-fact tone, that they had moved out of that house years before to a place of their own in the same vicinity, and that Pablito had also moved when they did and lived with Nestor and Benigno.

'But what's happened to you people? I thought that you were all together,' I said.

'Not any more,' Lidia replied. 'Since the Nagual left we have had separate tasks. The Nagual joined us and the Nagual took us apart.'

'And where's the Nagual now?' I asked in the most casual tone I could affect.

Both of them looked at me and then glanced at each other.

'Oh, we don't know,' Lidia said. 'He and Genaro left.'

She seemed to be telling the truth, but I insisted once more that they tell me what they knew.

'We really don't know anything,' Lidia snapped at me, obviously flustered by my questions. 'They moved to another area. You have to ask that question of la Gorda. She has something to tell you. She knew yesterday that you had come and we rushed all night to get here. We were afraid that you were dead. The Nagual told us that you are the only one we should help and trust. He said that you are himself.'

She covered her face and giggled and then added as an afterthought, 'But that's hard to believe.'

'We don't know you,' Rosa said. 'That's the trouble. The four of us feel the same way. We were afraid that you were dead and then when we saw you, we got mad at you for not being dead. Soledad is like our mother; maybe more than that.'

They exchanged conspiratorial looks with each other. I immediately interpreted that as a sign of trouble. They were up to no good. Lidia noticed my sudden distrust, which must have been written all over my face. She reacted with a series of assertions about their desire to help me. I really had no reason to doubt their sincerity. If they had wanted to hurt me they could have done so while I was asleep. She sounded so earnest that I felt petty. I decided to distribute the gifts I had brought for them. I told them that there were unimportant trinkets in the packages and that they could choose any one they liked. Lidia said that they would prefer it if I assigned the gifts myself. In a very polite tone she added that they would be grateful if I would also cure Soledad.

'What do you think I should do to cure her?' I asked her after a long silence.

'Use your double,' she said in a matter-of-fact tone.

I carefully went over the fact that doña Soledad had nearly assassinated me and that I had survived by the grace of something in me, which was neither my skill nor my knowledge. As far as I was concerned that undefined something that seemed to have delivered a blow to her was real, but unreachable. In short, I could not help doña Soledad any more than I could walk to the moon.

They listened to me attentively and remained quiet but agitated.

'Where is doña Soledad now?' I asked Lidia.

'She's with la Gorda,' she said in a despondent tone. 'La Gorda took her away and is trying to cure her, but we really don't know where they are. That's the truth.'

'And where's Josefina?'

'She went to get the Witness. He is the only one who can cure Soledad. Rosa thinks that you know more than the Witness, but since you're angry with Soledad, you want her dead. We don't blame you.'

I assured them that I was not angry with her, and above all I did not want her dead.

'Cure her, then!' Rosa said in an angry, high-pitched voice. 'The Witness has told us that you always know what to do, and the Witness can't be wrong.'

'And who in the devil is the Witness?'

'Nestor is the Witness,' Lidia said as if she were reluctant to voice his name. 'You know that. You have to.'

I remembered that during our last meeting don Genaro had called Nestor the Witness. I thought at the time that the name was a joke or a ploy that don Genaro was using to ease the gripping tension and the anguish of those last moments together.

'That was no joke,' Lidia said in a firm tone. 'Genaro and the Nagual followed a different path with the Witness. They took him along with them everywhere they went. And I mean everywhere! The Witness has witnessed all there is to witness.'

Obviously there was a tremendous misunderstanding between us. I laboured to explain that I was practically a stranger to them. Don Juan had kept me away from everyone, including Pablito and Nestor. Outside of the casual hellos and good-byes that all of them had exchanged with me over the years, we had never actually talked. I knew all of them mainly through the descriptions that don Juan had given me. Although I had once met Josefina I could not remember what she looked like, and all I had ever seen of la Gorda was her gigantic behind. I said to them that I had not even known, until the day before, that the four of them were don Juan's apprentices, and that Benigno was part of the group as well.

They exchanged a coy look with each other. Rosa moved her lips to say something but Lidia gave her a command with her feet. I felt that after my long and soulful explanation they should not still sneak messages to each other. My nerves were so taut that their covert foot movements were just the thing to send me into a rage. I yelled at them at the top of my lungs and banged on the table with my right hand. Rosa stood up with unbelievable speed, and I suppose as a response to her sudden movement, my body, by itself, without the notice of my reason, moved a step back, just in time to avoid by inches a blow from a massive stick or some heavy object that Rosa was wielding in her left hand. It came down on the table with a thunderous noise.

I heard again, as I had heard the night before while doña Soledad was choking me, a most peculiar and mysterious sound, a dry sound like a pipe breaking, right behind my windpipe at the base of my neck. My ears popped, and with the speed of lightning my left arm came down on top of Rosa's stick and crushed it. I saw the whole scene myself, as if I had been watching a movie.

Rosa screamed and I realized then that I had leaned forward with all my weight and had struck the back of her hand with my left fist. I was appalled. Whatever was happening to me was not real. It was a nightmare. Rosa kept on screaming. Lidia took her into don Juan's room. I heard her yells of pain for a few moments longer and then they stopped. I sat down at the table. My thoughts were dissociated and incoherent.

The peculiar sound at the base of my neck was something I had become keenly aware of. Don Juan had described it as the sound one makes at the moment of changing speed. I had the faint recollection of having experienced it in his company. Although I had become aware of it the previous night, I had not fully acknowledged it until it happened with Rosa. I realized then that the sound had created a special sensation of heat on the roof of my mouth and inside my ears. The force and dryness of the sound made me think of the peal of a large, cracked bell.

Lidia returned awhile later. She seemed more calm and collected. She even smiled. I asked her to please help me unravel that riddle and tell me what had happened. After a long vacillation she told me that when I had yelled and banged on the table Rosa got excited and nervous, and believing I was going to hurt them, she had tried to strike me with her 'dream hand'. I had dodged her blow and hit her on the back of her hand, the same way I had struck doña Soledad. Lidia said that Rosa's hand would be useless unless I found a way to help her.

Rosa walked into the room then. Her arm was wrapped with a piece of cloth. She looked at me. Her eyes were like those of a child. My feelings were at the height of turmoil. Some part of me felt ugly and guilty. But again another part remained unruffled. Had it not been for that part I would not have survived either doña Soledad's attack or Rosa's devastating blow.

After a long silence I told them that it was very petty of me to be annoyed by their foot messages, but that there was no comparison between yelling or banging on the table and what Rosa had done. In view of the fact that I had no familiarity with their practices, she could have severed my arm with her blow.

I demanded, in a very intimidating tone, to see her hand. She reluctantly unwrapped it. It was swollen and red. There was no doubt left in my mind that these people were carrying out some sort of test that don Juan had set up for me. By confronting them I was being hurled into a realm which was impossible to reach or accept in rational terms. He had said time and time again that my rationality comprised only a very small part of what he had called the totality of oneself. Under the impact of the unfamiliar and the altogether real danger of my physical annihilation, my body had had to make use of its hidden resources, or die. The trick seemed to be in the truthful acceptance of the possibility that such resources exist and can be reached. The years of training had been but the steps to arrive at that acceptance. Truthful to his premise of no compromise, don Juan had aimed at a total victory or a total defeat for me. If the training had failed to put me in contact with my hidden resources, the test would have made it evident, in which case there would have been very little I could have done. Don Juan had said to doña Soledad that I would have killed myself. Being such a profound connoisseur of human nature, he was probably right.

It was time to adopt a new course of action. Lidia had said that I could help Rosa and doña Soledad with the same force that had caused them injury; the problem, therefore, was to get the right sequence of feelings, or thoughts, or whatever, that led my body to unleash that force. I took Rosa's hand and rubbed it. I willed it to be cured. I had only the best feelings for her. I caressed her hand and hugged her for a long time. I rubbed her head and she fell asleep on my shoulder but there was no change in the redness or the swelling.

Lidia watched me without saying a word. She smiled at me. I wanted to tell her that I was a fiasco as a healer. Her eyes seemed to catch my mood and they held it until it froze.

Rosa wanted to sleep. She was either dead tired or ill. I did not want to find out which. I picked her up in my arms; she was lighter than I would have imagined. I took her to don Juan's bed and gently placed her on it. Lidia covered her. The room was very dark. I looked out of the window and saw a cloudless sky filled with stars. Up to that moment I had been oblivious to the fact that we were at a very high altitude.

As I looked at the sky, I felt a surge of optimism. Somehow the stars looked festive to me. The southeast was indeed a lovely direction to face.

I had a sudden urge that I felt obliged to satisfy. I wanted to see how different the view of the sky was from doña Soledad's window, which faced the north. I took Lidia by the hand with the intention of leading her there, but a ticklish sensation on top of my head stopped me. It went like a ripple down my back to my waist, and from there it went to the pit of my stomach. I sat down on the mat. I made an effort to think about my feelings. It seemed that at the very moment I had felt the tickling on my head my thoughts had diminished in strength and number. I tried, but I could not involve myself in the usual mental process that I call thinking.

My mental deliberations made me oblivious to Lidia. She had knelt on the floor, facing me. I became aware that her enormous eyes were scrutinizing me from a few inches away. I automatically took her hand again and walked to doña Soledad's room. As we reached the door I felt her whole body stiffening. I had to pull her. I was about to cross the threshold when I caught sight of the bulky, dark mass of a human body huddled against the wall opposite the door. The sight was so unexpected that I gasped and let go of Lidia's hand. It was doña Soledad. She was resting her head against the wall. I turned to Lidia. She had recoiled a couple of steps. I wanted to whisper that doña Soledad had returned, but there were no sounds to my words although I was sure I had vocalized them. I would have tried to talk again had it not been that I had an urge to act. It was as if words took too much time and I had very little of it. I stepped into the room and walked over to doña Soledad. She appeared to be in great pain. I squatted by her side, and rather than asking her anything, I lifted her face to look at her. I saw something on her forehead; it looked like the plaster of leaves that she had made for herself. It was dark, viscous to the touch. I felt the imperative need to peel it off her forehead. In a very bold fashion I grabbed her head, tilted it back and yanked the plaster off. It was like peeling off rubber. She did not move or complain about pain. Underneath the plaster there was a yellowish-green blotch. It moved, as if it were alive or imbued with energy. I looked at it for a moment, unable to do anything. I poked it with my finger and it stuck to it like glue. I did not panic as I ordinarily would have; I rather liked the stuff. I stirred it with the tips of my fingers and all of it came off her forehead. I stood up. The gooey substance felt warm. It was like a sticky paste for an instant and then it dried up between my fingers and on the palm of my hand. I then felt another jolt of apprehension and ran to don Juan's room. I grabbed Rosa's arm and wiped the same fluorescent, yellowish-green stuff from her hand that I had wiped from doña Soledad's forehead.

My heart was pounding so hard that I could hardly stand on my feet. I wanted to lie down, but something in me pushed me to the window and made me jog on the spot.

I cannot recall how long I jogged there. Suddenly I felt that someone was wiping my neck and shoulders. I became aware then that I was practically nude, perspiring profusely. Lidia had a cloth around my shoulders and was wiping the sweat off my face. My normal thought processes came back to me all at once. I looked around the room. Rosa was sound asleep. I ran to doña Soledad's room. I expected to find her also asleep, but there was no one there. Lidia had trailed behind me. I told her what had happened. She rushed to Rosa and woke her up while I put on my clothes. Rosa did not want to wake up. Lidia grabbed her injured hand and squeezed it. In one single, springing movement Rosa stood up and was fully awake.

They began to rush around the house turning off the lanterns. They seemed to be getting ready to run away. I wanted to ask them why they were in such a hurry, when I realized that I had dressed in a great hurry myself. We were rushing together; not only that, but they seemed to be waiting for direct commands from me.

We ran out of the house carrying all the packages I had brought. Lidia had advised me not to leave any of them behind; I had not yet assigned them and they still belonged to me. I threw them in the back seat of the car while the two girls crammed into the front. I started the car and backed up slowly, finding my way in the darkness.

Once we were on the road I was brought face to face with the most pressing issue. Both of them said in unison that I was the leader; their actions were dependent on my decisions. I was the Nagual. We could not just run out of the house and drive away aimlessly. I had to guide them. But the truth was that I had no idea where to go or what to do. I turned casually to look at them. The headlights cast a glare inside the car and their eyes were like mirrors that reflected it. I remembered that don Juan's eyes did the same; they seemed to reflect more light than the eyes of an average person.

I knew that the two girls were aware of my impasse. Rather than making a joke about it in order to cover up my incapacity, I bluntly put the responsibility of a solution in their laps. I said that I lacked practice as the Nagual and would appreciate it if they would oblige me with a suggestion or a hint as to where we should go. They seemed disgusted with me. They clicked their tongues and shook their heads. I mentally shuffled through various courses of action, none of which was feasible, such as driving them to town, or taking them to Nestor's house, or even taking them to Mexico City.

I stopped the car. I was driving towards town. I wanted more than anything else in the world to have a heart-to-heart talk with the girls. I opened my mouth to begin, but they turned away from me, faced each other and put their arms around each other's shoulders. That appeared to be an indication that they had locked themselves in and were not listening to me.

My frustration was enormous. What I craved for at that moment was don Juan's mastery over any situation at hand, his intellectual companionship, his humour. Instead I was in the company of two nincompoops.

I caught a gesture of dejection in Lidia's face and that stopped my avalanche of self-pity. I became overtly aware, for the first time, that there was no end to our mutual disappointment. Obviously they too were accustomed, although in a different manner, to the mastery of don Juan. For them the shift from the Nagual himself to me must have been disastrous.

I sat for a long while with the motor running. Then all at once I again had a bodily shiver that started on the top of my head as a ticklish sensation and I knew then what had happened when I had entered doña Soledad's room awhile before. I had not seen her in an ordinary sense. What I had thought was doña Soledad huddled against the wall was in fact the memory of her leaving her body the instant after I had hit her. I also knew that when I touched that gooey, phosphorescent substance I had cured her, and that it was some sort of energy I had left in her head and in Rosa's hand with my blows.

A vision of a particular ravine went through my mind. I became convinced that doña Soledad and la Gorda were there. My knowledge was not a mere conjecture, it was rather a truth that needed no further corroboration. La Gorda had taken doña Soledad to the bottom of that particular ravine and was at that precise moment attempting to cure her. I wanted to tell her that it was wrong to treat the swelling in doña Soledad's forehead and that there was no longer a need for them to stay there.

I described my vision to the girls. Both of them told me, the way don Juan used to tell me, not to indulge. With him, however, that reaction was more congruous. I had never really minded his criticisms or scorn, but the two girls were in a different league. I felt insulted.

'I'll take you home,' I said. 'Where do you live?'

Lidia turned to me and in a most furious tone said that both of them were my wards and that I had to deliver them to safety, since at the request of the Nagual they had relinquished their freedom to act in order to help me.

I had a fit of anger at that point. I wanted to slap the two girls, but then I felt the curious shiver running through my body once more. It started again as a tickling on top of my head which went down my back until it reached my umbilical region, and then I knew where they lived. The ticklishness was like a shield, a soft, warm sheet of film. I could sense it physically, covering the area between my pubis and the edge of my rib cage. My wrath disappeared and was replaced by a strange sobriety, an aloofness, and at the same time a desire to laugh. I knew then of something transcendental. Under the impact of doña Soledad and the little sisters' actions, my body had suspended judgement; I had, in don Juan's terms, stopped the world. I had amalgamated two dissociated sensations. The ticklishness on the very top of my head and the dry cracking sound at the base of my neck: between them lay the means to that suspension of judgement.

As I sat in my car with those two girls, on the side of a deserted mountain road, I knew for a fact that for the first time I had had a complete awareness of stopping the world. That feeling brought to my mind the memory of another, similar, first-time bodily awareness I had had years before. It had to do with the ticklishness on top of the head. Don Juan said that sorcerers had to cultivate such a sensation and he described it at great length. According to him, it was a sort of itching, which was neither pleasurable nor painful, and which occurred on the very top of one's head. In order to make me aware of it, on an intellectual level, he described and analysed its features and then, on the practical side, he attempted to guide me in developing the necessary bodily awareness and memory of this feeling by making me run under branches or rocks that protruded on a horizontal plane a few inches above my height.

For years I tried to follow what he was pointing out to me, but on the one hand I was incapable of understanding what he meant by his description, and on the other hand I was incapable of providing my body with the adequate memory by following his pragmatic steps. Never did I feel anything on top of my head as I ran underneath the branches or rocks he had selected for his demonstrations. But one day my body by itself discovered the sensation while I was driving a high panel truck into a three-storey parking structure. I entered the gate of the structure at the same speed I usually did in my small, two-door sedan; the result was that from the high seat of the truck I perceived the transverse cement beam of the roof coming at my head. I could not stop the truck in time and the feeling I got was that the cement beam was scalping me. I had never driven a motor vehicle which was as high as that truck, thus I was incapable of making the necessary perceptual adjustments. The space between the roof of the truck and the roof of the parking structure seemed nonexistent for me. I felt the beam with my scalp.

That day I drove for hours inside the structure, giving my

body a chance to store the memory of that ticklish sensation.

I faced the two girls and wanted to tell them that I had just found out where they lived. I desisted. There was no way of describing to them that the ticklish sensation had made me remember a casual remark that don Juan had once made as we passed a house on our way to Pablito's place. He had pointed out an unusual feature in the surroundings and said that that house was an ideal place for quietness but was not a place to rest. I drove them there.

Their house was rather big. It was also an adobe structure with a tile roof like doña Soledad's. It had one long room in the front, a roofed, open-air kitchen in back of the house, a huge patio next to the kitchen and an area for chickens beyond the patio. The most important part of their house, however, was a closed room with two doors, one opening to the front room and the other to the back. Lidia said that they had built it themselves. I wanted to see it, but both of them said that it was not the appropriate time because Josefina and la Gorda were not present to show me the parts of the room that belonged to them.

In the corner of the front room there was a sizeable, built-in brick platform. It was about eighteen inches high and had been constructed like a bed with one end against the wall. Lidia put some thick straw mats on its flat top and urged me to lie down and sleep while they watched over me.

Rosa had lit a lantern and hung it on a nail above the bed. There was enough light to write. I explained to them that writing eased my tension and asked if it bothered them.

'Why do you have to ask?' Lidia retorted. 'Just do it!'

In the vein of a perfunctory explanation I told them that I had always done some things, such as taking notes, which were strange even to don Juan and don Genaro and would perforce be strange to them.

'We all do strange things,' Lidia said dryly.

I sat down on the bed under the lantern, with my back against the wall. They lay down next to me, one on each side. Rosa covered herself with a blanket and went to sleep as if all she needed to do was to lie down. Lidia said that then was the appropriate time and place for us to talk, although she would prefer that I turn off the light because it made her sleepy.

Our conversation in the darkness centred around the whereabouts of the other two girls. She said that she could not even imagine where la Gorda was, but that Josefina was undoubtedly in the mountains, still looking for Nestor, even though it was dark. She explained that Josefina was the most capable one to take care of herself in eventualities such as being in a deserted place in the dark. That was the reason why la Gorda had selected her to run that errand.

I mentioned that in listening to them talk about la Gorda I had formed the opinion that she was the boss. Lidia replied that la Gorda was indeed in charge, and that the Nagual himself had put her in command. She added that even if he had not done so, la Gorda would have taken over, sooner or later, because she was the best.

I was compelled at that point to light the lantern in order to write. Lidia complained that the light made it impossible to stay awake, but I prevailed.

'What makes la Gorda the best?' I asked.

'She has more personal power,' she said. 'She knows everything. Besides, the Nagual taught her how to control people.'

'Do you envy la Gorda for being the best?'

'I used to, but not now.'

'Why did you change?'

'I finally accepted my fate, as the Nagual told me.'

'And what is your fate?'

'My fate . . . . my fate is to be the breeze. To be a dreamer. My fate is to be a warrior.'

'Do Rosa or Josefina envy la Gorda?'

'No, they don't. All of us have accepted our fates. The Nagual said that power comes only after we accept our fate without recriminations. I used to complain a lot and feel terrible because I liked the Nagual. I thought I was a woman. But he showed me that I was not. He showed me that I was a warrior. My life had ended before I met him. This body that you see here is new. The same thing happened to all of us. Perhaps you were not like us, but to us the Nagual was a new life.

'When he told us that he was going to leave, because he had to do other things, we thought we would die. But look at us now. We're alive, and do you know why? Because the Nagual showed us that we were himself. He's here with us. He'll always be here. We are his body and his spirit.'

'Do all four of you feel the same way?'

'We are not four. We are one. That is our fate. We have to carry each other. And you are the same. All of us are the same. Even Soledad is the same, although she goes in a different direction.'

'And Pablito, Nestor and Benigno? Where do they fit?'

'We don't know. We don't like them. Especially Pablito. He's a coward. He has not accepted his fate and wants to wriggle out of it. He even wants to chuck his chances as a sorcerer and live an ordinary life. That'll be great for Soledad. But the Nagual gave us orders to help him. We are getting tired of helping him, though. Maybe one of these days la Gorda will push him out of the way forever.'

'Can she do that?'

'Can she do that! Of course she can. She's got more of the Nagual than the rest of us. Perhaps even more than you.'

'Why do you think the Nagual never told me that you were his apprentices?'

'Because you're empty.'

'Did he say that I was empty?'

'Everyone knows you're empty. It is written on your body.'

'How can you tell that?'

'There is a hole in the middle.'

'In the middle of my body? Where?'

She very gently touched a spot on the right side of my stomach. She drew a circle with her finger as if she were following the edges of an invisible hole four or five inches in diameter.

'Are you empty yourself, Lidia?'

'Are you kidding? I am complete. Can't you *see*?'

Her answers to my questions were taking a turn that I had not expected. I did not want to antagonize her with my ignorance. I shook my head affirmatively.

'Why do you think I have a hole here that makes me empty?'
I asked after deliberating what the most innocent question would be.

She did not answer. She turned her back to me and complained that the light of the lantern bothered her eyes. I insisted on a response. She faced me defiantly.

'I don't want to talk to you any more,' she said. 'You are stupid. Not even Pablito is that stupid and he's the worst.'

I did not want to end up in another blind alley by pretending that I knew what she was talking about, so I asked her again what caused my emptiness. I coaxed her to talk, giving her ample assurances that don Juan had never explained that topic to me. He had said time and time again that I was empty and I understood him the way any Western man would understand that statement. I thought he meant that I was somehow void of determination, will, purpose or even intelligence. He had never spoken to me about a hole in my body.

'There is a hole there on the right side,' she said matter-of-factly. 'A hole that a woman made when she emptied you.'

'Would you know who the woman is?'

'Only you can tell that. The Nagual said that men, most of the time, cannot tell who had emptied them. Women are more fortunate; they know for a fact who emptied them.'

'Are your sisters empty, like me?'

'Don't be stupid. How can they be empty?'

'Doña Soledad said that she was empty. Does she look like me?'

'No. The hole in her stomach was enormous. It was on both sides, which meant that a man and a woman emptied her.'

'What did doña Soledad do with a man and a woman?'

'She gave her completeness to them.'

I vacillated for a moment before asking the next question. I wanted to assess all the implications of her statement.

'La Gorda was even worse than Soledad,' Lidia went on. 'Two women emptied her. The hole in her stomach was like a cavern. But now she has closed it. She is complete again.'

'Tell me about those two women.'

'I just can't tell you anything more,' she said in a most imperative tone. 'Only la Gorda can speak to you about this matter. Wait until she comes.'

'Why only la Gorda?'

'Because she knows everything.'

'Is she the only one who knows everything?'

'The Witness knows as much, maybe even more, but he is Genaro himself and that makes him very difficult to handle. We don't like him.'

'Why don't you like him?'

'Those three bums are awful. They are crazy like Genaro. Well, they are Genaro himself. They are always fighting us because they were afraid of the Nagual and now they are taking their revenge on us. That's what la Gorda says anyway.'

'And what makes la Gorda say that?'

'The Nagual told her things he didn't tell the rest of us. She *sees*. The Nagual said that you also *see*. Josefina, Rosa and I don't *see*, and yet all five of us are the same. We are the same.'

The phrase 'we are the same', which doña Soledad had used the night before, brought on an avalanche of thoughts and fears. I put my writing pad away. I looked around. I was in a strange world lying in a strange bed in between two young women I did not know. And yet I felt at ease there. My body experienced abandon and indifference. I trusted them.

'Are you going to sleep here?' I asked.

'Where else?'

'How about your own room?'

'We can't leave you alone. We feel the same way you do; you are a stranger, except that we are bound to help you. La Gorda said that no matter how stupid you are, we have to look after you. She said we have to sleep in the same bed with you as if you were the Nagual himself.'

Lidia turned off the lantern. I remained sitting with my back against the wall. I closed my eyes to think and I fell asleep instantly.

Lidia, Rosa and I had been sitting on a flat area just outside the front door for nearly two hours, since eight o'clock in the morning. I had tried to steer them into a conversation but they had refused to talk. They seemed to be very relaxed, almost asleep. Their mood of abandonment was not contagious, however. Sitting there in that forced silence had put me into a mood of my own. Their house sat on top of a small hill; the front door faced the east. From where I sat I could see almost the entire narrow valley that ran from east to west. I could not see the town but I could see the green areas of cultivated fields on the floor of the valley. On the other side and flanking the valley in every direction, there were gigantic, round, eroded hills. There were no high mountains in the vicinity of the valley, only those enormous, eroded, round hills, the sight of which created in me the most intense feeling of oppression. I had the sensation that those hills were about to transport me to another time.

Lidia spoke to me all of a sudden and her voice disrupted my reverie. She pulled my sleeve.

'Here comes Josefina,' she said.

I looked at the winding trail that led from the valley to the house. I saw a woman walking slowly up the trail, perhaps fifty yards away. I noticed immediately the remarkable difference in age between Lidia and Rosa and the approaching woman. I looked at her again. I would never have thought Josefina to be that old. Judging by her slow gait and the posture of her body, she seemed to be a woman in her mid-fifties. She was thin, wore a long, dark skirt and was carrying a load of firewood on her back. She had a bundle tied around her waist; it looked as though she had a bundled-up child riding on her left hip. She seemed to be breast-feeding it as she walked. Her steps were almost feeble. She could barely make the last steep slope before reaching the house. When she finally stood in front of us, a few yards away, she was panting so heavily that I attempted to help her sit down. She made a gesture that seemed to say that she was all right.

I heard Lidia and Rosa giggling. I did not look at them because my total attention had been taken by assault. The woman in front of me was absolutely the most disgusting, foul creature I had ever seen. She untied the bundle of firewood and dropped it on the floor with a loud clatter. I jumped involuntarily, due in part to the loud noise and in part to the fact that the woman nearly fell on my lap, pulled by the weight of the wood.

She looked at me for an instant and then lowered her eyes, seemingly embarrassed by her clumsiness. She straightened her back and sighed with apparent relief. Obviously, the load had been too great for her old body.

As she stretched her arms, her hair fell partially loose. She was wearing a soiled headband tied over her forehead. Her hair was long and greying and seemed dirty and matted. I could see the white hairs against the dark brown of the headband. She smiled at me and sort of nodded her head. All her teeth seemed to be missing; I could see the black hole of her toothless mouth. She covered her face with her hand and laughed. She took off her sandals and walked into the house without giving me time to say anything. Rosa followed her.

I was dumbfounded. Doña Soledad had implied that Josefina was the same age as Lidia and Rosa. I turned to Lidia. She was peering at me.

'I had no idea she was that old,' I said.

'Yes, she's pretty old,' she said in a matter-of-fact tone.

'Does she have a child?' I asked.

'Yes, and she takes him everywhere. She never leaves him with us. She's afraid we are going to eat him.'

'Is it a boy?'

'A boy.'

'How old is he?'

'She's had him for some time. But I don't know his age. We thought that she shouldn't have a child at her age. But she didn't pay any attention to us.'

'Whose child is he?'

'Josefina's, of course.'

'I mean, who's the father?'

'The Nagual, who else?'

I thought that that development was quite extravagant and very unnerving.

'I suppose anything is possible in the Nagual's world,' I said.

I meant it more as a thought to myself than a statement made to Lidia.

'You bet,' she said, and laughed.

The oppressiveness of those eroded hills became unbearable. There was something truly abhorrent about that area, and Josefina had been the final blow. On top of having an ugly, old, smelly body and no teeth, she also seemed to have some sort of facial paralysis. The muscles on the left side of her face appeared to be injured, a condition which created a most unpleasant distortion of her left eye and the left side of her mouth. My oppressive mood plummeted to one of sheer anguish. For an instant I toyed with the idea, so familiar by then, of running to my car and driving away.

I complained to Lidia that I did not feel well. She laughed and said that Josefina had no doubt scared me.

'She has that effect on people,' she said. 'Everybody hates her guts. She's uglier than a cockroach.'

'I remember seeing her once,' I said, 'but she was young.'

'Things change,' Lidia said philosophically, 'one way or another. Look at Soledad. What a change, eh? And you yourself have changed. You look more massive than I remember you. You are looking more and more like the Nagual.'

I wanted to say that the change in Josefina was abhorrent but I was afraid that she might overhear me.

I looked at the eroded hills across the valley. I felt like fleeing from them.

'The Nagual gave us this house,' she said, 'but it is not a house for rest. We had another house before that was truly beautiful. This is a place to steam up. Those mountains over there will drive you nuts.'

Her boldness in reading my feelings gave me a respite. I did not know what to say.

'We are all naturally lazy,' she went on. 'We don't like to strain ourselves. The Nagual knew that, so he must have figured that this place would drive us up the wall.'

She stood up abruptly and said that she wanted something to eat. We went to the kitchen, a semi-enclosed area with only two walls. At the open end, to the right of the door, there was an earthen stove; at the other end, where the two walls met, there was a large dining area with a long table and three benches. The floor was paved with smooth river rocks. The flat roof was about ten feet high and was resting on the two walls and on thick supporting beams on the open sides.

Lidia poured me a bowl of beans and meat from a pot which cooked on a very low fire. She heated up some tortillas over the fire. Rosa came in and sat down next to me and asked Lidia to serve her some food.

I became immersed in watching Lidia use a ladle to scoop the beans and meat. She seemed to have an eye for the exact amount. She must have been aware that I was admiring her manoeuvres. She took two or three beans from Rosa's bowl and returned them to the pot.

Out of the corner of my eye I saw Josefina coming into the kitchen. I did not look at her, though. She sat facing me across the table. I had a squeamish feeling in my stomach. I felt that I could not eat with that woman looking at me. To ease my tension I joked with Lidia that there were still two extra beans in Rosa's bowl that she had overlooked. She scooped up two beans with the ladle with a precision that made me gasp. I laughed nervously, knowing that once Lidia sat down I would have to move my eyes from the stove and acknowledge the presence of Josefina.

I finally and reluctantly had to look across the table at Josefina. There was a dead silence. I stared at her incredulously. My mouth fell open. I heard the loud laughter of Lidia and Rosa. It took an endless moment for me to put my thoughts and feelings in some sort of order. Whoever was facing me was not the Josefina I had seen just awhile ago, but a very pretty girl. She did not have Indian features as Lidia and Rosa did. She seemed to be more Latin than Indian. She had a light olive complexion, a very small mouth and a finely chiselled nose, small white teeth and short, black, curly hair. She had a dimple on the left side of her face, which gave a definite cockiness to her smile.

She was the girl I had met briefly years ago. She held my scrutiny. Her eyes were friendly. I became possessed by degrees with some uncontrollable nervousness. I ended up desperately clowning about my genuine bewilderment.

They laughed like children. After their laughter had subsided I wanted to know what was the point of Josefina's histrionic display.

'She's practising the art of stalking,' Lidia said. 'The Nagual taught us to baffle people so they wouldn't notice us. Josefina is very pretty and if she walks alone at night, no one will bother her if she is ugly and smelly, but if she goes out as she really is, well, you yourself can tell what would happen.'

Josefina nodded affirmatively and then contorted her face into the ugliest grimace possible.

'She can hold that face all day,' Lidia said.

I contended that if I lived around that area I would certainly notice Josefina in her disguise more readily than if she did not have one.

'That disguise was just for you,' Lidia said, and all three of them laughed. 'And look how it baffled you. You noticed her child even more than you noticed her.'

Lidia went into their room and brought out a package of rags that looked like a bundled-up child and threw it on the table in front of me. I laughed uproariously with them.

'Do all of you have particular disguises?' I asked.

'No. Only Josefina. No one around here knows her as she really is,' Lidia replied.

Josefina nodded and smiled but she remained silent. I liked her tremendously. There was something so very innocent and sweet about her.

'Say something, Josefina,' I said, grabbing her by her forearms.

She looked at me bewildered, and recoiled. I thought that I had gotten carried away by my elation and perhaps grabbed her too hard. I let her go. She sat up straight. She contorted her small mouth and thin lips and produced a most grotesque outburst of grunts and shrieks.

Her whole face suddenly changed. A series of ugly, involuntary spasms marred her tranquil expression of a moment before.

I looked at her, horrified. Lidia pulled me by the sleeve.

'Why do you have to scare her, stupid?' she whispered. 'Don't you know that she became mute and can't talk at all?'

Josefina obviously understood her and seemed bent on protesting. She clenched her fist at Lidia and let out another outburst of extremely loud and horrifying shrieks, and then choked and coughed. Rosa began to rub her back. Lidia tried to do the same but Josefina nearly hit her in the face.

Lidia sat down next to me and made a gesture of impotence. She shrugged her shoulders.

'She's that way,' Lidia whispered to me.

Josefina turned to her. Her face was contorted in a most ugly grimace of anger. She opened her mouth and bellowed at the top of her voice some more frightening, guttural sounds.

Lidia slid off the bench and in a most unobtrusive manner left the kitchen area.

Rosa held Josefina by the arm. Josefina seemed to be the epitome of fury. She moved her mouth and contorted her face. In a matter of minutes she had lost all the beauty and innocence that had enchanted me. I did not know what to do. I tried to apologize but Josefina's inhuman sounds drowned out my words. Finally Rosa took her into the house.

Lidia returned and sat across the table from me.

'Something went wrong up here,' she said, touching her head.

'When did it happen?' I asked.

'A long time ago. The Nagual must have done something to her, because all of a sudden she lost her speech.'

Lidia seemed sad. I had the impression that her sadness showed against her desire. I even felt tempted to tell her not to struggle so hard to hide her emotions.

'How does Josefina communicate with you people?' I asked. 'Does she write?'

'Come on, don't be silly. She doesn't write. She's not you. She uses her hands and feet to tell us what she wants.'

Josefina and Rosa came back to the kitchen. They stood by my side. I thought that Josefina was again the picture of innocence and candour. Her beatific expression did not give the slightest inkling of the fact that she could become so ugly, so fast. Looking at her I had the sudden realization that her fabulous ability for gestures undoubtedly was intimately linked to her aphasia. I reasoned that only a person who had lost her capacity to verbalize could be so versed in mimicry.

Rosa said to me that Josefina had confided that she wished she could talk, because she liked me very much.

'Until you came she was happy the way she was,' Lidia said in a harsh voice.

Josefina shook her head affirmatively, corroborating Lidia's statement, and went into a mild outburst of sounds.

'I wish la Gorda was here,' Rosa said. 'Lidia always gets Josefina angry.'

'I don't mean to!' Lidia protested.

Josefina smiled at her and extended her arm to touch her. It seemed as if she were attempting to apologize. Lidia brushed her hand away.

'Why, you mute imbecile,' she muttered.

Josefina did not get angry. She looked away. There was so much sadness in her eyes that I did not want to look at her. I felt compelled to intercede.

'She thinks she's the only woman in the world who has problems,' Lidia snapped at me. 'The Nagual told us to drive her hard and without mercy until she no longer feels sorry for herself.'

Rosa looked at me and reaffirmed Lidia's claim with a nod of her head.

Lidia turned to Rosa and ordered her to leave Josefina's side. Rosa moved away complyingly and sat on the bench next to me.

'The Nagual said that one of these days she will talk again,' Lidia said to me.

'Hey!' Rosa said, pulling my sleeve. 'Maybe you're the one who'll make her talk.'

'Yes!' Lidia exclaimed as if she had had the same thought. 'Maybe that's why we had to wait for you.'

'It's so clear!' Rosa added with the expression of having had a true revelation.

Both of them jumped to their feet and embraced Josefina.

'You're going to talk again!' Rosa exclaimed as she shook Josefina by the shoulders.

Josefina opened her eyes and rolled them. She started making faint, muffled sighs, as if she were sobbing, and ended up running back and forth, crying like an animal. Her excitation was so great that she seemed to have locked her jaws open. I honestly thought that she was on the brink of a nervous breakdown. Lidia and Rosa ran to her side and helped her close her mouth. But they did not try to calm her down.

'You're going to talk again! You're going to talk again!' they shouted.

Josefina sobbed and howled in a manner that sent chills down my spine.

I was absolutely confounded. I tried to talk sense to them. I appealed to their reason, but then I realized that they had very little of it, by my standards. I paced back and forth in front of them, trying to figure out what to do.

'You are going to help her, aren't you?' Lidia demanded.

'Please, sir, please,' Rosa pleaded with me.

I told them that they were crazy, that I could not possibly know what to do. And yet, as I talked I noticed that there was a funny feeling of optimism and certainty in the back of my mind. I wanted to discard it at first, but it took hold of me. Once before I had had a similar feeling in relation to a dear friend of mine who was mortally ill. I thought I could make her well and actually leave the hospital where she lay dying. I even consulted don Juan about it.

'Sure. You can cure her and make her walk out of that death trap,' he said.

'How?' I asked him.

'It's a very simple procedure,' he said. 'All you have to do is remind her that she's an incurable patient. Since she's a terminal case she has power. She has nothing to lose any more. She's lost everything already. When one has nothing to lose, one becomes courageous. We are timid only when there is something we can still cling to.'

'But is it enough just to remind her of that?'

'No. That will give her the boost she needs. Then she has

to push the disease away with her left hand. She must push her arm out in front of her with her hand clenched as if she were holding a knob. She must push on and on as she says out, out, out. Tell her that, since she has nothing else to do, she must dedicate every second of her remaining life to performing that movement. I assure you that she can get up and walk away, if she wants to.'

'It sounds so simple,' I said.

Don Juan chuckled.

'It seems simple,' he said, 'but it isn't. In order to do this your friend needs an impeccable spirit.'

He looked at me for a long time. He seemed to be measuring the concern and sadness I felt for my friend.

'Of course,' he added, 'if your friend had an impeccable spirit she wouldn't be there in the first place.'

I told my friend what don Juan had said. But she was already too weak even to attempt to move her arm.

In Josefina's case my rationale for my secret confidence was the fact that she was a warrior with an impeccable spirit. Would it be possible, I silently asked myself, to apply the same hand movement to her?

I told Josefina that her incapacity to speak was due to some sort of blockage.

'Yes, yes, it's a blockage,' Lidia and Rosa repeated after me.

I explained to Josefina the arm movement and told her that she had to push that blockage by moving her arm in that fashion.

Josefina's eyes were transfixed. She seemed to be in a trance. She moved her mouth, making barely audible sounds. She tried moving her arm, but her excitation was so intense that she flung her arm without any coordination. I tried to redirect her movements, but she appeared to be so thoroughly befuddled that she could not even hear what I was saying. Her eyes went out of focus and I knew she was going to faint. Rosa apparently realized what was happening; she jumped away and grabbed a cup of water and sprinkled it over Josefina's face. Josefina's eyes rolled back, showing the whites of her eyes. She blinked repeatedly until she could focus her eyes again. She moved her mouth, but she made no sound.

'Touch her throat!' Rosa yelled at me.

'No! No!' Lidia shouted back. 'Touch her head. It's in her head, you dummy!'

She grabbed my hand and I reluctantly let her place it on Josefina's head.

Josefina shivered, and little by little she let out a series of faint sounds. Somehow they seemed to me more melodious than the inhuman sounds she made before.

Rosa also must have noticed the difference.

'Did you hear that? Did you hear that?' she asked me in a whisper.

But whatever the difference might have been, Josefina let out another series of sounds more grotesque than ever. When she quietened down, she sobbed for a moment and then entered into another state of euphoria. Lidia and Rosa finally quietened her. She plunked down on the bench, apparently exhausted. She could barely lift her eyelids to look at me. She smiled meekly.

'I am so very, very sorry,' I said and held her hand.

Her whole body vibrated. She lowered her head and began to weep again. I felt a surge of ultimate empathy for her. At that moment I would have given my life to help her.

She sobbed uncontrollably as she tried to speak to me. Lidia and Rosa appeared to be so caught up in her drama that they were making the same gestures with their mouths.

'For heaven's sake, do something!' Rosa exclaimed in a pleading voice.

I experienced an unbearable anxiety. Josefina stood up and embraced me, or rather clung to me in a frenzy and pushed me away from the table. At that instant Lidia and Rosa, with astounding agility, speed and control, grabbed me by the shoulders with both hands and at the same time hooked the heels of my feet with their feet. The weight of Josefina's body and her embrace, plus the speed of Lidia's and Rosa's man-oeuvre, rendered me helpless. They all moved at once, and before I knew what was happening, they had laid me on the floor with Josefina on top of me. I felt her heart pounding. She held on to me with great force; the sound of her heart reverberated in my ears. I felt it pounding in my own chest. I tried to push her away but she held on fast. Rosa and Lidia had me pinned down on the floor with their weight on my arms and legs. Rosa cackled insanely and began nibbling on my side. Her small, sharp teeth chattered as her jaws snapped open and shut with nervous spasms.

All at once I had a monstrous sensation of pain, physical revulsion and terror. I lost my breath. My eyes could not focus. I knew that I was passing out. I heard then the dry, cracking sound of a pipe breaking at the base of my neck and felt the ticklish sensation on top of my head, running like a shiver through my entire body. The next thing I knew I was looking at them from the other side of the kitchen. The three girls were staring at me while they lay on the floor.

'What are you people doing?' I heard someone say in a loud, harsh, commanding voice.

I then had an inconceivable feeling. I felt Josefina let go of me and stand up. I was lying on the floor, and yet I was also standing a distance away from them, looking at a woman I had never seen before. She was by the door. She walked towards me and stopped six or seven feet away. She stared at me for a moment. I knew immediately that she was la Gorda. She demanded to know what was going on.

'We were just playing a little joke on him,' Josefina said clearing her throat. 'I was pretending to be mute.'

The three girls huddled up close together and began to laugh. La Gorda remained impassive, looking at me.

They had tricked me! I found my stupidity and gullibility so outrageous that I had a fit of hysterical laughter, which was almost out of control. My body shivered.

I knew that Josefina had not just been playing, as she had claimed. The three of them had meant business. I had actually felt Josefina's body as a force that, in fact, was getting inside my own body. Rosa's nibbling on my side, which undoubtedly was a ruse to distract my attention, coincided with the sensation I had had that Josefina's heart was pounding inside my chest.

I heard la Gorda urging me to calm down.

I had a nervous flutter in my midsection and then a quiet, calm anger swept over me. I loathed them. I had had enough of them. I would have picked up my jacket and writing pad and walked out of the house had it not been that I was not quite myself yet. I was somewhat dizzy and my senses were definitely out of line. I had had the sensation that when I had first looked at the girls from across the kitchen, I was actually viewing them from a position above my eye level, from a place close to the ceiling. But something even more disconcerting was that I had actually perceived that the ticklish sensation on top of my head was what scooped me from Josefina's embrace. It was not as if something came out from the top of my head; something actually did come out from the top of my head.

A few years before, don Juan and don Genaro had manoeuvred my perception and I had had an impossible double sensation: I felt that don Juan had fallen on top of me and pinned me to the ground, while at the same time I felt I was still standing up. I was actually in both places at once. In sorcerers' terms I could say that my body had stored the memory of that double perception and seemed to have repeated it. There were, however, two new things that had been added to my bodily memory this time. One was that the ticklish sensation I had become so aware of during the course of my confrontations with those women was the vehicle to arriving at that double perception; and the other was that the sound at the base of my neck let loose something in me that was capable of coming out of the top of my head.

After a minute or two I definitely felt that I was coming down from near the ceiling until I was standing on the floor. It took a while for my eyes to adjust to seeing at my normal eye level.

As I looked at the four women I felt naked and vulnerable. I then had an instant of dissociation, or lack of perceptual continuity. It was as if I had shut my eyes, and some force suddenly had made me twirl a couple of times. When I opened my eyes the girls were staring at me with their mouths open. But somehow I was myself again.

3 LA GORDA

The first thing I noticed about la Gorda was her eyes: very dark and calm. She seemed to be examining me from head to toe. Her eyes scanned my body the same way don Juan's used to. In fact, her eyes had the same calmness and force. I knew why she was the best. The thought that came to my mind was that don Juan must have left her his eyes.

She was slightly taller than the other three girls. She had a lean, dark body and a superb back. I noticed the graceful line of her broad shoulders when she half turned her upper body to face the three girls.

She gave them an unintelligible command and the three of them sat down on a bench, right behind her. She was actually shielding them from me with her body.

She turned to face me again. Her expression was one of utmost seriousness, but without a trace of gloom or heaviness. She did not smile and yet she was friendly. She had very pleasant features: a nicely shaped face, neither round nor angular; a small mouth with thin lips; a broad nose; high cheekbones; and long, jet-black hair.

I could not help noticing her beautiful, muscular hands which she kept clasped in front of her, over her umbilical region. The backs of her hands were turned to me. I could see her muscles being contracted rhythmically as she clasped her palms.

She was wearing a long, faded orange cotton dress with long sleeves and a brown shawl. There was something terribly calming and final about her. I felt the presence of don Juan. My body relaxed.

'Sit down, sit down,' she said to me in a coaxing tone.

I walked back to the table. She pointed out a place for me to sit, but I remained standing.

She smiled for the first time and her eyes became softer and shinier. She was not as pretty as Josefina, and yet she was the most beautiful of all of them.

We were quiet for a moment. In terms of an explanation she said that they had done their best in the years since the Nagual left, and that because of their dedication they had become accustomed to the task that he had left for them to perform.

I did not quite understand what she was talking about, but as she spoke I felt more than ever the presence of don Juan. It was not that she was copying his manners, or the inflection of his voice. She had an inner control that made her act the way don Juan did. Their similarity was from the inside out.

I told her that I had come because I needed Pablito's and Nestor's help. I said that I was rather slow or even stupid in understanding the ways of sorcerers, but that I was sincere, and yet all of them had treated me with malice and deceitfulness.

She began to apologize but I did not let her finish. I picked up my things and went out the front door. She ran after me. She was not preventing me from leaving but rather she was talking very fast, as if she needed to say all she could before I drove away.

She said that I had to hear her out, and that she was willing to ride with me until she had told me everything the Nagual had entrusted her to tell me.

'I'm going to Mexico City,' I said.

'I'll ride with you to Los Angeles if necessary,' she said, and I knew that she meant it.

'All right,' I said just to test her, 'get in the car.'

She vacillated for an instant, then she stood silently and faced her house. She put her clasped hands just below her navel. She turned and faced the valley and did the same movement with her hands.

I knew what she was doing. She was saying good-bye to

her house and to those awesome round hills that surrounded it.

Don Juan had taught me that good-bye gesture years before. He had stressed that it was an extremely powerful gesture, and that a warrior had to use it sparingly. I had had very few occasions to perform it myself.

The good-bye movement la Gorda was executing was a variant of the one don Juan had taught me. He had said that the hands were clasped as in prayer, either gently or with great speed, even producing a clapping sound. Done either way, the purpose of clasping the hands was to imprison the feeling that the warrior did not wish to leave behind. As soon as the hands had closed in and captured that feeling, they were taken with great force to the middle of the chest, at the level of the heart. There the feeling became a dagger and the warrior stabbed himself with it, as if holding the dagger with both hands.

Don Juan had told me that a warrior said good-bye in that fashion only when he had reason to feel he might not come back.

La Gorda's good-bye enthralled me.

'Are you saying good-bye?' I asked out of curiosity.

'Yes,' she said dryly.

'Don't you put your hands to your chest?' I asked.

'Men do that. Women have wombs. They store their feelings there.'

'Aren't you supposed to say good-bye like that only when you're not coming back?' I asked.

'Chances are I may not come back,' she replied. 'I'm going with you.'

I had an attack of unwarranted sadness, unwarranted in the sense that I did not know that woman at all. I had only doubts and suspicions about her. But as I peered into her clear eyes I had a sense of ultimate kinship with her. I mellowed. My anger had disappeared and given way to a strange sadness. I looked around, and I knew that those mysterious, enormous, round hills were ripping me apart.

'Those hills over there are alive,' she said, reading my thoughts.

I turned to her and told her that both the place and the women had affected me at a very deep level, a level I could not ordinarily conceive. I did not know which was more devastating, the place or the women. The women's onslaughts had been direct and terrifying, but the effect of those hills was a constant, nagging apprehension, a desire to flee from them. When I told that to la Gorda she said that I was correct in assessing the effect of that place, that the Nagual had left them there because of that effect, and that I should not blame anyone for what had happened, because the Nagual himself had given those women orders to try to do away with me.

'Did he give orders like that to you too?' I asked.

'No, not to me. I'm different than they are,' she said. 'They are sisters. They are the same, exactly the same. Just like Pablito, Nestor and Benigno are the same. Only you and I can be exactly the same. We are not now because you're still incomplete. But someday we will be the same, exactly the same.'

'I've been told that you're the only one who knows where the Nagual and Genaro are now,' I said.

She peered at me for a moment and shook her head affirmatively.

'That's right,' she said. 'I know where they are. The Nagual told me to take you there if I can.'

I told her to stop beating around the bush and to reveal their exact whereabouts to me immediately. My demand seemed to plunge her into chaos. She apologized and reassured me that later on, when we were on our way, she would disclose everything to me. She begged me not to ask her about them any more because she had strict orders not to mention anything until the right moment.

Lidia and Josefina came to the door and stared at me. I hurriedly got in the car. La Gorda got in after me, and as she did I could not help observing that she had entered the car as she would have entered a tunnel. She sort of crawled in. Don Juan used to do that. I jokingly said once, after I had seen him do it scores of times, that it was more functional to get in the way I did. I thought that perhaps his lack of familiarity with automobiles was responsible for his strange way of entering. He explained then that the car was a cave and that caves had to be entered in that fashion if we were going to use them. There was an inherent spirit to caves, whether they were natural or man-made, and that that spirit had to be approached with respect. Crawling was the only way of showing that respect.

I was wondering whether or not to ask la Gorda if don Juan had instructed her about such details, but she spoke first. She said that the Nagual had given her specific instructions about what to do in case I would survive the attacks of doña Soledad and the three girls. Then she casually added that before I headed for Mexico City we had to go to a specific place in the mountains where don Juan and I used to go, and that there she would reveal all the information the Nagual had never disclosed to me.

I had a moment of indecision, and then something in me which was not my reason made me head for the mountains. We drove in complete silence. I attempted at various opportune moments to start up a conversation, but she turned me down every time with a strong shake of her head. Finally she seemed to have gotten tired of my trying and said forcefully that what she had to say required a place of power and until we were in one we had to abstain from draining ourselves with useless talk.

After a long drive and an exhausting hike away from the road, we finally reached our destination. It was late afternoon. We were in a deep canyon. The bottom of it was already dark, while the sun was still shining on the top of the mountains above it. We walked until we came to a small cave a few feet up the north side of the canyon, which ran from east to west. I used to spend a great deal of time there with don Juan.

Before we entered the cave, la Gorda carefully swept the floor with branches, the way don Juan used to, in order to clear the ticks and parasites from the rocks. Then she cut a large heap of small branches with soft leaves from the surrounding bushes and placed them on the rock floor like a mat.

She motioned me to enter. I had always let don Juan enter

first as a sign of respect. I wanted to do the same with her, but she declined. She said I was the Nagual. I crawled into the cave the same way she had crawled into my car. I laughed at my inconsistency. I had never been able to treat my car as a cave.

She coaxed me to relax and make myself comfortable.

'The reason the Nagual could not reveal all his designs to you was because you're incomplete,' la Gorda said all of a sudden. 'You still are, but now after your bouts with Soledad and the sisters, you are stronger than before.'

'What's the meaning of being incomplete? Everyone has told me that you're the only one who can explain that,' I said.

'It's a very simple matter,' she said. 'A complete person is one who has never had children.'

She paused as if she were allowing me time to write down what she had said. I looked up from my notes. She was staring at me, judging the effect of her words.

'I know that the Nagual told you exactly what I've just said,' she continued. 'You didn't pay any attention to him and you probably haven't paid any attention to me, either.'

I read my notes out loud and repeated what she had said. She giggled.

'The Nagual said that an incomplete person is one who has had children,' she said as if dictating to me.

She scrutinized me, apparently waiting for a question or a comment. I had none.

'Now I've told you everything about being complete and incomplete,' she said. 'And I've told you just like the Nagual told me. It didn't mean anything to me at that time, and it doesn't mean anything to you now.'

I had to laugh at the way she patterned herself after don Juan.

'An incomplete person has a hole in the stomach,' she went on. 'A sorcerer can *see* it as plainly as you can see my head. When the hole is on the left side of one's stomach, the child who created that hole is of the same sex. If it is on the right side, the child is of the opposite sex. The hole on the left side is black, the one on the right is dark brown.'

'Can you see that hole in anyone who has had children?'

'Sure. There are two ways of *seeing* it. A sorcerer may *see* it in *dreaming* or by looking directly at a person. A sorcerer who *sees* has no problems in viewing the luminous being to find out if there is a hole in the luminosity of the body. But even if the sorcerer doesn't know how to *see*, he can look and actually distinguish the darkness of the hole through the clothing.'

She stopped talking. I urged her to go on.

'The Nagual told me that you write and then you don't remember what you wrote,' she said with a tone of accusation.

I became entangled in words trying to defend myself. Nonetheless, what she had said was the truth. Don Juan's words always had had a double effect on me: once when I heard for the first time whatever he had said, and then when I read at home whatever I had written down and had forgotten about.

Talking to la Gorda, however, was intrinsically different. Don Juan's apprentices were not in any way as engulfing as he was. Their revelations, although extraordinary, were only missing pieces to a jigsaw puzzle. The unusual character of those pieces was that with them the picture did not become clearer but that it became more and more complex.

'You had a brown hole in the right side of your stomach,' she continued. 'That means that a woman emptied you. You made a female child.

'The Nagual said that I had a huge black hole myself, because I made two women. I never saw the hole, but I've seen other people with holes like mine.'

'You said that I had a hole; don't I have it any more?'

'No. It's been patched. The Nagual helped you to patch it. Without his help you would be more empty than you are now.'

'What kind of patch is it?'

'A patch in your luminosity. There is no other way of saying it. The Nagual said that a sorcerer like himself can fill up the hole anytime. But that that filling is only a patch without luminosity. Anyone who *sees* or does *dreaming* can tell that it looks like a lead patch on the yellow luminosity of the rest of the body.

'The Nagual patched you and me and Soledad. But then he left it up to us to put back the shine, the luminosity.'

'How did he patch us?'

'He's a sorcerer, he put things in our bodies. He replaced us. We are no longer the same. The patch is what he put there himself.'

'But how did he put those things there and what were they?'

'What he put in our bodies was his own luminosity and he used his hand to do that. He simply reached into our bodies and left his fibres there. He did the same with all of his six children and also with Soledad. All of them are the same. Except Soledad; she's something else.'

La Gorda seemed unwilling to go on. She vacillated and almost began to stutter.

'What is doña Soledad?' I insisted.

'It's very hard to tell,' she said after considerable coaxing. 'She is the same as you and me, and yet she's different. She has the same luminosity, but she's not together with us. She goes in the opposite direction. Right now she's more like you. Both of you have patches that look like lead. Mine is gone and I'm again a complete, luminous egg. That is the reason I said that you and I will be exactly the same someday when you become complete again. Right now what makes us almost the same is the Nagual's luminosity and the fact that both of us are going in the same direction and that we both were empty.'

'What does a complete person look like to a sorcerer?' I asked.

'Like a luminous egg made out of fibres,' she said. 'All the fibres are complete; they look like strings, taut strings. It looks as if the strings have been tightened like a drum is tightened.

'On an empty person, on the other hand, the fibres are crumpled up at the edges of the hole. When they have had many children, the fibres don't look like fibres any more. Those people look like two chunks of luminosity, separated by blackness. It is an awesome sight. The Nagual made me *see* them one day when we were in a park in the city.'

'Why do you think the Nagual never told me about all this?'

'He told you everything, but you never understood him correctly. As soon as he realized that you were not understanding what he was saying, he was compelled to change the subject. Your emptiness prevented you from understanding. The Nagual said that it was perfectly natural for you not to understand. Once a person becomes incomplete he's actually empty like a gourd that has been hollowed out. It didn't matter to you how many times he told you that you were empty; it didn't matter that he even explained it to you. You never knew what he meant, or worse yet, you didn't want to know.'

La Gorda was treading on dangerous ground. I tried to head her off with another question, but she rebuffed me.

'You love a little boy and you don't want to understand what the Nagual meant,' she said accusingly. 'The Nagual told me that you have a daughter you've never seen, and that you love that little boy. One took your edge, the other pinned you down. You have welded them together.'

I had to stop writing. I crawled out of the cave and stood up. I began to walk down the steep incline to the floor of the gully. La Gorda followed me. She asked me if I was upset by her directness. I did not want to lie.

'What do you think?' I asked.

'You're fuming!' she exclaimed and giggled with an abandon that I had witnessed only in don Juan and don Genaro.

She seemed about to lose her balance and grabbed my left arm. In order to help her get down to the floor of the gully, I lifted her up by her waist. I thought that she could not have weighed more than a hundred pounds. She puckered her lips the way don Genaro used to and said that her weight was a hundred and fifteen. We both laughed at once. It was a moment of direct, instant communication.

'Why does it bother you so much to talk about these things?' she asked.

I told her that once I had had a little boy whom I had loved immensely. I felt the imperative to tell her about him. Some extravagant need beyond my comprehension made me open up with that woman who was a total stranger to me.

As I began to talk about that little boy, a wave of nostalgia enveloped me; perhaps it was the place or the situation or the time of the day. Somehow I had merged the memory of that little boy with the memory of don Juan, and for the first time in all the time I had not seen him I missed don Juan. Lidia had said that they never missed him because he was always with them; he was their bodies and their spirits. I had known instantly what she meant. I felt the same way myself. In that gully, however, an unknown feeling had overtaken me. I told la Gorda that I had never missed don Juan until that moment. She did not answer. She looked away.

Possibly my feeling of longing for those two people had to do with the fact that both of them had produced catharses in my life. And both of them were gone. I had not realized until that moment how final that separation was. I said to la Gorda that that little boy had been, more than anything else, my friend, and that one day he was whisked away by forces I could not control. That was perhaps one of the greatest blows I had ever received. I even went to see don Juan to ask his assistance. It was the only time I had ever asked him for help. He listened to my plea and then he broke into uproarious laughter. His reaction was so unexpected that I could not even get angry. I could only comment on what I thought was his insensitivity.

'What do you want me to do?' he asked.

I said that since he was a sorcerer perhaps he could help me to regain my little friend for my solace.

'You're wrong. A warrior doesn't seek anything for his solace,' he said in a tone that did not admit reproach.

Then he proceeded to smash my arguments. He said that a warrior could not possibly leave anything to chance, that a warrior actually affected the outcome of events by the force of his awareness and his unbending intent. He said that if I would have had the unbending intent to keep and help that child, I would have taken measures to assure his stay with me. But as it was, my love was merely a word, a useless outburst of an empty man. He then told me something about emptiness and completeness, but I did not want to hear it. All I felt was a sense of loss, and the emptiness that he had mentioned, I was

sure, referred to the feeling of having lost someone irreplace-
able.

'You loved him, you honoured his spirit, you wished him
well, now you must forget him,' he said.

But I had not been able to do so. There was something
terribly alive in my emotions even though time had mellowed
them. At one point I thought I had forgotten, but then one
night an incident produced the deepest emotional upheaval in
me. I was walking to my office when a young Mexican woman
approached me. She had been sitting on a bench, waiting for a
bus. She wanted to know if that particular bus went to a children's hospital. I did not know. She explained that her little
boy had had a high temperature for a long time and she was
worried because she did not have any money. I moved towards
the bench and saw a little boy standing on the seat with his
head against the back of the bench. He was wearing a jacket
and short pants and a cap. He could not have been more than
two years old. He must have seen me, for he walked to the
edge of the bench and put his head against my leg.

'My little head hurts,' he said to me in Spanish.

His voice was so tiny and his dark eyes so sad that a wave
of irrepressible anguish welled up in me. I picked him up and
drove him and his mother to the nearest hospital. I left them
there and gave the mother enough money to pay the bill. But I
did not want to stay or to know any more about him. I wanted
to believe that I had helped him, and that by doing so I had
paid back to the spirit of man.

I had learned the magical act of 'paying back to the spirit
of man' from don Juan. I had asked him once, overwhelmed
by the realization that I could never pay him back for all he
had done for me, if there was anything in the world I could
do to even the score. We were leaving a bank, after exchanging
some Mexican currency.

'I don't need you to pay me back,' he said, 'but if you still
want to pay back, make your deposit to the spirit of man.
That's always a very small account, and whatever one puts in
it is more than enough.'

By helping that sick child I had merely paid back to the

spirit of man for any help that my little boy may receive from strangers along his path.

I told la Gorda that my love for him would remain alive for the rest of my life even though I would never see him again. I wanted to tell her that the memory I had of him was buried so deep that nothing could touch it, but I desisted. I felt it would have been superfluous to talk about it. Besides, it was getting dark and I wanted to get out of that gully.

'We better go,' I said. 'I'll take you home. Maybe some other time we can talk about these things again.'

She laughed the way don Juan used to laugh at me. I had apparently said something utterly funny.

'Why do you laugh, Gorda?' I asked.

'Because you know yourself that we can't leave this place just like that,' she said. 'You have an appointment with power here. And so do I.'

She walked back to the cave and crawled in.

'Come on in,' she yelled from inside. 'There is no way to leave.'

I reacted most incongruously. I crawled in and sat next to her again. It was evident that she too had tricked me. I had not come there to have any confrontations. I should have been furious. I was indifferent instead. I could not lie to myself that I had only stopped there on my way to Mexico City. I had gone there compelled by something beyond my comprehension.

She handed me my notebook and motioned me to write. She said that if I wrote I would not only relax myself but I would also relax her.

'What is this appointment with power?' I asked.

'The Nagual told me that you and I have an appointment here with something out there. You first had an appointment with Soledad and then one with the little sisters. They were supposed to destroy you. The Nagual said that if you survived their assaults I had to bring you here so that we together could keep the third appointment.'

'What kind of appointment is it?'

'I really don't know. Like everything else, it depends on us.

Right now there are some things out there that have been waiting for you. I say that they have been waiting for you because I come here by myself all the time and nothing ever happens. But tonight is different. You are here and those things will come.'

'Why is the Nagual trying to destroy me?' I asked.

'He's not trying to destroy anybody!' la Gorda exclaimed in protest. 'You are his child. Now he wants you to be himself. More himself than any of us. But to be a true Nagual you have to claim your power. Otherwise he wouldn't have been so careful in setting up Soledad and the little sisters to stalk you. He taught Soledad how to change her shape and rejuvenate herself. He made her construct a devilish floor in her room. A floor no one can oppose. You see, Soledad is empty, so the Nagual set her up to do something gigantic. He gave her a task, a most difficult and dangerous task, but the only one which was suited for her, and that was to finish you off. He told her that nothing could be more difficult than for one sorcerer to kill another. It's easier for an average man to kill a sorcerer or for a sorcerer to kill an average man, but two sorcerers don't fit well at all. The Nagual told Soledad that her best bet was to surprise you and scare you. And that's what she did. The Nagual set her up to be a desirable woman so she could lure you into her room, and there her floor would have bewitched you, because as I've said, no one, but no one, can stand up to that floor. That floor was the Nagual's masterpiece for Soledad. But you did something to her floor and Soledad had to change her tactics in accordance with the Nagual's instructions. He told her that if her floor failed and she could not frighten and surprise you, she had to talk to you and tell you everything you wanted to know. The Nagual trained her to talk very well as her last resource. But Soledad could not overpower you even with that.'

'Why was it so important to overpower me?'

She paused and peered at me. She cleared her throat and sat up straight. She looked up at the low roof of the cave and exhaled noisily through her nose.

'Soledad is a woman like myself,' she said. 'I'll tell you something about my own life and maybe you'll understand her.

'I had a man once. He got me pregnant when I was very young and I had two daughters with him. One after the other. My life was hell. That man was a drunkard and beat me day and night. And I hated him and he hated me. And I got fat like a pig. One day another man came along and told me that he liked me and wanted me to go with him to work in the city as a paid servant. He knew I was a hardworking woman and only wanted to exploit me. But my life was so miserable that I fell for it and went with him. He was worse than the first man, mean and fearsome. He couldn't stand me after a week or so. And he used to give me the worst beatings you can imagine. I thought he was going to kill me and he wasn't even drunk, and all because I hadn't found work. Then he sent me to beg on the streets with a sick baby. He would pay the child's mother something from the money I got. And then he would beat me because I hadn't made enough. The child got sicker and sicker and I knew that if it died while I was begging, the man would kill me. So one day when I knew that he was not there I went to the child's mother and gave her her baby and some of the money I had made that day That was a lucky day for me; a kind foreign lady had given me fifty pesos to buy medicine for the baby.

'I had been with that horrible man for three months and I thought it had been twenty years. I used the money to go back to my home. I was pregnant again. The man had wanted me to have a child of my own, so that he would not have to pay for one. When I got to my hometown I tried to go back to see my children, but they had been taken away by their father's family. All the family got together under the pretence that they wanted to talk to me, but instead they took me to a deserted place and beat me with sticks and rocks and left me for dead.'

La Gorda showed me the many scars on her scalp.

'To this day I don't know how I made it back to town. I even lost the child I had in my womb. I went to an aunt I still had; my parents were dead. She gave me a place to rest and she tended to me. She fed me, the poor soul, for two months before I could get up.

'Then one day my aunt told me that that man was in town looking for me. He had talked to the police and had said that he had given me money in advance to work and that I had run away, stealing the money after I had killed a woman's baby. I knew that the end had come for me. But my luck turned right again and I caught a ride in the truck of an American. I saw the truck coming on the road and I lifted my hand in desperation and the man stopped and let me get on. He drove me all the way to this part of Mexico. He dropped me in the city. I didn't know a soul. I roamed all over the place for days like a crazy dog, eating garbage from the street. That was when my luck turned for the last time.

'I met Pablito, with whom I have a debt that I can't pay back. Pablito took me to his carpentry shop and gave me a corner there to put my bed. He did that because he felt sorry for me. He found me in the market after he stumbled and fell on top of me. I was sitting there begging. A moth or a bee, I don't know which, flew to him and hit him in the eye. He turned around on his heels and stumbled and fell right on top of me. I thought he would be so mad that he would hit me, but he gave me some money instead. I asked him if he could give me work. That was when he took me to his shop and set me up with an iron and an ironing board to do laundry.

'I did very well. Except that I got fatter, because most of the people I washed for fed me with their leftovers. Sometimes I ate sixteen times a day. I did nothing else but eat. Kids in the street used to taunt me and sneak behind me and step on my heels and then someone would push me and I would fall. Those kids made me cry with their cruel jokes, especially when they used to spoil my wash on purpose.

'One day, very late in the afternoon, a weird old man came over to see Pablito. I had never seen that man before. I had never known that Pablito was in cahoots with such a scary, awesome man. I turned my back to him and kept on working. I was alone there. Suddenly I felt the hands of that man on my neck. My heart stopped. I could not scream, I couldn't even breathe. I fell down and that awful man held my head, maybe for an hour. Then he left. I was so frightened that I stayed where I had fallen until the next morning. Pablito found me there; he laughed and said that I should be very proud and happy because that old man was a powerful sorcerer and was one of his teachers. I was dumbfounded; I couldn't believe Pablito was a sorcerer. He said that his teacher had seen a perfect circle of moths flying over my head. He had also seen my death circling around me. And that was why he had acted like lightning and had changed the direction of my eyes. Pablito also said that the Nagual had laid his hands on me and had reached into my body and that soon I would be different. I had no idea what he was talking about. I had no idea what that crazy old man had done, either. But it didn't matter to me. I was like a dog that everyone kicked around. Pablito had been the only person who had been kind to me. At first I had thought he wanted me for his woman. But I was too ugly and fat and smelly. He just wanted to be kind to me.

'The crazy old man came back another night and grabbed me again by the neck from behind. He hurt me terribly. I cried and screamed. I didn't know what he was doing. He never said a word to me. I was deathly afraid of him. Then, later on he began to talk to me and told me what to do with my life. I liked what he said. He took me everywhere with him. But my emptiness was my worst enemy. I couldn't accept his ways, so one day he got sick and tired of pampering me and sent the wind after me. I was in the back of Soledad's house by myself that day, and I felt the wind getting very strong. It was blowing through the fence. It got into my eyes. I wanted to get inside the house, but my body was frightened and instead of walking through the door I walked through the gate in the fence. The wind pushed me and made me twirl. I tried to go back to the house, but it was useless. I couldn't break the force of the wind. It pushed me over the hills and off the road and I ended up in a deep hole, a hole like a tomb. The wind kept me there for days and days, until I had decided to change and accept my fate without recrimination. Then the wind stopped and the Nagual found me and took me back to the house. He told me that my task was to give what I didn't have, love and affection, and that I had to take care of the sisters, Lidia and Josefina, better than if they were myself. I understood then what the Nagual had been saying to me for years. My life had been over a long time ago. He had offered me a new life and that life had to be completely new. I couldn't bring to that new life my ugly old ways. That first night he found me, the moths had pointed me out to him; I had no business rebelling against my fate.

'I began my change by taking care of Lidia and Josefina better than I took care of myself. I did everything the Nagual told me, and one night in this very gully in this very cave I found my completeness. I had fallen asleep right here where I am now and then a noise woke me up. I looked up and saw myself as I had once been, thin, young, fresh. It was my spirit that was coming back to me. At first it didn't want to come closer because I still looked pretty awful. But then it couldn't help itself and came to me. I knew right then, and all at once, what the Nagual had struggled for years to tell me. He had said that when one has a child that child takes the edge of our spirit. For a woman to have a girl means the end of that edge. To have had two as I did meant the end of me. The best of my strength and my illusions went to those girls. They stole my edge, the Nagual said, in the same way I had stolen it from my parents. That's our fate. A boy steals the biggest part of his edge from his father, a girl from her mother. The Nagual said that people who have had children, could tell, if they aren't as stubborn as you, that something is missing in them. Some craziness, some nervousness, some power that they had before is gone. They used to have it, but where is it now? The Nagual said that it is in the little child running around the house, full of energy, full of illusions. In other words, complete. He said that if we watch children we can tell that they are daring, they move in leaps. If we watch their parents we can see that they are cautious and timid. They don't leap any more. The Nagual told me we explain that by saying that the parents are grown-ups and have responsibilities. But that's not true. The truth of the matter is that they have lost their edge.'

I asked la Gorda what the Nagual would have said if I had told him that I knew parents with much more spirit and edge than their children.

She laughed, covering her face in a gesture of sham embarrassment.

'You can ask me,' she said giggling. 'You want to hear what I think?'

'Of course I want to hear it.'

'Those people don't have more spirit, they merely had a lot of vigour to begin with and have trained their children to be obedient and meek. They have frightened their children all their lives, that's all.'

I described to her the case of a man I knew, a father of four, who at the age of fifty-three changed his life completely. That entailed leaving his wife and his executive job in a large corporation after more than twenty-five years of building a career and a family. He chucked it all very daringly and went to live on an island in the Pacific.

'You mean he went there all by himself?' la Gorda asked with a tone of surprise.

She had destroyed my argument. I had to admit that the man had gone there with his twenty-three-year-old bride.

'Who no doubt is complete,' la Gorda added.

I had to agree with her again.

'An empty man uses the completeness of a woman all the time,' she went on. 'A complete woman is dangerous in her completeness, more so than a man. She is unreliable, moody, nervous, but also capable of great changes. Women like that can pick themselves up and go anywhere. They'll do nothing there, but that's because they had nothing going to begin with. Empty people, on the other hand, can't jump like that any more, but they're more reliable. The Nagual said that empty people are like worms that look around before moving a bit and then they back up and then they move a little bit more again. Complete people always jump, somersault and almost always land on their heads, but it doesn't matter to them.

'The Nagual said that to enter into the other world one has

to be complete. To be a sorcerer one has to have all of one's luminosity: no holes, no patches and all the edge of the spirit. So a sorcerer who is empty has to regain completeness. Man or woman, they must be complete to enter into that world out there, that eternity where the Nagual and Genaro are now waiting for us.'

She stopped talking and stared at me for a long moment. There was barely enough light to write.

'But how did you regain your completeness?' I asked.

She jumped at the sound of my voice. I repeated my question. She stared up at the roof of the cave before answering me.

'I had to refuse those two girls,' she said. 'The Nagual once told you how to do that but you didn't want to hear it. His point was that one has to steal that edge back. He said that we got it the hard way by stealing it and that we must recover it the same way, the hard way.

'He guided me to do that, and the first thing he made me do was to refuse my love for those two children. I had to do that in *dreaming*. Little by little I learned not to like them, but the Nagual said that that was useless, one has to learn not to care and not not to like. Whenever those girls meant nothing to me I had to see them again, lay my eyes and my hands on them. I had to pat them gently on the head and let my left side snatch the edge out of them.'

'What happened to them?'

'Nothing. They never felt a thing. They went home and are now like two grown-up persons. Empty like most people around them. They don't like the company of children because they have no use for them. I would say that they are better off. I took the craziness out of them. They didn't need it, while I did. I didn't know what I was doing when I gave it to them. Besides, they still retain the edge they stole from their father. The Nagual was right: no one noticed the loss, but I did notice my gain. As I looked out of this cave I saw all my illusions lined up like a row of soldiers. The world was bright and new. The heaviness of my body and my spirit had been lifted off and I was truly a new being.'

'Do you know how you took your edge from your children?'

'They are not my children! I have never had any. Look at me.'

She crawled out of the cave, lifted her skirt and showed me her naked body. The first thing I noticed was how slender and muscular she was.

She urged me to come closer and examine her. Her body was so lean and firm that I had to conclude she could not possibly have had children. She put her right leg on a high rock and showed me her vagina. Her drive to prove her change was so intense that I had to laugh to bridge my nervousness. I said that I was not a doctor and therefore I could not tell, but that I was sure she must be right.

'Of course I'm right,' she said as she crawled back into the cave. 'Nothing has ever come out of this womb.'

After a moment's pause she answered my question, which I had already forgotten under the onslaught of her display.

'My left side took my edge back,' she said. 'All I did was to go and visit the girls. I went there four or five times to allow them time to feel at ease with me. They were big girls and were going to school. I thought I would have to fight not to like them, but the Nagual said that it didn't matter, that I should like them if I wanted to. So I liked them. But my liking them was just like liking a stranger. My mind was made up, my purpose was unbending. I want to enter into the other world while I'm still alive, as the Nagual told me. In order to do that I need all the edge of my spirit. I need my completeness. Nothing can turn me away from that world! Nothing!'

She stared at me defiantly.

'You have to refuse both, the woman who emptied you and the little boy who has your love, if you are seeking your completeness. The woman you can easily refuse. The little boy is something else. Do you think that your useless affection for that child is so worthy as to keep you from entering into that realm?'

I had no answer. It was not that I wanted to think it over. It was rather that I had become utterly confused.

'Soledad has to take her edge out of Pablito if she wants to enter into the Nagual,' she went on. 'How in the hell is she going to do that? Pablito, no matter how weak he is, is a sorcerer. But the Nagual gave Soledad a unique chance. He said to her that her only moment would come when you walked into the house, and for that moment he not only made us move out into the other house, but he made us help her widen the path to the house, so you could drive your car to the very door. He told her that if she lived an impeccable life she would bag you, and suck away all your luminosity, which is all the power the Nagual left inside your body. That would not be difficult for her to do. Since she's going in the opposite direction, she could drain you to nothing. Her great feat was to lead you to a moment of helplessness.

'Once she had killed you, your luminosity would have increased her power and she would then have come after us. I was the only one who knew that. Lidia, Josefina and Rosa love her. I don't. I knew what her designs were. She would have taken us one by one, in her own time, since she had nothing to lose and everything to gain. The Nagual said to me that there was no other way for her. He entrusted me with the girls and told me what to do in case Soledad killed you and came after our luminosity. He figured that I had a chance to save myself and to save perhaps one of the three. You see, Soledad is not a bad woman at all; she's simply doing what an impeccable warrior would do. The little sisters like her more than they like their own mothers. She's a real mother to them. That was, the Nagual said, the point of her advantage. I haven't been able to pull the little sisters away from her, no matter what I do. So if she had killed you, she would then have taken at least two of those three trusting souls. Then without you in the picture Pablito is nothing. Soledad would have squashed him like a bug. And then with all her completeness and power she would have entered into that world out there. If I had been in her place I would've tried to do exactly as she did.

'So you see, it was all or nothing for her. When you first arrived everyone was gone. It looked as if it was the end for you and for some of us. But then at the end it was nothing for her and a chance for the sisters. The moment I knew that you had succeeded I told the three girls that now it was their turn. The Nagual had said that they should wait until the morning to catch you unawares. He said that the morning was not a good time for you. He commanded me to stay away and not interfere with the sisters and to come in only if you would try to injure their luminosity.'

'Were they supposed to kill me, too?'

'Well, yes. You are the male side of their luminosity. Their completeness is at times their disadvantage. The Nagual ruled them with an iron hand and balanced them, but now that he's gone they have no way of levelling off. Your luminosity could do that for them.'

'How about you, Gorda? Are you supposed to finish me off too?'

'I've told you already that I'm different. I am balanced. My emptiness, which was my disadvantage, is now my advantage. Once a sorcerer regains his completeness he's balanced, while a sorcerer who was always complete is a bit off. Like Genaro was a bit off. But the Nagual was balanced because he had been incomplete, like you and me, even more so than you and me. He had three sons and one daughter.

'The little sisters are like Genaro, a bit off. And most of the times so taut that they have no measure.'

'How about me, Gorda? Do I also have to go after them?'

'No. Only they could have profited by sucking away your luminosity. You can't profit at all by anyone's death. The Nagual left a special power with you, a balance of some kind, which none of us has.'

'Can't they learn to have that balance?'

'Sure they can. But that has nothing to do with the task the little sisters had to perform. Their task was to steal your power. For that, they became so united that they are now one single being. They trained themselves to sip you up like a glass of soda. The Nagual set them up to be deceivers of the highest order, especially Josefina. She put on a show that was peerless. Compared to their art, Soledad's attempt was child's play. She's a crude woman. The little sisters are true sorceresses. Two of them gained your confidence, while the third shocked you and rendered you helpless. They played their cards to perfection. You fell for it all and nearly succumbed. The only flaw was that you injured and cured Rosa's luminosity the night before and that made her jumpy. Had it not been for her nervousness and her biting your side so hard, chances are you wouldn't be here now. I saw everything from the door. I came in at the precise moment you were about to annihilate them.'

'But what could I do to annihilate them?'

'How could I know that? I'm not you.'

'I mean what did you see me doing?'

'I saw your double coming out of you.'

'What did it look like?'

'It looked like you, what else? But it was very big and menacing. Your double would have killed them. So I came in and interfered with it. It took the best of my power to calm you down. The sisters were no help. They were lost. And you were furious and violent. You changed colours right in front of us twice. One colour was so violent that I feared you would kill me too.'

'What colour was it, Gorda?'

'White, what else? The double is white, yellowish white, like the sun.'

I stared at her. The simile was very new to me.

'Yes,' she continued, 'we are pieces of the sun. That is why we are luminous beings. But our eyes can't see that luminosity because it is very faint. Only the eyes of a sorcerer can *see* it, and that happens after a lifetime struggle.'

Her revelation had taken me by total surprise. I tried to re-organize my thoughts in order to ask the most appropriate question.

'Did the Nagual ever tell you anything about the sun?' I asked.

'Yes. We are all like the sun but very, very faint. Our light is too weak, but it is light anyway.'

'But, did he say that the sun was perhaps the Nagual?' I insisted desperately.

La Gorda did not answer. She made a series of involuntary noises with her lips. She was apparently thinking how to answer my probe. I waited, ready to write it down. After a long pause she crawled out of the cave.

'I'll show you my faint light,' she said matter-of-factly.

She walked to the centre of the narrow gully in front of the cave and squatted. From where I was I could not see what she was doing so I had to get out of the cave myself. I stood ten or twelve feet away from her. She put her hands under her skirt, while she was still squatting. Suddenly, she stood up. Her hands were loosely clasped into fists; she raised them over her head and snapped her fingers open. I heard a quick, bursting sound and I saw sparks flying from her fingers. She again clasped her hands and then snapped them open and another volley of much larger sparks flew out of them. She squatted once more and reached under her skirt. She seemed to be pulling something from her pubis. She repeated the snapping movement of her fingers as she threw her hands over her head, and I saw a spray of long, luminous fibres flying away from her fingers. I had to tilt my head up to see them against the already dark sky. They appeared to be long, fine filaments of a reddish light. After a while they faded and disappeared.

She squatted once again, and when she let her fingers open a most astonishing display of lights emanated from them. The sky was filled with thick rays of light. It was a spellbinding sight. I became engrossed in it; my eyes were fixed. I was not paying attention to la Gorda. I was looking at the lights. I heard a sudden outcry that forced me to look at her, just in time to see her grab one of the lines she was creating and spin to the very top of the canyon. She hovered there for an instant like a dark, huge shadow against the sky, and then descended to the bottom of the gully in spurts or small leaps or as if she were coming down a stairway on her belly.

I suddenly saw her standing over me. I had not realized that I had fallen on my seat. I stood up. She was soaked in perspiration and was panting, trying to catch her breath. She could not speak for a long time. She began to jog in place. I did not dare to touch her. Finally she seemed to have calmed down enough to crawl back into the cave. She rested for a few minutes.

Her actions had been so fast that I had hardly had any time to evaluate what had happened. At the moment of her display I had felt an unbearable, ticklish pain in the area just below my navel. I had not physically exerted myself and yet I was also panting.

'I think it's time to go to our appointment,' she said, out of breath. 'My flying·opened us both. You felt my flying in your belly; that means you are open and ready to meet the four forces.'

'What four forces are you talking about?'

'The Nagual's and Genaro's allies. You've seen them. They are horrendous. Now they are free from the Nagual's and Genaro's gourds. You heard one of them around Soledad's house the other night. They are waiting for you. The moment the darkness of the day sets in, they'll be uncontainable. One of them even came after you in the daytime at Soledad's place. Those allies now belong to you and me. We will take two each. I don't know which ones. And I don't know how, either. All the Nagual told me was that you and I would have to tackle them by ourselves.'

'Wait, wait!' I shouted.

She did not let me speak. She gently put her hand over my mouth. I felt a pang of terror in the pit of my stomach. I had been confronted in the past with some inexplicable phenomena which don Juan and don Genaro had called their allies. There were four of them and they were entities, as real as anything in the world. Their presence was so outlandish that it would create an unparalleled state of fear in me every time I perceived them. The first one I had encountered was don Juan's; it was a dark, rectangular mass, eight or nine feet high and four or five feet across. It moved with the crushing weight of a giant boulder and breathed so heavily that it reminded me of the sound of bellows. I had always encountered it at night, in the darkness. I had fancied it to be like a door that walked by pivoting on one corner and then on the other.

The second ally I came across was don Genaro's. It was a long-faced, bald-headed, extraordinarily tall, glowing man, with thick lips and enormous, droopy eyes. He always wore pants that were too short for his long, skinny legs.

I had seen those two allies a great many times while in the company of don Juan and don Genaro. The sight of them would invariably cause an irreconcilable separation between my reason and my perception. On the one hand, I had no rational ground whatsoever to believe that what was happening to me was actually taking place, and on the other hand, there was no possible way of discarding the truthfulness of my perception.

Since they had always appeared while don Juan and don Genaro were around, I had filed them away as products of the powerful influence that those two men had had on my suggestible personality. In my understanding it was either that, or that don Juan and don Genaro had in their possession forces they called their allies, forces which were capable of manifesting themselves to me as those horrendous entities.

A feature of the allies was that they never allowed me to scrutinize them thoroughly. I had tried various times to focus my undivided attention on them, but every time I would get dizzy and dissociated.

The other two allies were more elusive. I had seen them only once, a gigantic black jaguar with yellow glowing eyes, and a ravenous, enormous coyote. The two beasts were ultimately aggressive and overpowering. The jaguar was don Genaro's and the coyote was don Juan's.

La Gorda crawled out of the cave. I followed her. She led the way. We walked out of the gully and reached a long, rocky plain. She stopped and let me step ahead. I told her that if she was going to let me lead us I was going to try to get to the car. She shook her head affirmatively and clung to me. I could feel her clammy skin. She seemed to be in a state of great agitation. It was perhaps a mile to where we had left the car, and to reach it we had to cross the deserted, rocky plain. Don Juan had shown me a hidden trail among some big boulders, almost on the side of the mountain that flanked the plain towards the east. I headed for that trail. Some unknown urge was guiding me; otherwise

I would have taken the same trail we had taken before when we had crossed the plain on the level ground.

La Gorda seemed to be anticipating something awesome. She grabbed on to me. Her eyes were wild.

'Are we going the right way?' I asked.

She did not answer. She pulled her shawl and twisted it until it looked like a long, thick rope. She encircled my waist with it, crossed over the ends and encircled herself. She tied a knot and thus had us bound together in a band that looked like a figure eight.

'What did you do this for?' I asked.

She shook her head. Her teeth chattered but she could not say a word. Her fright seemed to be extreme. She pushed me to keep on walking. I could not help wondering why I was not scared out of my wits myself.

As we reached the high trail the physical exertion began to take its toll on me. I was wheezing and had to breathe through my mouth. I could see the shape of the big boulders. There was no moon but the sky was so clear that there was enough light to distinguish shapes. I could hear la Gorda also wheezing.

I tried to stop to catch my breath but she pushed me gently as she shook her head negatively. I wanted to make a joke to break the tension when I heard a strange thumping noise. My head moved involuntarily to my right to allow my left ear to scan the area. I stopped breathing for an instant and then I clearly heard that someone else besides la Gorda and myself was breathing heavily. I checked again to make sure before I told her. There was no doubt that that massive shape was there among the boulders. I put my hand on la Gorda's mouth as we kept on moving and signalled her to hold her breath. I could tell that the massive shape was very close. It seemed to be sliding as quietly as it could. It was wheezing softly.

La Gorda was startled. She squatted and pulled me down with her by the shawl tied around my waist. She put her hands under her skirt for a moment and then stood up; her hands were clasped and when she snapped her fingers open a volley of sparks flew from them.

'Piss in your hands,' la Gorda whispered through clenched teeth.

'Huh?' I said, unable to comprehend what she wanted me to do.

She whispered her order three or four times with increasing urgency. She must have realized I did not know what she wanted, for she squatted again and showed that she was urinating in her hands. I stared at her dumbfounded as she made her urine fly like reddish sparks.

My mind went blank. I did not know which was more absorbing, the sight la Gorda was creating with her urine, or the wheezing of the approaching entity. I could not decide on which of the two stimuli to focus my attention; both were enthralling.

'Quickly! Do it in your hands!' la Gorda grumbled between her teeth.

I heard her, but my attention was dislocated. With an imploring voice la Gorda added that my sparks would make the approaching creature, whatever it was, retreat. She began to whine and I began to feel desperate. I could not only hear but I could sense with my whole body the approaching entity. I tried to urinate in my hands; my effort was useless. I was too self-conscious and nervous. I became possessed by la Gorda's agitation and struggled desperately to urinate. I finally did it. I snapped my fingers three or four times, but nothing flew out of them.

'Do it again,' la Gorda said. 'It takes a while to make sparks.'

I told her that I had used up all the urine I had. There was the most intense look of despair in her eyes.

At that instant I saw the massive, rectangular shape moving towards us. Somehow it did not seem menacing to me, although la Gorda was about to faint out of fear.

Suddenly she untied her shawl and leaped on to a small rock that was behind me and hugged me from behind, putting her chin on my head. She had practically climbed on my shoulders. The instant that we adopted that position the shape ceased moving. It kept on wheezing, perhaps twenty feet away from us.

I felt a giant tension that seemed to be focused in my mid-section. After a while I knew without the shadow of a doubt that if we remained in that position we would have drained our energy and fallen prey to whatever was stalking us.

I told her that we were going to run for our lives. She shook her head negatively. She seemed to have regained her strength and confidence. She said then that we had to bury our heads in our arms and lie down with our thighs against our stomachs. I remembered then that years before don Juan had made me do the same thing one night when I was caught in a deserted field in northern Mexico by something equally unknown and yet equally real to my senses. At that time don Juan had said that fleeing was useless and the only thing one could do was to remain on the spot in the position la Gorda had just prescribed.

I was about to kneel down when I had the unexpected feeling that we had made a terrible mistake in leaving the cave. We had to go back to it at any cost.

I looped la Gorda's shawl over my shoulders and under my arms. I asked her to hold the tips above my head, climb to my shoulders and stand on them, bracing herself by pulling up the ends of the shawl and fastening it like a harness. Years before don Juan had told me that one should meet strange events, such as the rectangular shape in front of us, with unexpected actions. He said that once he himself stumbled upon a deer that 'talked' to him, and he stood on his head for the duration of that event, as a means of assuring his survival and to ease the strain of such an encounter.

My idea was to try to walk around the rectangular shape, back to the cave, with la Gorda standing on my shoulders.

She whispered that the cave was out of the question. The Nagual had told her not to remain there at all. I argued, as I fixed the shawl for her, that my body had the certainty that in the cave we would be all right. She replied that that was true, and it would work except that we had no means whatever to control those forces. We needed a special container, a gourd of some sort, like those I had seen dangling from don Juan's and don Genaro's belts.

She took off her shoes and climbed on my shoulders and stood there. I held her by her calves. As she pulled on the ends of the shawl I felt the tension of the band under my armpits. I waited until she had gained her balance. To walk in the darkness carrying one hundred and fifteen pounds on my shoulders was no mean feat. I went very slowly. I counted twenty-three paces and I had to put her down. The pain on my shoulder blades was unbearable. I told her that although she was very slender, her weight was crushing my collarbone.

The interesting part, however, was that the rectangular shape was no longer in sight. Our strategy had worked. La Gorda suggested that she carry me on her shoulders for a stretch. I found the idea ludicrous; my weight was more than what her small frame could stand. We decided to walk for a while and see what happened.

There was a dead silence around us. We walked slowly, bracing each other. We had moved no more than a few yards when I again began to hear strange breathing noises, a soft, prolonged hissing like the hissing of a feline. I hurriedly helped her to get back on my shoulders and walked another ten paces.

I knew we had to maintain the unexpected as a tactic if we wanted to get out of that place. I was trying to figure out another set of unexpected actions we could use instead of la Gorda standing on my shoulders, when she took off her long dress. In one single movement she was naked. She scrambled on the ground looking for something. I heard a cracking sound and she stood up holding a branch from a low bush. She manoeuvred her shawl around my shoulders and neck and made a sort of riding support where she could sit with her legs wrapped around my waist, like a child riding piggyback. She then put the branch inside her dress and held it above her head. She began to twirl the branch, giving the dress a strange bounce. To that effect she added a whistle, imitating the peculiar cry of a night owl.

After a hundred yards or so I heard the same sounds coming from behind us and from the sides. She changed to another birdcall, a piercing sound similar to that made by a peacock. A few minutes later the same birdcalls were echoing all around us.

I had witnessed a similar phenomenon of birdcalls being answered, years before with don Juan. I had thought at the time that perhaps the sounds were being produced by don Juan who was hiding nearby in the darkness, or even by someone closely associated with him, such as don Genaro, who was aiding him in creating an insurmountable fear in me, a fear that made me run in total darkness without even stumbling. Don Juan had called that particular action of running in darkness the gait of power.

I asked la Gorda if she knew how to do the gait of power. She said yes. I told her that we were going to try it, even though I was not at all sure I could do it. She said that it was neither the time nor the place for that and pointed in front of us. My heart, which had been beating fast all along, began to pound wildly inside my chest. Right ahead of us, perhaps ten feet away, and smack in the middle of the trail was one of don Genaro's allies, the strange glowing man, with the long face and the bald head. I froze on the spot. I heard la Gorda's shriek as though it were coming from far away. She frantically pounded on my sides with her fists. Her action broke my fixation on the man. She turned my head to the left and then to the right. On my left side, almost touching my leg, was the black mass of a giant feline with glaring yellow eyes. To my right I saw an enormous phosphorescent coyote. Behind us, almost touching la Gorda's back, was the dark rectangular shape.

The man turned his back to us and began to move on the trail. I also began to walk. La Gorda kept on shrieking and whining. The rectangular shape was almost grabbing her back. I heard it moving with crushing thumps. The sound of its steps reverberated on the hills around us. I could feel its cold breath on my neck. I knew that la Gorda was about to go mad. And so was I. The feline and the coyote were almost rubbing my legs. I could hear their hissing and growling increasing in volume. I had, at that moment, the irrational urge to make a certain sound don Juan had taught me. The allies answered me. I kept on frantically making the sound and they answered me back. The tension diminished by degrees, and before we reached the road I was part of a most extravagant scene. La Gorda was riding piggyback, happily bouncing her dress over her head as if nothing had ever happened, keeping the bounces in rhythm with the sound I was making, while four creatures of another world answered me back as they moved at my pace, flanking us on all four sides.

We got to the road in that fashion. But I did not want to leave. There seemed to be something missing. I stayed motionless with la Gorda on my back and made a very special tapping sound don Juan had taught me. He had said that it was the call of moths. In order to produce it one had to use the inside edge of the left hand and the lips.

As soon as I made it everything seemed to come to rest peacefully. The four entities answered me, and as they did I knew which were the ones that would go with me.

I then walked to the car and eased la Gorda off my back on to the driver's seat and pushed her over to her side. We drove away in absolute silence. Something had touched me somewhere and my thoughts had been turned off.

La Gorda suggested that we go to don Genaro's place instead of driving to her house. She said that Benigno, Nestor and Pablito lived there but they were out of town. Her suggestion appealed to me.

Once we were in the house la Gorda lit a lantern. The place looked just as it had the last time I had visited don Genaro. We sat on the floor. I pulled up a bench and put my writing pad on it. I was not tired and I wanted to write but I could not do it. I could not write at all.

'What did the Nagual tell you about the allies?' I asked.

My question seemed to catch her off guard. She did not know how to answer.

'I can't think,' she finally said.

It was as though she had never experienced that state before. She paced back and forth in front of me. Tiny beads of perspiration had formed on the tip of her nose and on her upper lip.

She suddenly grabbed me by the hand and practically pulled me out of the house. She led me to a nearby ravine and there she got sick.

My stomach felt queasy. She said that the pull of the allies had been too great and that I should force myself to throw up. I stared at her, waiting for a further explanation. She took my head in her hands and stuck her finger down my throat, with the certainty of a nurse dealing with a child, and actually made me vomit. She explained that human beings had a very delicate glow around the stomach and that that glow was always being pulled by everything around. At times when the pull was too great, as in the case of contact with the allies, or even in the case of contact with strong people, the glow would become agitated, change colour or even fade altogether. In such instances the only thing one could do was simply to throw up.

I felt better but not quite myself yet. I had a sense of tiredness, of heaviness around my eyes. We walked back to the house. As we reached the door la Gorda sniffed the air like a dog and said that she knew which allies were mine. Her statement, which ordinarily would have had no other significance than the one she alluded to, or the one I myself read into it, had the special quality of a cathartic device. It made me explode into thoughts. All at once, my usual intellectual deliberations came into being. I felt myself leaping in the air, as if thoughts had an energy of their own.

The first thought that came to my mind was that the allies were actual entities, as I had suspected without ever daring to admit it, even to myself. I had seen them and felt them and communicated with them. I was euphoric. I embraced la Gorda and began to explain to her the crux of my intellectual dilemma. I had seen the allies without the aid of don Juan or don Genaro and that act made all the difference in the world to me. I told la Gorda that once when I had reported to don Juan that I had seen one of the allies he had laughed and urged me not to take myself so seriously and to disregard what I had seen.

I had never wanted to believe I was having hallucinations, but I did not want to accept that there were allies, either. My rational background was unbending. I could not bridge the gap. This time, however, everything was different, and the thought that there were actually beings on this earth that were from another world without being aliens to the earth was more than I could bear. I said to la Gorda, half in jest, that secretly I would have given anything to be crazy. That would have absolved some part of me from the crushing responsibility of revamping my understanding of the world. The irony of it was that I could not have been more willing to revamp my understanding of the world, on an intellectual level, that is. But that was not enough. That had never been enough. And that had been my insurmountable obstacle all along, my deadly flaw. I had been willing to dally in don Juan's world in a semi-convinced fashion; therefore, I had been a quasi-sorcerer. All my efforts had been no more than my inane eagerness to fence with the intellect, as if I were in academia where one can do that very thing from 8.00 a.m. to 5.00 p.m., at which time, duly tired, one goes home. Don Juan used to say as a joke that, after arranging the world in a most beautiful and enlightened manner, the scholar goes home at five o'clock in order to forget his beautiful arrangement.

While la Gorda made us some food I worked feverishly on my notes. I felt much more relaxed after eating. La Gorda was in the best of spirits. She clowned, the way don Genaro used to, imitating the gestures I made while I wrote.

'What do you know about the allies, Gorda?' I asked.

'Only what the Nagual told me,' she replied. 'He said that the allies were forces that a sorcerer learns to control. He had two inside his gourd and so did Genaro.'

'How did they keep them inside their gourds?'

'No one knows that. All the Nagual knew was that a tiny, perfect gourd with a neck must be found before one could harness the allies.'

'Where can one find that kind of gourd?'

'Anywhere. The Nagual left word with me, in case we survived the attack of the allies, that we should start looking for the perfect gourd, which must be the size of the thumb of the left hand. That was the size of the Nagual's gourd.'

'Have you seen his gourd?'

'No. Never. The Nagual said that a gourd of that kind is

not in the world of men. It's like a little bundle that one can distinguish hanging from their belts. But if you deliberately look at it you will see nothing.

'The gourd, once it is found, must be groomed with great care. Usually sorcerers find gourds like that on vines in the woods. They pick them and dry them and then they hollow them out. And then they smooth them and polish them. Once the sorcerer has his gourd he must offer it to the allies and entice them to live there. If the allies consent, the gourd disappears from the world of men and the allies become an aid to the sorcerer. The Nagual and Genaro could make their allies do anything that needed to be done. Things they themselves could not do. Such as, for instance, sending the wind to chase me or sending that chicken to run inside Lidia's blouse.'

I heard a peculiar, prolonged hissing sound outside the door. It was the exact sound I had heard in doña Soledad's house two days before. This time I knew it was the jaguar. The sound did not scare me. In fact, I would have stepped out to see the jaguar had la Gorda not stopped me.

'You're still incomplete,' she said. 'The allies would feast on you if you go out by yourself. Especially that daring one that's prowling out there now.'

'My body feels very safe,' I protested.

She patted my back and held me down against the bench on which I was writing.

'You're not a complete sorcerer yet,' she said. 'You have a huge patch in your middle and the force of those allies would yank it out of place. They are no joke.'

'What are you supposed to do when an ally comes to you in this fashion?'

'I don't bother with them one way or another. The Nagual taught me to be balanced and not to seek anything eagerly. Tonight, for instance, I knew which allies would go to you, if you can ever get a gourd and groom it. You may be eager to get them. I'm not. Chances are I'll never get them myself. They are a pain in the neck.'

'Why?'

'Because they are forces and as such they can drain you to

nothing. The Nagual said that one is better off with nothing except one's purpose and freedom. Someday when you're complete, perhaps we'll have to choose whether or not to keep them.'

I told her that I personally liked the jaguar even though there was something overbearing about it.

She peered at me. There was a look of surprise and bewilderment in her eyes.

'I really like that one,' I said.

'Tell me what you saw,' she said.

I realized at that moment that I had automatically assumed that she had seen the same things I had. I described in great detail the four allies as I had seen them. She listened more than attentively; she appeared to be spellbound by my description.

'The allies have no form,' she said when I had finished. 'They are like a presence, like a wind, like a glow. The first one we found tonight was a blackness that wanted to get inside my body. That's why I screamed. I felt it reaching up my legs. The others were just colours. Their glow was so strong, though, that it made the trail look as if it were daytime.'

Her statements astounded me. I had finally accepted, after years of struggle and purely on the basis of our encounter with them that night, that the allies had a consensual form, a substance which could be perceived equally by everyone's senses.

I jokingly told la Gorda that I had already written in my notes that they were creatures with form.

'What am I going to do now?' I asked in a rhetorical sense.

'It's very simple,' she said. 'Write that they are not.'

I thought that she was absolutely right.

'Why do I see them as monsters?' I asked.

'That's no mystery,' she said. 'You haven't lost your human form yet. The same thing happened to me. I used to see the allies as people; all of them were Indian men with horrible faces and mean looks. They used to wait for me in deserted places. I thought they were after me as a woman. The Nagual used to laugh his head off at my fears. But still I was half dead with fright. One of them used to come and sit on my bed and shake it until I would wake up. The fright that that ally used to give me was something that I don't want repeated, even now that I'm changed. Tonight I think I was as afraid of the allies as I used to be.'

'You mean that you don't see them as human beings any more?'

'No. Not any more. The Nagual told you that an ally is formless. He is right. An ally is only a presence, a helper that is nothing and yet it is as real as you and me.'

'Have the little sisters seen the allies?'

'Everybody has seen them one time or another.'

'Are the allies just a force for them too?'

'No. They are like you; they haven't lost their human form yet. None of them has. For all of them, the little sisters, the Genaros and Soledad, the allies are horrendous things; with them the allies are malevolent, dreadful creatures of the night. The sole mention of the allies sends Lidia and Josefina and Pablito into a frenzy. Rosa and Nestor are not that afraid of them, but they don't want to have anything to do with them, either. Benigno has his own designs so he's not concerned with them. They don't bother him, or me, for that matter. But the others are easy prey for the allies, especially now that the allies are out of the Nagual's and Genaro's gourds. They come all the time looking for you.

'The Nagual told me that as long as one clings to the human form, one can only reflect that form, and since the allies feed directly on to our life-force in the middle of the stomach, they usually make us sick, and then we see them as heavy, ugly creatures.'

'Is there something that we can do to protect ourselves, or to change the shape of those creatures?'

'What all of you have to do is lose your human forms.'

'What do you mean?'

My question did not seem to have any meaning for her. She stared at me blankly as if waiting for me to clarify what I had just said. She closed her eyes for a moment.

'You don't know about the human mould and the human form, do you?' she asked.

I stared at her.

'I've just *seen* that you know nothing about them,' she said and smiled.

'You are absolutely right,' I said.

'The Nagual told me that the human form is a force,' she said. 'And the human mould is ... well ... a mould. He said that everything has a particular mould. Plants have moulds, animals have moulds, worms have moulds. Are you sure the Nagual never showed you the human mould?'

I told her that he had sketched the concept, but in a very brief manner, once when he had tried to explain something about a dream I had had. In the dream in question I had seen a man who seemed to be concealing himself in the darkness of a narrow gully. To find him there scared me. I looked at him for a moment and then the man stepped forward and made himself visible to me. He was naked and his body glowed. He seemed to be delicate, almost frail. I liked his eyes. They were friendly and profound. I thought that they were very kind. But then he stepped back into the darkness of the gully and his eyes became like two mirrors, like the eyes of a ferocious animal.

Don Juan said that I had encountered the human mould in 'dreaming'. He explained that sorcerers have the avenue of their 'dreaming' to lead them to the mould, and that the mould of men was definitely an entity, an entity which could be seen by some of us at certain times when we are imbued with power, and by all of us for sure at the moment of our death. He described the mould as being the source, the origin of man, since, without the mould to group together the force of life, there was no way for that force to assemble itself into the shape of man.

He interpreted my dream as a brief and extraordinarily simplistic glance at the mould. He said that my dream had re-stated the fact that I was a simpleminded and very earthy man.

La Gorda laughed and said that she would have said the same thing herself. To see the mould as an average naked man and then as an animal had been indeed a very simplistic view of the mould.

'Perhaps it was just a stupid, ordinary dream,' I said, trying to defend myself.

'No,' she said with a large grin. 'You see, the human mould

glows and it is always found in water holes and narrow gullies.'

'Why in gullies and water holes?' I asked.

'It feeds on water. Without water there is no mould,' she replied. 'I know that the Nagual took you to water holes regularly in hopes of showing you the mould. But your emptiness prevented you from seeing anything. The same thing happened to me. He used to make me lie naked on a rock in the very centre of a particular dried-up water hole, but all I did was to feel the presence of something that scared me out of my wits.'

'Why does emptiness prevent one from seeing the mould?'

'The Nagual said that everything in the world is a force, a pull or a push. In order for us to be pushed or pulled we need to be like a sail, like a kite in the wind. But if we have a hole in the middle of our luminosity, the force goes through it and never acts upon us.

'The Nagual told me that Genaro liked you very much and tried to make you aware of the hole in your middle. He used to fly his sombrero as a kite to tease you; he even pulled you from that hole until you had diarrhoea, but you never caught on to what he was doing.'

'Why didn't they tell me as plainly as you have told me?'

'They did, but you didn't notice their words.'

I found her statement impossible to believe. To accept that they had told me about it and I had not acknowledged it was unthinkable.

'Did you ever see the mould, Gorda?' I asked.

'Sure, when I became complete again. I went to that particular water hole one day by myself and there it was. It was a radiant, luminous being. I could not look at it. It blinded me. But being in its presence was enough. I felt happy and strong. And nothing else mattered, nothing. Just being there was all I wanted. The Nagual said that sometimes if we have enough personal power we can catch a glimpse of the mould even though we are not sorcerers; when that happens we say that we have seen God. He said that if we call it God it is the truth. The mould is God.

'I had a dreadful time understanding the Nagual, because I was a very religious woman. I had nothing else in the world but my religion. So to hear the Nagual say the things he used to say made me shiver. But then I became complete and the forces of the world began to pull me, and I knew that the Nagual was right. The mould is God. What do you think?

'The day I see it I'll tell you, Gorda,' I said.

She laughed, and said that the Nagual used to make fun of me, saying that the day I would see the mould I would probably become a Franciscan friar, because in the depths of me I was a religious soul.

'Was the mould you saw a man or a woman?' I asked.

'Neither. It was simply a luminous human. The Nagual said that I could have asked something for myself. That a warrior cannot let that chance pass. But I could not think of anything to ask for. It was better that way. I have the most beautiful memory of it. The Nagual said that a warrior with enough power can *see* the mould, many, many times. What a great fortune that must be!'

'But if the human mould is what puts us together, what is the human form?'

'Something sticky, a sticky force that makes us the people we are. The Nagual told me that the human form has no form. Like the allies that he carried in his gourd, it's anything, but in spite of not having form, it possesses us during our lives and doesn't leave us until we die. I've never seen the human form but I have felt it in my body.'

She then described a very complex series of sensations that she had had over a period of years that culminated in a serious illness, the climax of which was a bodily state that reminded me of descriptions I had read of a massive heart attack. She said that the human form, as the force that it is, left her body after a serious internal battle that manifested itself as illness.

'It sounds as if you had a heart attack,' I said.

'Maybe I did,' she replied, 'but one thing I know for sure. The day I had it, I lost my human form. I became so weak that for days I couldn't even get out of my bed. Since that day I haven't had the energy to be my old self. From time to time I have tried to get into my old habits, but I didn't have the strength to enjoy them the way I used to. Finally I gave up trying.'

'What is the point of losing your form?'

'A warrior must drop the human form in order to change, to really change. Otherwise there is only talk about change, like in your case. The Nagual said that it is useless to think or hope that one can change one's habits. One cannot change one iota as long as one holds on to the human form. The Nagual told me that a warrior knows that he cannot change, and yet he makes it his business to try to change, even though he knows that he won't be able to. That's the only advantage a warrior has over the average man. The warrior is never disappointed when he fails to change.'

'But you are still yourself, Gorda, aren't you?'

'No. Not any more. The only thing that makes you think you are yourself is the form. Once it leaves, you are nothing.'

'But you still talk and think and feel as you always did, don't you?'

'Not at all. I'm new.'

She laughed and hugged me as if she were consoling a child.

'Only Eligio and I have lost our form,' she went on. 'It was our great fortune that we lost it while the Nagual was among us. You people will have a horrid time. That is your fate. Whoever loses it next will have only me as a companion. I already feel sorry for whoever it will be.'

'What else did you feel, Gorda, when you lost your form, besides not having enough energy?'

'The Nagual told me that a warrior without form begins to see an eye. I saw an eye in front of me every time I closed my eyes. It got so bad that I couldn't rest any more; the eye followed me wherever I went. I nearly went mad. Finally, I suppose, I became used to it. Now I don't even notice it because it has become part of me.

'The formless warrior uses that eye to start *dreaming*. If you don't have a form, you don't have to go to sleep to do *dreaming*. The eye in front of you pulls you every time you want to go.'

'Where exactly is that eye, Gorda?'

She closed her eyes and moved her hand from side to side, right in front of her eyes, covering the span of her face.

'Sometimes the eye is very small and other times it is enormous,' she went on. 'When it's small your *dreaming* is precise. If it's big your *dreaming* is like flying over the mountains and not really seeing much. I haven't done enough *dreaming* yet, but the Nagual told me that that eye is my trump card. One day when I become truly formless I won't see the eye any more; the eye will become just like me, nothing, and yet it'll be there like the allies. The Nagual said that everything has to be sifted through our human form. When we have no form, then nothing has form and yet everything is present. I couldn't understand what he meant by that, but now I see that he was absolutely right. The allies are only a presence and so will be the eye. But at this time that eye is everything to me. In fact, in having that eye I should need nothing else in order to call up my *dreaming*, even when I'm awake. I haven't been able to do that yet. Perhaps I'm like you, a bit stubborn and lazy.'

'How did you do the flying you showed me tonight?'

'The Nagual taught me how to use my body to make lights, because we are light anyway, so I make sparks and lights and they in turn lure the lines of the world. Once I *see* one, it's easy to hook myself to it.'

'How do you hook yourself?'

'I grab it.'

She made a gesture with her hands. She clawed them and then placed them together joined at the wrists, forming a sort of bowl, with the clawed fingers upright.

'You have to grab the line like a jaguar,' she went on, 'and never separate the wrists. If you do, you'll fall down and break your neck.'

She paused and that forced me to look at her, waiting for more of her revelations.

'You don't believe me, do you?' she asked.

Without giving me time to answer, she squatted and began again to produce her display of sparks. I was calm and collected and could place my undivided attention on her actions. When she snapped her fingers open, every fibre of her muscles seemed to tense at once. That tension seemed to be focused on the very tips of her fingers and was projected out like rays of light. The moisture in her fingertips was actually a vehicle to carry some sort of energy emanating from her body.

'How did you do that, Gorda?' I asked, truly marvelling at her.

'I really don't know,' she said. 'I simply do it. I've done it lots and lots of times and yet I don't know how I do it. When I grab one of those rays I feel that I'm being pulled by something. I really don't do anything else except let the lines I've grabbed pull me. When I want to get back through, I feel that the line doesn't want to let me free and I get frantic. The Nagual said that that was my worst feature. I get so frightened that one of these days I'm going to injure my body. But I figure that one of these days I'll be even more formless and then I won't get frightened, so as long as I hold on until that day, I'm all right.'

'Tell me then, Gorda, how do you let the lines pull you?'

'We're back again in the same spot. I don't know. The Nagual warned me about you. You want to know things that cannot be known.'

I struggled to make clear to her that what I was after were the procedures. I had really given up looking for an explanation from all of them because their explanations explained nothing to me. To describe to me the steps that were followed was something altogether different.

'How did you learn to let your body hold on to the lines of the world?' I asked.

'I learned that in *dreaming*,' she said, 'but I really don't know how. Everything for a woman warrior starts in *dreaming*. The Nagual told me, just as he told you, first to look for my hands in my dreams. I couldn't find them at all. In my dreams I had no hands. I tried and tried for years to find them. Every night I used to give myself the command to find my hands but it was to no avail. I never found anything in my dreams. The Nagual was merciless with me. He said that I had to find them or perish. So I lied to him that I had found my hands in my dreams. The Nagual didn't say a word but Genaro threw his hat on the floor and danced on it. He patted my head and said that I was really a great warrior. The more he praised me the worse I felt. I was about to tell the Nagual the truth when crazy Genaro aimed his behind at me and let out the loudest and longest fart I had ever heard. He actually pushed me backwards with it. It was like a hot, foul wind, disgusting and smelly, just like me. The Nagual was choking with laughter.

'I ran to the house and hid there. I was very fat then, I used to eat a great deal and I had a lot of gas. So I decided not to eat for a while. Lidia and Josefina helped me. I didn't eat anything for twenty-three days, and then one night I found my hands in my dreams. They were old and ugly and green, but they were mine. So that was the beginning. The rest was easy.'

'And what was the rest, Gorda?'

'The next thing the Nagual wanted me to do was to try to find houses or buildings in my dreams and look at them, trying not to dissolve the images. He said that the art of the dreamer is to hold the image of his dream. Because that's what we do any way during all our lives.'

'What did he mean by that?'

'Our art as ordinary people is that we know how to hold the image of what we are looking at. The Nagual said that we do that but we don't know how. We just do it; that is, our bodies do it. In *dreaming* we have to do the same thing, except that in *dreaming* we have to learn how to do it. We have to struggle not to look but merely to glance and yet hold the image.

'The Nagual told me to find in my dreams a brace for my belly button. It took a long time because I didn't understand what he meant. He said that in *dreaming* we pay attention with the belly button; therefore it has to be protected. We need a little warmth or a feeling that something is pressing the belly button in order to hold the images in our dreams.

'I found a pebble in my dreams that fit my belly button, and the Nagual made me look for it day after day in water holes and canyons, until I found it. I made a belt for it and I still wear it day and night. Wearing it made it easier for me to hold images in my dreams.

'Then the Nagual gave me the task of going to specific places in my *dreaming*. I was doing really well with my task but at that time I lost my form and I began to see the eye in front of me. The Nagual said that the eye had changed everything and he gave me orders to begin using the eye to pull myself away. He said that I didn't have time to get to my double in *dreaming*, but that the eye was even better. I felt cheated. Now I don't care. I've used that eye the best way I could. I let it pull me in my *dreaming*. I close my eyes and fall asleep like nothing, even in the daytime or anywhere. The eye pulls me and I enter into another world. Most of the time I just wander around in it. The Nagual told me and the little sisters that during our menstrual periods *dreaming* becomes power. I get a little crazy for one thing. I become more daring. And like the Nagual showed us, a crack opens in front of us during those days. You're not a woman so it can't make any sense to you, but two days before her period a woman can open that crack and step through it into another world.'

With her left hand she followed the contour of an invisible line that seemed to run vertically in front of her at arm's length.

'During that time a woman, if she wants to, can let go of the images of the world,' la Gorda went on. 'That's the crack between the worlds, and as the Nagual said, it is right in front of all of us women.

'The reason the Nagual believes women are better sorcerers than men is because they always have the crack in front of them, while a man has to make it.

'Well, it was during my periods that I learned in *dreaming* to fly with the lines of the world. I learned to make sparks with my body to entice the lines and then I learned to grab them. And that's all I have learned in *dreaming* so far.'

I laughed and told her that I had nothing to show for my years of 'dreaming'.

'You've learned how to call the allies in *dreaming*,' she said with great assurance.

I told her that don Juan had taught me to make those sounds. She did not seem to believe me.

'The allies must come to you, then, because they're seeking his luminosity,' she said, 'the luminosity he left with you. He told me that every sorcerer has only so much luminosity to give away. So he parcels it out to all his children in accordance with an order that comes to him from somewhere out there in that vastness. In your case he even gave you his own call.'

She clicked her tongue and winked at me.

'If you don't believe me,' she went on, 'why don't you make the sound the Nagual taught you and see if the allies come to you?'

I felt reluctant to do it. Not because I believed that my sound would bring anything, but because I did not want to humour her.

She waited for a moment, and when she was sure I was not going to try, she put her hand to her mouth and imitated my tapping sound to perfection. She played it for five or six minutes, stopping only to breathe.

'See what I mean?' she asked smiling. 'The allies don't give a fig about my calling, no matter how close it is to yours. Now try it yourself.'

I tried. After a few seconds I heard the call being answered. La Gorda jumped to her feet. I had the clear impression that she was more surprised than I was. She hurriedly made me stop, turned off the lantern and gathered up my notes.

She was about to open the front door, but she stopped short; a most frightening sound came from just outside the door. It sounded to me like a growl. It was so horrendous and ominous that it made us both jump back, away from the door. My physical alarm was so intense that I would have fled if I had had a place to go.

Something heavy was leaning against the door; it made the

door creak. I looked at la Gorda. She seemed to be even more alarmed. She was still standing with her arm outstretched as if to open the door. Her mouth was open. She seemed to have been frozen in mid-action.

The door was about to be sprung open any moment. There were no bangs on it, just a terrifying pressure, not only on the door but all around the house.

La Gorda stood up and told me to embrace her quickly from behind, locking my hands around her waist over her belly button. She performed then a strange movement with her hands. It was as though she were flipping a towel while holding it at the level of her eyes. She did it four times. Then she made another strange movement. She placed her hands at the middle of her chest with the palms up, one above the other without touching. Her elbows were straight out to her sides. She clasped her hands as if she had suddenly grabbed two unseen bars. She slowly turned her hands over until the palms were facing down and then she made a most beautiful, exertive movement, a movement that seemed to engage every muscle in her body. It was as though she were opening a heavy sliding door that offered a great resistance. Her body shivered with the exertion. Her arms moved slowly, as if opening a very, very heavy door, until they were fully extended laterally.

I had the clear impression that as soon as she opened that door a wind rushed through. That wind pulled us and we actually went through the wall. Or rather, the walls of the house went through us, or perhaps all three, la Gorda, the house and myself, went through the door she had opened. All of a sudden I was out in an open field. I could see the dark shapes of the surrounding mountains and trees. I was no longer holding on to la Gorda's waist. A noise above me made me look up, and I saw her hovering perhaps ten feet above me like the black shape of a giant kite. I felt a terrible itch in my belly button and then la Gorda plummeted down to the ground at top speed, but instead of crashing she came to a soft, total halt.

At the moment that la Gorda landed, the itch in my umbilical region turned into a horribly exhausting nervous pain. It was as if her landing were pulling my insides out. I screamed in pain at the top of my voice.

Then la Gorda was standing next to me, desperately out of breath. I was sitting down. We were again in the room of don Genaro's house where we had been.

La Gorda seemed unable to catch her breath. She was drenched in perspiration.

'We've got to get out of here,' she muttered.

It was a short drive to the little sisters' house. None of them was around. La Gorda lit a lantern and led me directly to the open-air kitchen in back. There she undressed herself and asked me to bathe her like a horse, by throwing water on her body. I took a small tub full of water and proceeded to pour it gently on her, but she wanted me to drench her.

She explained that a contact with the allies, like the one we had, produced a most injurious perspiration that had to be washed off immediately. She made me take off my clothes and then drenched me in ice-cold water. Then she handed me a clean piece of cloth and we dried ourselves as we walked back into the house. She sat on the big bed in the front room after hanging the lantern on the wall above it. Her knees were up and I could see every part of her body. I hugged her naked body, and it was then that I realized what doña Soledad had meant when she said that la Gorda was the Nagual's woman. She was formless like don Juan. I could not possibly think of her as a woman.

I started to put on my clothes. She took them away from me. She said that before I could wear them again I had to sun them. She gave me a blanket to put over my shoulders and got another one for herself.

'That attack of the allies was truly scary,' she said as we sat down on the bed. 'We were really lucky that we could get out of their grip. I had no idea why the Nagual told me to go to Genaro's with you. Now I know. That house is where the allies are the strongest. They missed us by the skin of our teeth. We were lucky that I knew how to get out.'

'How did you do it, Gorda?'

'I really don't know,' she said. 'I simply did it. My body knew how, I suppose, but when I want to think how I did it, I can't.

'This was a great test for both of us. Until tonight I didn't know that I could open the eye, but look what I did. I actually opened the eye, just as the Nagual said I could. I've never been able to do it until you came along. I've tried but it never worked. This time the fear of those allies made me just grab the eye the way the Nagual told me to, by shaking it four times in its four directions. He said that I should shake it as I shake a bed sheet, and then I should open it as a door, by holding it right at the middle. The rest was very easy. Once the door was opened I felt a strong wind pulling me instead of blowing me away. The trouble, the Nagual said, is to return. You have to be very strong to do that. The Nagual and Genaro and Eligio could go in and out of that eye like nothing. For them the eye was not even an eye; they said it was an orange light, like the sun. And so were the Nagual and Genaro an orange light when they flew. I'm still very low on the scale; the Nagual said that when I do my flying I spread out and look like a pile of cow dung in the sky. I have no light. That's why the return is so dreadful for me. Tonight you helped me and pulled me back twice. The reason I showed you my flying tonight was because the Nagual gave me orders to let you *see* it no matter how difficult or crummy it is. With my flying I was supposed to be helping you, the same way you were supposed to be helping me when you showed me your double. I *saw* your whole manoeuvre from the door. You were so busy feeling sorry for Josefina that your body didn't notice my presence. I *saw* how your double came out from the top of your head. It wriggled out like a worm. I *saw* a shiver that began in your feet and went through your body and then your double came out. It was like you, but very shiny. It was like the Nagual himself. That's why the sisters were petrified. I knew they thought that it was the Nagual himself. But I couldn't *see* all of it. I missed the sound because I have no attention for it.'

'I beg your pardon?'

'The double needs a tremendous amount of attention. The

Nagual gave that attention to you but not to me. He told me that he had run out of time.'

She said something else about a certain kind of attention but I was very tired. I fell asleep so suddenly that I did not even have time to put my notes away.

4 THE GENAROS

I woke up around eight the next morning and found that la
Gorda had sunned my clothes and made breakfast. We ate in
the kitchen, in the dining area. When we had finished I asked
her about Lidia, Rosa and Josefina. They seemed to have vanished from the house.

'They are helping Soledad,' she said. 'She's getting ready to
leave.'

'Where is she going?'

'Somewhere away from here. She has no more reason to
stay. She was waiting for you and you have already come.'

'Are the little sisters going with her?'

'No. They just don't want to be here today. It looks as if
today is not a good day for them to stick around.'

'Why isn't it a good day?'

'The Genaros are coming to see you today and the girls
don't get along with them. If all of them are here together,
they'll get into a most dreadful fight. The last time that happened they nearly killed one another.'

'Do they fight physically?'

'You bet they do. All of them are very strong and none of
them wants to take second place. The Nagual told me that
that would happen, but I am powerless to stop them; and not
only that but I have to take sides, so it's a mess.'

'How do you know that the Genaros are coming today?'

'I haven't talked to them. I just know that they will be here
today, that's all.'

'Do you know that because you *see*, Gorda?'

'That's right. I *see* them coming. And one of them is coming directly to you because you're pulling him.'

I assured her that I was not pulling anyone in particular. I said that I had not revealed to anyone the purpose of my trip, but that it had to do with something I had to ask Pablito and Nestor.

She smiled coyly and said that fate had paired me with Pablito, that we were very alike, and that undoubtedly he was going to see me first. She added that everything that happened to a warrior could be interpreted as an omen; thus my encounter with Soledad was an omen of what I was going to find out on my visit. I asked her to explain her point.

'The men will give you very little this time,' she said. 'It's the women who will rip you to shreds, as Soledad did. That's what I would say if I read the omen. You're waiting for the Genaros, but they are men like you. And look at this other omen; they are a little bit behind. I would say a couple of days behind. That's your fate as well as theirs, as men, to be always a couple of days behind.'

'Behind what, Gorda?'

'Behind everything. Behind us women, for instance.'

She laughed and patted my head.

'No matter how stubborn you are,' she went on, 'you have to admit that I'm right. Wait and see.'

'Did the Nagual tell you that men are behind women?' I asked.

'Sure he did,' she replied. 'All you have to do is look around.'

'I do, Gorda. But I don't see any such thing. Women are always behind. They are dependent on men.'

She laughed. Her laughter was not scornful or bitter; it was rather a clear sound of joyfulness.

'You know the world of people better than I do,' she said forcefully. 'But right now I'm formless and you're not. I'm telling you, women are better sorcerers because there is a crack in front of our eyes and there is none in front of yours.'

She did not seem angry, but I felt obliged to explain that I asked questions and made comments not because I was attacking or defending any given point, but because I wanted her to talk.

She said that she had done nothing else but talk since the moment we met, and that the Nagual had trained her to talk because her task was the same as mine, to be in the world of people.

'Everything we say', she went on, 'is a reflection of the world of people. You will find out before your visit is over that you talk and act the way you do because you're clinging to the human form, just as the Genaros and the little sisters are clinging to the human form when they fight to kill one another.'

'But aren't all of you supposed to cooperate with Pablito, Nestor and Benigno?'

'Genaro and the Nagual told every one of us that we should live in harmony and help and protect one another, because we are alone in the world. Pablito was left in charge of us four, but he's a coward. If it were left up to him, he would let us die like dogs. When the Nagual was around, though, Pablito was very nice to us and took very good care of us. Everyone used to tease him and joke that he took care of us as if we were his wives. The Nagual and Genaro told him, not too long before they left, that he had a real chance to become the Nagual someday, because we might become his four winds, his four corners. Pablito understood it to be his task and from that day on he changed. He became insufferable. He began to order us around as if we were really his wives.

'I asked the Nagual about Pablito's chances and he told me that I should know that everything in a warrior's world depends on personal power and personal power depends on impeccability. If Pablito were impeccable he would have a chance. I laughed when he told me that. I know Pablito very well. But the Nagual explained to me that I shouldn't take it so lightly. He said that warriors always have a chance, no matter how slim. He made me see that I was a warrior myself and that I shouldn't hinder Pablito with my thoughts. He said that I should turn them off and let Pablito be; that the impeccable thing for me to do was to help Pablito in spite of what I knew about him.

'I understood what the Nagual said. Besides, I have my own debt with Pablito, and I welcomed the opportunity to help him. But I also knew that no matter how I helped him he was going to fail. I knew all along that he didn't have what it takes to be like the Nagual. Pablito is very childish and he won't accept his defeat. He's miserable because he's not impeccable, and yet he's still trying in his thoughts to be like the Nagual.'

'How did he fail?'

'As soon as the Nagual left, Pablito had a deadly run-in with Lidia. Years ago the Nagual had given him the task of being Lidia's husband, just for appearances. The people around here thought that she was his wife. Lidia didn't like that one bit. She's very tough. The truth of the matter is that Pablito has always been scared to death of her. They could never get along together and they tolerated each other only because the Nagual was around; but when he left, Pablito got crazier than he already was and became convinced that he had enough personal power to take us as his wives. The three Genaros got together and discussed what Pablito should do and decided that he should take the toughest woman first, Lidia. They waited until she was alone and then all three of them came into the house and grabbed her by the arms and threw her on the bed. Pablito got on top of her. She thought at first that the Genaros were joking. But when she realized that they were serious, she hit Pablito with her head in the middle of his forehead and nearly killed him. The Genaros fled and Nestor had to tend to Pablito's wounds for months.'

'Is there something that I can do to help them understand?'

'No. Unfortunately, understanding is not their problem. All six of them understand very well. The real trouble is something else, something very ugly that no one can help them with. They indulge in not trying to change. Since they know they won't succeed in changing no matter how much they try, or want to, or need to, they have given up trying altogether. That's as wrong as feeling disappointed with our failures. The Nagual told each of them that warriors, both men and women, must be impeccable in their effort to change, in order to scare

the human form and shake it away. After years of impeccability a moment will come, the Nagual said, when the form
cannot stand it any longer and it leaves, just as it left me. In
doing so, of course, it injures the body and can even make it
die, but an impeccable warrior survives, always.'

A sudden knock at the front door interrupted her. La Gorda
stood up and went over to unlatch the door. It was Lidia. She
greeted me very formally and asked la Gorda to go with her.
They left together.

I welcomed being alone. I worked on my notes for hours.
The open-air dining area was cool and had very good light.

La Gorda returned around noon. She asked me if I wanted
to eat. I was not hungry, but she insisted that I eat. She said
that contacts with the allies were very debilitating, and that
she felt very weak herself.

After eating I sat down with la Gorda and was getting ready
to ask her about 'dreaming' when the front door opened
loudly and Pablito walked in. He was panting. He obviously
had been running and appeared to be in a state of great excitation. He stood at the door for a moment, catching his breath.
He hadn't changed much. He seemed a bit older, or heavier, or
perhaps only more muscular. He was, however, still very lean
and wiry. His complexion was pale, as if he had not been in
the sun for a long time. The brownness of his eyes was accen-
tuated by a faint mark of weariness in his face. I remembered
Pablito as having a beguiling smile; as he stood there looking
at me, his smile was as charming as ever. He ran over to where
I was sitting and grasped my forearms for a moment, without
saying a word. I stood up. He then shook me gently and embraced me. I myself was utterly delighted to see him. I was
jumping up and down with an infantile joy. I did not know
what to say to him. He finally broke the silence.

'Maestro,' he said softly, nodding his head slightly as if he
were bowing to me.

The title of 'maestro', teacher, caught me by surprise. I
turned around as if I were looking for someone else who was
just behind me. I deliberately exaggerated my movements to
let him know that I was mystified. He smiled, and the only

thing that occurred to me was to ask him how he knew I was there.

He said that he, Nestor and Benigno had been forced to return because of a most unusual apprehension, which made them run day and night without any pause. Nestor had gone to their own house to find out if there was something there that would account for the feeling that had driven them. Benigno had gone to Soledad's place and he himself had come to the girls' house.

'You hit the jackpot, Pablito,' la Gorda said, and laughed.

Pablito did not answer. He glared at her.

'I'll bet that you're working yourself up to throw me out,' he said in a tone of great anger.

'Don't fight with me, Pablito,' la Gorda said, unruffled.

Pablito turned to me and apologized, and then added in a very loud voice, as if he wanted someone else in the house to hear him, that he had brought his own chair to sit on and that he could put it wherever he pleased.

'There's no one else around here except us,' la Gorda said softly, and chuckled.

'I'll bring in my chair anyway,' Pablito said. 'You don't mind, Maestro, do you?'

I looked at la Gorda. She gave me an almost imperceptible go-ahead sign with the tip of her foot.

'Bring it in. Bring anything you want,' I said.

Pablito stepped out of the house.

'They're all that way,' la Gorda said, 'all three of them.'

Pablito came back a moment later carrying an unusual-looking chair on his shoulders. The chair was shaped to follow the contour of his back, so when he had it on his shoulders, upside down, it looked like a backpack.

'May I put it down?' he asked me.

'Of course,' I replied, moving the bench over to make room.

He laughed with exaggerated ease.

'Aren't you the Nagual?' he asked me, and then looked at la Gorda and added, 'Or do you have to wait for orders?'

'I am the Nagual,' I said facetiously in order to humour him.

I sensed that he was about to pick a fight with la Gorda; she must have sensed it too, for she excused herself and went out the back.

Pablito put his chair down and slowly circled around me as if he were inspecting my body. Then he took his low-back narrow chair in one hand, turned it around and sat down, resting his folded arms on the back of the chair that was made to allow him the maximum comfort as he sat astride it. I sat down facing him. His mood had changed completely the instant la Gorda left.

'I must ask you to forgive me for acting the way I did,' he said smiling. 'But I had to get rid of that witch.'

'Is she that bad, Pablito?'

'You can bet on that,' he replied.

To change the subject I told him that he looked very fine and prosperous.

'You look very fine yourself, Maestro,' he said.

'What's this nonsense of calling me Maestro?' I asked in a joking tone.

'Things are not the same as before,' he replied. 'We are in a new realm, and the Witness says that you're a maestro now, and the Witness cannot be wrong. But he will tell you the whole story himself. He'll be here shortly, and will he be glad to see you again. I think that by now he must have felt that you are here. As we were coming back, all of us had the feeling that you might be on your way, but none of us felt that you had already arrived.'

I told him then that I had come for the sole purpose of seeing him and Nestor, that they were the only two people in the world with whom I could talk about our last meeting with don Juan and don Genaro, and that I needed more than anything else to clear up the uncertainties that that last meeting had created in me.

'We're bound to one another,' he said. 'I'll do anything I can to help. You know that. But I must warn you that I'm not as strong as you would want me to be. Perhaps it would be better if we didn't talk at all. But, on the other hand, if we don't talk we'll never understand anything.'

In a careful and deliberate manner I formulated my query. I explained that there was one single issue at the crux of my rational predicament.

'Tell me, Pablito,' I said, 'did we truly jump with our bodies into the abyss?'

'I don't know,' he said. 'I really don't know.'

'But you were there with me.'

'That's the point. Was I really there?'

I felt annoyed at his cryptic replies. I had the sensation that if I would shake him or squeeze him, something in him would be set free. It was apparent to me that he was deliberately withholding something of great value. I protested that he would choose to be secretive with me when we had a bond of total trust.

Pablito shook his head as if silently objecting to my accusation.

I asked him to recount to me his whole experience, starting from the time prior to our jump, when don Juan and don Genaro had prepared us together for the final onslaught.

Pablito's account was muddled and inconsistent. All he could remember about the last moments before we jumped into the abyss was that after don Juan and don Genaro had said good-bye to both of us and had disappeared into the darkness, his strength waned, he was about to fall on his face, but I held him by his arm and carried him to the edge of the abyss and there he blacked out.

'What happened after you blacked out, Pablito?'

'I don't know.'

'Did you have dreams or visions? What did you see?'

'As far as I'm concerned I had no visions, or if I did I couldn't pay any attention to them. My lack of impeccability makes it impossible for me to remember them.'

'And then what happened?'

'I woke up at Genaro's old place. I don't know how I got there.'

He remained quiet, while I frantically searched in my mind for a question, a comment, a critical statement or anything that would add extra breadth to his statements. As it was, nothing in Pablito's account was usable to buttress what had happened to me. I felt cheated. I was almost angry with him. My feelings were a mixture of pity for Pablito and myself and at the same time a most intense disappointment.

'I'm sorry I'm such a letdown to you,' Pablito said.

My immediate reaction to his words was to cover up my feelings and assure him that I was not disappointed at all.

'I am a sorcerer,' he said, laughing, 'a poor one, but enough of a one to know what my body tells me. And right now it tells me that you are angry with me.'

'I'm not angry, Pablito!' I exclaimed.

'That's what your reason says, but not your body,' he said. 'Your body is angry. Your reason, however, finds no reason to feel anger towards me, so you're caught in a cross fire. The least I can do for you is to untangle this. Your body is angry because it knows that I am not impeccable and that only an impeccable warrior can help you. Your body is angry because it feels that I am wasting myself. It knew all that the minute I walked through that door.'

I did not know what to say. I felt a flood of post-fact realizations. Perhaps he was right in saying that my body knew all that. At any rate, his directness in confronting me with my feelings had blunted the edge of my frustration. I began to wonder if Pablito was not just playing a game with me. I told him that being so direct and bold he could not possibly be as weak as he pictured himself to be.

'My weakness is that I'm made to have longings,' he said almost in a whisper. 'I'm even to the point where I long for my life as an ordinary man. Can you believe that?'

'You can't be serious, Pablito!' I exclaimed.

'I am,' he replied. 'I long for the grand privilege of walking the face of the earth as an ordinary man, without this awesome burden.'

I found his stand simply preposterous and caught myself exclaiming over and over that he could not possibly be serious. Pablito looked at me and sighed. I was overtaken by a sudden apprehension. He seemed to be on the verge of tears. My apprehension gave way to an intense feeling of empathy. Neither of us could help each other.

La Gorda came back to the kitchen at that moment. Pablito seemed to experience an instantaneous revitalization. He jumped to his feet and stomped on the floor.

'What the hell do you want?' he yelled in a shrill, nervous voice. 'Why are you snooping around?'

La Gorda addressed me as if he did not exist. She politely said that she was going to Soledad's house.

'What the hell do we care where you go?' he yelled. 'You can go to hell for that matter.'

He stomped on the floor like a spoiled child while la Gorda stood there laughing.

'Let's get out of this house, Maestro,' he said loudly.

His sudden shift from sadness to anger fascinated me. I became engrossed in watching him. One of the features that I had always admired was his nimbleness; even when he stomped his feet his movements had grace.

He suddenly reached across the table and nearly snatched my writing pad away from me. He grabbed it with the thumb and index finger of his left hand. I had to hold on to it with both hands, using all my strength. There was such an extraordinary force in his pull that if he had really wanted to take it he could have easily jerked it away from my grip. He let go, and as he retrieved his hand I saw a fleeting image of an extension to it. It happened so fast that I could have explained it as a visual distortion on my part, a product of the jolt of having to stand up halfway, drawn by the force of his pull. But I had learned by then that I could neither behave with those people in my accustomed manner, nor could I explain anything in my accustomed manner, so I did not even try.

'What's that in your hand, Pablito?' I asked.

He recoiled in surprise and hid his hand behind his back. He had a blank expression and mumbled that he wanted us to leave that house because he was becoming dizzy.

La Gorda began to laugh loudly and said that Pablito was

as good a deceiver as Josefina, maybe even better, and that if I pressed him to tell me what was in his hand he would faint and Nestor would have to tend to him for months.

Pablito began to choke. His face became almost purple. La Gorda told him in a nonchalant tone to cut out the acting because he had no audience; she was leaving and I did not have much patience. She then turned to me and told me in a most commanding tone to stay there and not go to the Genaros' house.

'Why in the hell not?' Pablito yelled and jumped in front of her as if trying to stop her from leaving. 'What gall! Telling the Maestro what to do!'

'We had a bout with the allies in your house last night,' la Gorda said to Pablito matter-of-factly. 'The Nagual and I are still weak from that. If I were you, Pablito, I would put my attention to work. Things have changed. Everything has changed since he came.'

La Gorda left through the front door. I became aware then that indeed she looked very tired. Her shoes seemed too tight, or perhaps she was so weak that her feet dragged a little bit. She seemed small and frail.

I thought that I must have looked as tired. Since there were no mirrors in their house, I had the urge to go outside and look at myself in the side mirror of my car. I perhaps would have done it but Pablito thwarted me. He asked me in the most earnest tone not to believe a word of what she had said about his being a deceiver. I told him not to worry about that.

'You don't like la Gorda at all, do you?' I asked.

'You can say that again,' he replied with a fierce look. 'You know better than anyone alive the kind of monsters those women are. The Nagual told us that one day you were going to come here just to fall into their trap. He begged us to be on the alert and warn you about their designs. The Nagual said that you had one out of four chances. If our power was high we could bring you here ourselves and warn you and save you; if our power was low we ourselves would arrive here just in time to see your corpse; the third chance was to find you either the slave to the witch Soledad or the slave of those disgusting, mannish women; the fourth chance and the faintest one of all was to find you alive and well.

'The Nagual told us that in case you survived, you would then be the Nagual and we should trust you because only you could help us.'

'I'll do anything for you, Pablito. You know that.'

'Not just for me. I'm not alone. The Witness and Benigno are with me. We are together and you have to help all of us.'

'Of course, Pablito. That goes without saying.'

'People around here have never bothered us. Our problems are with those ugly, mannish freaks. We don't know what to do with them. The Nagual gave us orders to stay around them no matter what. He gave me a personal task but I've failed at it. I was very happy before. You remember. Now I can't seem to manage my life any more.'

'What happned, Pablito?'

'Those witches drove me from my house. They took over and pushed me out like trash. I now live in Genaro's house with Nestor and Benigno. We even have to cook our own meals. The Nagual knew that this might happen and gave la Gorda the task of mediating between us and those three bitches. But la Gorda is still what the Nagual used to call her, Two Hundred and Twenty Buttocks. That was her nickname for years and years, because she tipped the scales at two hundred and twenty pounds.'

Pablito chuckled at his recollection of la Gorda.

'She was the fattest, smelliest slob you'd ever want to see,' he went on. 'Today she's half her real size, but she's still the same fat, slow woman up there in her head, and she can't do a thing for us. But you're here now, Maestro, and our worries are over. Now we are four against four.'

I wanted to interject a comment but he stopped me.

'Let me finish what I have to say before that witch comes back to throw me out,' he said as he nervously looked at the door.

'I know that they have told you that the five of you are the same because you are the Nagual's children. That's a lie!

You're also like us, the Genaros, because Genaro also helped to make your luminosity. You're one of us too. See what I mean? So, don't you believe what they tell you. You also belong to us. The witches don't know that the Nagual told us everything. They think that they are the only ones who know. It took two Toltecs to make us. We are the children of both. Those witches . . .'

'Wait, wait, Pablito,' I said, putting my hand over his mouth. He stood up, apparently frightened by my sudden movement.

'What do you mean that it took two Toltecs to make us?'

'The Nagual told us that we are Toltecs. All of us are Toltecs. He said that a Toltec is the receiver and holder of mysteries. The Nagual and Genaro are Toltecs. They gave us their special luminosity and their mysteries. We received their mysteries and now we hold them.'

His usage of the word Toltec baffled me. I was familiar only with its anthropological meaning. In that context, it always refers to a culture of Nahuatl-speaking people in central and southern Mexico which was already extinct at the time of the Conquest.

'Why did he call us Toltecs?' I asked, not knowing what else to say.

'Because that's what we are. Instead of saying that we are sorcerers or witches, he said that we are Toltecs.'

'If that's the case, why do you call the little sisters witches?'

'Oh, that's because I hate them. That has nothing to do with what we are.'

'Did the Nagual tell that to everyone?'

'Why, certainly. Everyone knows.'

'But he never told me that.'

'Oh, that's because you are a very educated man and are always discussing stupid things.'

He laughed in a forced, high-pitched tone and patted me on the back.

'Did the Nagual by any chance tell you that the Toltecs were ancient people that lived in this part of Mexico?' I asked.

'See, there you go. That's why he didn't tell you. The old crow probably didn't know that they were ancient people.'

He rocked in his chair as he laughed. His laughter was very pleasing and very contagious.

'We are the Toltecs, Maestro,' he said. 'Rest assured that we are. That's all I know. But you can ask the Witness. He knows. I lost my interest a long time ago.'

He stood up and went over to the stove. I followed him. He examined a pot of food cooking on a low fire. He asked me if I knew who had made that food. I was pretty sure that la Gorda had made it, but I said that I did not know. He sniffed it four or five times in short inhalations, like a dog. Then he announced that his nose told him that la Gorda had cooked it. He asked me if I had had some, and when I said that I had finished eating just before he arrived, he took a bowl from a shelf and helped himself to an enormous portion. He recommended in very strong terms that I should eat food cooked only by la Gorda and that I should only use her bowl, as he himself was doing. I told him that la Gorda and the little sisters had served me my food in a dark bowl that they kept on a shelf apart from the others. He said that that bowl belonged to the Nagual. We went back to the table. He ate very slowly and did not talk at all. His total absorption in eating made me realize that all of them did the same thing: they ate in complete silence.

'La Gorda is a great cook,' he said as he finished his food. 'She used to feed me. That was ages ago, before she hated me, before she became a witch, I mean a Toltec.'

He looked at me with a glint in his eye and winked.

I felt obligated to comment that la Gorda did not strike me as being capable of hating anyone. I asked him if he knew that she had lost her form.

'That's a lot of baloney!' he exclaimed.

He stared at me as if measuring my look of surprise and then hid his face under his arm and giggled like an embarrassed child.

'Well, she actually did do that,' he added. 'She's just great.'

'Why do you dislike her, then?'

'I'm going to tell you something, Maestro, because I trust you. I don't dislike her at all. She's the very best. She's the

Nagual's woman. I just act that way with her because I like her to pamper me, and she does. She never gets mad at me. I could do anything. Sometimes I get carried away and I get physical with her and want to strike her. When that happens she just jumps out of the way, like the Nagual used to do. The next minute she doesn't even remember what I did. That's a true formless warrior for you. She does the same thing with everyone. But the rest of us are a sorry mess. We are truly bad. Those three witches hate us and we hate them back.'

'You are sorcerers, Pablito; can't you stop all this bickering?'

'Sure we can, but we don't want to. What do you expect us to do, be like brothers and sisters?'

I did not know what to say.

'They were the Nagual's women,' he went on. 'And yet everybody expected me to take them. How in heaven's name am I going to do that! I tried with one of them and instead of helping me the bastardly witch nearly killed me. So now every one of those women is after my hide as if I had committed a crime. All I did was to follow the Nagual's instructions. He told me that I had to be intimate with each of them, one by one, until I could hold all of them at once. But I couldn't be intimate with even one.'

I wanted to ask him about his mother, doña Soledad, but I could not figure out a way to bring her into the conversation at that point. We were quiet for a moment.

'Do you hate them for what they tried to do to you?' he asked all of a sudden.

I saw my chance.

'No, not at all,' I said. 'La Gorda explained to me their reasons. But doña Soledad's attack was very scary. Do you see much of her?'

He did not answer. He looked at the ceiling. I repeated my question. I noticed then that his eyes were filled with tears. His body shook, convulsed by quiet sobs.

He said that once he had had a beautiful mother, whom, no doubt, I could still remember. Her name was Manuelita, a saintly woman who raised two children, working like a mule to support them. He felt the most profound veneration for that mother who had loved and reared him. But one horrible day his fate was fulfilled and he had the misfortune to meet Genaro and the Nagual, and between the two of them they destroyed his life. In a very emotional tone Pablito said that the two devils took his soul and his mother's soul. They killed his Manuelita and left behind that horrendous witch, Soledad. He peered at me with eyes flooded with tears and said that that hideous woman was not his mother. She could not possibly be his Manuelita.

He sobbed uncontrollably. I did not know what to say. His emotional outburst was so genuine and his contentions so truthful that I felt swayed by a tide of sentiment. Thinking as an average civilized man I had to agree with him. It certainly looked as if it was a great misfortune for Pablito to have crossed the path of don Juan and don Genaro.

I put my arm around his shoulders and almost wept myself. After a long silence he stood up and went out to the back. I heard him blowing his nose and washing his face in a pail of water. When he returned he was calmer. He was even smiling.

'Don't get me wrong, Maestro,' he said. 'I don't blame anyone for what has happened to me. It was my fate. Genaro and the Nagual acted like the impeccable warriors they were. I'm just weak, that's all. And I have failed in my task. The Nagual said that my only chance to avoid the attack of that horrendous witch was to corral the four winds, and make them into my four corners. But I failed. Those women were in cahoots with that witch Soledad and didn't want to help me. They wanted me dead.

'The Nagual also told me that if I failed, you wouldn't stand a chance yourself. He said that if she killed you, I had to flee and run for my life. He doubted that I could even get as far as the road. He said that with your power and with what the witch already knows, she would have been peerless. So, when I felt I had failed to corral the four winds, I considered myself dead. And of course, I hated those women. But today, Maestro, you bring me new hope.'

I told him that his feelings for his mother had touched me very deeply. I was in fact appalled by all that had happened but I doubted intensely that I had brought hope of any kind to him.

'You have!' he exclaimed with great certainty. 'I've felt terrible all this time. To have your own mother coming after you with an axe is nothing anyone can feel happy about. But now she's out of the way, thanks to you and whatever you did.

'Those women hate me because they're convinced I'm a coward. They just can't get it through their thick heads that we are different. You and those four women are different from me and the Witness and Benigno in one important way. All five of you were pretty much dead before the Nagual found you. He told us that once you had even tried to kill yourself. We were not that way. We were well and alive and happy. We are the opposite of you. You are desperate people; we are not. If Genaro hadn't come my way I would be a happy carpenter today. Or perhaps I would have died. It doesn't matter. I would've done what I could and that would have been fine.'

His words plunged me into a curious mood. I had to admit that he was right in that those women and myself were indeed desperate people. If I had not met don Juan I would no doubt be dead, but I could not say, as Pablito had, that it would have been fine with me either way. Don Juan had brought life and vigour to my body and freedom to my spirit.

Pablito's statements made me remember something don Juan had told me once when we were talking about an old man, a friend of mine. Don Juan had said in very emphatic terms that the old man's life or death had no significance whatsoever. I felt a bit cross at what I thought to be redundance on don Juan's part. I told him that it went without saying that the life and death of that old man had no significance, since nothing in the world could possibly have any significance except to each one of us personally.

'You said it!' he exclaimed, and laughed. 'That's exactly what I mean. That old man's life and death have no significance to him personally. He could have died in nineteen twenty-nine, or in nineteen fifty, or he could live until nineteen ninety-five. It doesn't matter. Everything is stupidly the same to him.'

My life before I met don Juan had been that way. Nothing

had ever mattered to me. I used to act as if certain things affected me, but that was only a calculated ploy to appear as a sensitive man.

Pablito spoke to me and disrupted my reflections. He wanted to know if he had hurt my feelings. I assured him that it was nothing. In order to start up the conversation again, I asked him where he had met don Genaro.

'My fate was that my boss got ill,' he said. 'And I had to go to the city market in his place to build a new section of clothing booths. I worked there for two months. While I was there I met the daughter of the owner of one of the booths. We fell in love. I built her father's stand a little bigger than the others so I could make love to her under the counter while her sister took care of the customers.

'One day Genaro brought a sack of medicinal plants to a retailer across the aisle, and while they were talking he noticed that the clothing stand was shaking. He looked carefully at the stand but he only saw the sister sitting on a chair half-asleep. The man told Genaro that every day the stand shook like that around that hour. The next day Genaro brought the Nagual to watch the stand shaking, and sure enough that day it shook. They came back the next day and it shook again. So they waited there until I came out. That day I made their acquaintance, and soon after Genaro told me that he was a herbalist and proposed to make me a potion that no woman could resist. I liked women so I fell for it. He certainly made the potion for me, but it took him ten years. In the meantime I got to know him very well, and I grew to love him more than if he were my own brother. And now I miss him like hell. So you see, he tricked me. Sometimes I'm glad that he did; most of the time I resent it though.'

'Don Juan told me that sorcerers have to have an omen before they choose someone. Was there something of that sort with you, Pablito?'

'Yes. Genaro said that he got curious watching the stand shaking and then he *saw* that two people were making love under the counter. So he sat down to wait for the people to come out; he wanted to see who they were. After a while the girl appeared in the stand but he missed me. He thought it was very strange that he would miss me after being so determined to set eyes on me. The next day he came back with the Nagual. He also *saw* that two people were making love, but when it was time to catch me, they both missed me. They came back again the next day; Genaro went around to the back of the stand while the Nagual stayed out in front. I bumped into Genaro while I was crawling out. I thought he hadn't seen me because I was still behind the piece of cloth that covered a small square opening I had made on the side wall. I began to bark to make him think there was a small dog under the drape. He growled and barked back at me and really made me believe that there was a huge mad dog on the other side. I got so scared I ran out the other way and crashed into the Nagual. If he would have been an ordinary man, I would have thrown him to the ground because I ran right into him, but instead, he lifted me up like a child. I was absolutely flabbergasted. For being such an old man he was truly strong. I thought I could use a strong man like that to carry lumber for me. Besides I didn't want to lose face with the people who had seen me running out from under the counter. I asked him if he would like to work for me. He said yes. That same day he went to the shop and started to work as my assistant. He worked there every day for two months. I didn't have a chance with those two devils.'

The incongruous image of don Juan working for Pablito was extremely humorous to me. Pablito began to imitate the way don Juan carried lumber on his shoulders. I had to agree with la Gorda that Pablito was as good an actor as Josefina.

'Why did they go to all that trouble, Pablito?'

'They had to trick me. You don't think that I would go with them just like that, do you? I've heard all my life about sorcerers and curers and witches and spirits, and I never believed a word of it. Those who talked about things like that were just ignorant people. If Genaro had told me that he and his friend were sorcerers, I would've walked out on them. But they were too clever for me. Those two foxes were really sly. They were in no hurry. Genaro said that he would've waited for me if it took him twenty years. That's why the Nagual went to work for me. I asked him to, so it was really me who gave them the key.

'The Nagual was a diligent worker. I was a little bit of a rascal in those days and I thought I was the one playing a trick on him. I believed that the Nagual was just a stupid old Indian so I told him that I was going to tell the boss that he was my grandpa, otherwise they wouldn't hire him, but I had to get a percentage of his salary. The Nagual said that it was fine with him. He gave me something out of the few pesos he made each day.

'My boss was very impressed with my grandpa because he was such a hard worker. But the other guys made fun of him. As you know, he had the habit of cracking all his joints from time to time. In the shop he cracked them every time he carried anything. People naturally thought that he was so old that when he carried something on his back his whole body creaked.

'I was pretty miserable with the Nagual as my grandpa. But by then Genaro had already prevailed on my greedy side. He had told me that he was feeding the Nagual a special formula made out of plants and that it made him strong as a bull. Every day he used to bring a small bundle of mashed-up green leaves and feed it to him. Genaro said that his friend was nothing without his concoction, and to prove it to me he didn't give it to him for two days. Without the green stuff the Nagual seemed to be just a plain, ordinary old man. Genaro told me that I could also use his concoction to make women love me. I got very interested in it and he said that we could be partners if I would help him prepare his formula and give it to his friend. One day he showed me some American money and told me he had sold his first batch to an American. That hooked me and I became his partner.

'My partner Genaro and I had great designs. He said that I should have my own shop, because with the money that we were going to make with his formula, I could afford anything. I bought a shop and my partner paid for it. So I went wild. I knew that my partner was for real and I began to work making his green stuff.'

I had the strange conviction at that point that don Genaro must have used psychotropic plants in making his concoction. I reasoned that he must have tricked Pablito into ingesting it in order to assure his compliance.

'Did he give you power plants, Pablito?' I asked.

'Sure,' he replied. 'He gave me his green stuff. I ate tons of it.'

He described and imitated how don Juan would sit by the front door of don Genaro's house in a state of profound lethargy and then spring to life as soon as his lips touched the concoction. Pablito said that in view of such a transformation he was forced to try it himself.

'What was in that formula?' I asked.

'Green leaves,' he replied. 'Any green leaves he could get a hold of. That was the kind of devil Genaro was. He used to talk about his formula and make me laugh until I was as high as a kite. God, I really loved those days.'

I laughed out of nervousness. Pablito shook his head from side to side and cleared his throat two or three times. He seemed to be struggling not to weep.

'As I've already said, Maestro,' he went on, 'I was driven by greed. I secretly planned to dump my partner once I had learned how to make the green stuff myself. Genaro must have always known the designs I had in those days, and just before he left he hugged me and told me that it was time to fulfil my wish; it was time to dump my partner, for I had already learned to make the green stuff.'

Pablito stood up. His eyes were filled with tears.

'That son of a gun Genaro,' he said softly. 'That rotten devil. I truly loved him, and if I weren't the coward I am, I would be making his green stuff today.'

I didn't want to write any more. To dispel my sadness I told Pablito that we should go look for Nestor.

I was arranging my notebooks in order to leave when the front door was flung open with a loud bang. Pablito and I jumped up involuntarily and quickly turned to look. Nestor was standing at the door. I ran to him. We met in the middle of the front room. He sort of leaped on me and shook me by the shoulders. He looked taller and stronger than the last time I had seen him. His long, lean body had acquired an almost feline smoothness. Somehow, the person facing me, peering at me, was not the Nestor I had known. I remembered him as a very shy man who was embarrassed to smile because of crooked teeth, a man who was entrusted to Pablito for his care. The Nestor who was looking at me was a mixture of don Juan and don Genaro. He was wiry and agile like don Genaro, but had the mesmeric command that don Juan had. I wanted to indulge in being perplexed, but all I could do was laugh with him. He patted me on the back. He took off his hat. Only then did I realize that Pablito did not have one. I also noticed that Nestor was much darker, and more rugged. Next to him Pablito looked almost frail. Both of them wore American Levi's, heavy jackets and crepe-soled shoes.

Nestor's presence in the house lightened up the oppressive mood instantly. I asked him to join us in the kitchen.

'You came right in time,' Pablito said to Nestor with an enormous smile as we sat down. 'The Maestro and I were weeping here, remembering the Toltec devils.'

'Were you really crying, Maestro?' Nestor asked with a malicious grin on his face.

'You bet he was,' Pablito replied.

A very soft cracking noise at the front door made Pablito and Nestor stop talking. If I had been by myself I would not have noticed or heard anything. Pablito and Nestor stood up; I did the same. We looked at the front door; it was being opened in a most careful manner. I thought that perhaps la Gorda had returned and was quietly opening the door so as not to disturb us. When the door was finally opened wide enough to allow one person to go through, Benigno came in as if he were sneaking into a dark room. His eyes were shut and he was walking on the tips of his toes. He reminded me of a kid sneaking into a movie theatre through an unlocked exit door in order to see a matinee, not daring to make any noise and at the same time not capable of seeing a thing in the dark.

Everybody was quietly looking at Benigno. He opened one eye just enough to peek out of it and orient himself and then he tiptoed across the front room to the kitchen. He stood by the table for a moment with his eyes closed. Pablito and Nestor sat down and signalled me to do the same. Benigno then slid next to me on the bench. He gently shoved my shoulder with his head; it was a light tap in order for me to move over to make room for him on the bench; then he sat down comfortably with his eyes still closed.

He was dressed in Levi's like Pablito and Nestor. His face had filled out a bit since the last time I had seen him, years before, and his hairline was different, but I could not tell how. He had a lighter complexion than I remembered, very small teeth, full lips, high cheekbones, a small nose and big ears. He had always seemed to me like a child whose features had not matured.

Pablito and Nestor, who had interrupted what they were saying to watch Benigno's entrance, resumed talking as soon as he sat down as though nothing had happened.

'Sure, he was crying with me,' Pablito said.

'He's not a crybaby like you,' Nestor said to Pablito.

Then he turned to me and embraced me.

'I'm so glad you're alive,' he said. 'We've just talked to la Gorda and she said that you were the Nagual, but she didn't tell us how you survived. How did you survive, Maestro?'

At that point I had a strange choice. I could have followed my rational path, as I had always done, and said that I did not have the vaguest idea, and I would have been truthful at that. Or I could have said that my double had extricated me from the grip of those women. I was measuring in my mind the possible effect of each alternative when I was distracted by Benigno. He opened one eye a little bit and looked at me and then giggled and buried his head in his arms.

'Benigno, don't you want to talk to me?' I asked.

He shook his head negatively.

I felt self-conscious with him next to me and decided to ask what was the matter with him.

'What's he doing?' I asked Nestor in a low voice.

Nestor rubbed Benigno's head and shook him. Benigno opened his eyes and then closed them again.

'He's that way, you know,' Nestor said to me. 'He's extremely shy. He'll open his eyes sooner or later. Don't pay any attention to him. If he gets bored he'll go to sleep.'

Benigno shook his head affirmatively without opening his eyes.

'Well, how did you get out?' Nestor insisted.

'Don't you want to tell us?' Pablito asked.

I deliberately said that my double had come out from the top of my head three times. I gave them an account of what had happened.

They did not seem in the least surprised and took my account as a matter of course. Pablito became delighted with his own speculations that doña Soledad might not recover and might eventually die. He wanted to know if I had struck Lidia as well. Nestor made an imperative gesture for him to be quiet and Pablito meekly stopped in the middle of a sentence.

'I'm sorry, Maestro,' Nestor said, 'but that was not your double.'

'But everyone said that it was my double.'

'I know for a fact that you misunderstood la Gorda, because as Benigno and I were walking to Genaro's house, la Gorda overtook us on the road and told us that you and Pablito were here in this house. She called you the Nagual. Do you know why?'

I laughed and said that I believed it was due to her notion that I had gotten most of the Nagual's luminosity.

'One of us here is a fool!' Benigno said in a booming voice without opening his eyes.

The sound of his voice was so outlandish that I jumped away from him. His thoroughly unexpected statement, plus my reaction to it, made all of them laugh. Benigno opened one eye and looked at me for an instant and then buried his face in his arms.

'Do you know why we called Juan Matus the Nagual?' Nestor asked me.

I said that I had always thought that that was their nice way of calling don Juan a sorcerer.

Benigno laughed so loudly that the sound of his laughter drowned out everybody else's. He seemed to be enjoying himself immensely. He rested his head on my shoulder as if it were a heavy object he could no longer support.

'The reason we called him the Nagual,' Nestor went on, 'is because he was split in two. In other words, any time he needed to, he could get into another track that we don't have ourselves; something would come out of him, something that was not a double but a horrendous, menacing shape that looked like him but was twice his size. We call that shape the nagual and anybody who has it is, of course, the Nagual.

'The Nagual told us that all of us can have that shape coming out of our heads if we wanted to, but chances are that none of us would want to. Genaro didn't want it, so I think we don't want it, either. So it appears that you're the one who's stuck with it.'

They cackled and yelled as if they were corralling a herd of cattle. Benigno put his arms around my shoulders without opening his eyes and laughed until tears were rolling down his cheeks.

'Why do you say that I am stuck with it?' I asked Nestor.

'It takes too much energy,' he said, 'too much work. I don't know how you can still be standing.

'The Nagual and Genaro split you once in the eucalyptus grove. They took you there because eucalyptuses are your trees. I was there myself and I witnessed when they split you and pulled your nagual out. They pulled you apart by the ears until they had split your luminosity and you were not an egg any more, but two long chunks of luminosity. Then they put you together again, but any sorcerer that *sees* can tell that there is a huge gap in the middle.'

'What's the advantage of being split?'

'You have one ear that hears everything and one eye that *sees* everything and you will always be able to go an extra mile in a moment of need. That splitting is also the reason why they told us that you are the Maestro.

'They tried to split Pablito but it looks like it failed. He's too pampered and has always indulged like a bastard. That's why he's so screwed up now.'

'What's a double then?'

'A double is the other, the body that one gets in *dreaming*. It looks exactly like oneself.'

'Do all of you have a double?'

Nestor scrutinized me with a look of surprise.

'Hey, Pablito, tell the Maestro about our doubles,' he said laughing.

Pablito reached across the table and shook Benigno.

'You tell him, Benigno,' he said. 'Better yet, show it to him.'

Benigno stood up, opened his eyes as wide as he could and looked at the roof, then he pulled down his pants and showed me his penis.

The Genaros went wild with laughter.

'Did you really mean it when you asked that, Maestro?' Nestor asked me with a nervous expression.

I assured him that I was deadly serious in my desire to know anything related to their knowledge. I went into a long elucidation of how don Juan had kept me outside of their realm for reasons I could not fathom, thus preventing me from knowing more about them.

'Think of this,' I said. 'I didn't know until three days ago that those four girls were the Nagual's apprentices, or that Benigno was don Genaro's apprentice.'

Benigno opened his eyes.

'Think of this yourself,' he said. 'I didn't know until now that you were so stupid.'

He closed his eyes again and all of them laughed insanely. I had no choice but to join them.

'We were just teasing you, Maestro,' Nestor said in way of an apology. 'We thought that you were teasing us, rubbing it in. The Nagual told us that you *see*. If you do, you can tell that we are a sorry lot. We don't have the body of *dreaming*. None of us has a double.'

In a very serious and earnest manner Nestor said that something had come in between them and their desire to have a double. I understood him as saying that a sort of barrier had been created since don Juan and don Genaro had left. He thought that it might be the result of Pablito flubbing his task. Pablito added that since the Nagual and Genaro had gone, something seemed to be chasing them, and even Benigno, who was living in the southernmost tip of Mexico at that time, had to return. Only when the three of them were together did they feel at ease.

'What do you think it is?' I asked Nestor.

'There is something out there in that immensity that's pulling us,' he replied. 'Pablito thinks it's his fault for antagonizing those women.'

Pablito turned to me. There was an intense glare in his eyes.

'They've put a curse on me, Maestro,' he said. 'I know that the cause of all our trouble is me. I wanted to disappear from these parts after my fight with Lidia, and a few months later I took off for Veracruz. I was actually very happy there with a girl I wanted to marry. I got a job and was doing fine until one day I came home and found that those four mannish freaks, like beasts of prey, had tracked me down by my scent. They were in my house tormenting my woman. That bitch Rosa put her ugly hand on my woman's belly and made her shit in the bed, just like that. Their leader, Two Hundred and Twenty Buttocks, told me that they had walked across the continent looking for me. She just grabbed me by the belt and pulled me out. They pushed me to the bus depot to bring me here. I got madder than the devil but I was no match for Two Hundred and Twenty Buttocks. She put me on the bus. But on our way here I ran away. I ran through bushes and over hills until my feet got so swollen that I couldn't get my shoes off. I nearly died. I was ill for nine months. If the Witness hadn't found me, I would have died.'

'I didn't find him,' Nestor said to me. 'La Gorda found him. She took me to where he was and between the two of us we carried him to the bus and brought him here. He was delirious and we had to pay an extra fare so that the bus driver would let him stay on the bus.'

In a most dramatic tone Pablito said that he had not changed his mind; he still wanted to die.

'But why?' I asked him.

Benigno answered for him in a booming, guttural voice.

'Because his pecker doesn't work,' he said.

The sound of his voice was so extraordinary that for an instant I had the impression that he was talking inside a cavern. It was at once frightening and incongruous. I laughed almost out of control.

Nestor said that Pablito had attempted to fulfil his task of establishing sexual relations with the women, in accordance with the Nagual's instructions. He had told Pablito that the four corners of his world were already set in position and all he had to do was to claim them. But when Pablito went to claim his first corner, Lidia, she nearly killed him. Nestor added that it was his personal opinion as a witness of the event that the reason Lidia rammed him with her head was because Pablito could not perform as a man, and rather than being embarrassed by the whole thing, she hit him.

'Did Pablito really get sick as a result of that blow or was he pretending?' I asked half in jest.

Benigno answered again in the same booming voice.

'He was just pretending!' he said. 'All he got was a bump on the head!'

Pablito and Nestor cackled and yelled.

'We don't blame Pablito for being afraid of those women,' Nestor said. 'They are all like the Nagual himself, fearsome warriors. They're mean and crazy.'

'Do you really think they're that bad?' I asked him.

'To say they're bad is only one part of the whole truth,' Nestor said. 'They're just like the Nagual. They're serious and gloomy. When the Nagual was around, they used to sit close to him and stare into the distance with half-closed eyes for hours, sometimes for days.'

'Is it true that Josefina was really crazy a long time ago?' I asked.

'That's a laugh,' Pablito said. 'Not a long time ago; she's crazy now. She's the most insane of the bunch.'

I told them what she had done to me. I thought that they would appreciate the humour of her magnificent performance. But my story seemed to affect them the wrong way. They listened to me like frightened children; even Benigno opened his eyes to listen to my account.

'Wow!' Pablito exclaimed. 'Those bitches are really awful. And you know that their leader is Two Hundred and Twenty Buttocks. She's the one that throws the rock and then hides her hand and pretends to be an innocent little girl. Be careful of her, Maestro.'

'The Nagual trained Josefina to be anything,' Nestor said. 'She can do anything you want: cry, laugh, get angry, anything.'

'But what is she like when she is not acting?' I asked Nestor.

'She's just crazier than a bat,' Benigno answered in a soft voice. 'I met Josefina the first day she arrived. I had to carry her into the house. The Nagual and I used to tie her down to her bed all the time. Once she began to cry for her friend, a little girl she used to play with. She cried for three days. Pablito consoled her and fed her like a baby. She's like him. Both of them don't know how to stop once they begin.'

Benigno suddenly began to sniff the air. He stood up and went over to the stove.

'Is he really shy?' I asked Nestor.

'He's shy and eccentric,' Pablito answered. 'He'll be that way until he loses his form. Genaro told us that we will lose our form sooner or later, so there is no point in making ourselves miserable in trying to change ourselves the way the Nagual told us to. Genaro told us to enjoy ourselves and not worry about anything. You and the women worry and try; we on the other hand, enjoy. You don't know how to enjoy things and we don't know how to make ourselves miserable. The Nagual called making yourself miserable, impeccability; we call it stupidity, don't we?'

'You are speaking for yourself, Pablito,' Nestor said. 'Benigno and I don't feel that way.'

Benigno brought a bowl of food over and placed it in front of me. He served everyone. Pablito examined the bowls and asked Benigno where he had found them. Benigno said that they were in a box where la Gorda had told him she had stored them. Pablito confided in me that those bowls used to belong to them before their split.

'We have to be careful,' Pablito said in a nervous tone.

'These bowls are no doubt bewitched. Those bitches put something in them. I'd rather eat out of la Gorda's bowl.'

Nestor and Benigno began to eat. I noticed then that Benigno had given me the brown bowl. Pablito seemed to be in a great turmoil. I wanted to put him at ease but Nestor stopped me.

'Don't take him so seriously,' he said. 'He loves to be that way. He'll sit down and eat. This is where you and the women fail. There is no way for you to understand that Pablito is like that. You expect everybody to be like the Nagual. La Gorda is the only one who's unruffled by him, not because she understands but because she has lost her form.'

Pablito sat down to eat and among the four of us we finished a whole pot of food. Benigno washed the bowls and carefully put them back in the box and then all of us sat down comfortably around the table.

Nestor proposed that as soon as it got dark we should all go for a walk in a ravine nearby, where don Juan, don Genaro and I used to go. I felt somehow reluctant. I did not feel confident enough in their company. Nestor said that they were used to walking in the darkness and that the art of a sorcerer was to be inconspicuous even in the midst of people. I told him what don Juan had once said to me, before he had left me in a deserted place in the mountains not too far from there. He had demanded that I concentrate totally on trying not to be obvious. He said that the people of the area knew everyone by sight. There were not very many people, but those who lived there walked around all the time and could spot a stranger from miles away. He told me that many of those people had firearms and would have thought nothing of shooting me.

'Don't be concerned with beings from the other world,' don Juan had said laughing. 'The dangerous ones are the Mexicans.'

'That's still valid,' Nestor said. 'That has been valid all the time. That's why the Nagual and Genaro were the artists they were. They learned to become unnoticeable in the middle of all this. They knew the art of stalking.'

It was still too early for our walk in the dark. I wanted to use the time to ask Nestor my critical question. I had been avoiding it all along; some strange feeling had prevented me from asking. It was as if I had exhausted my interest after Pablito's reply. But Pablito himself came to my aid and all of a sudden he brought up the subject as if he had been reading my mind.

'Nestor also jumped into the abyss the same day we did,' he said. 'And in that way he became the Witness, you became the Maestro and I became the village idiot.'

In a casual manner I asked Nestor to tell me about his jump into the abyss. I tried to sound only mildly interested. But Pablito was aware of the true nature of my forced indifference. He laughed and told Nestor that I was being cautious because I had been deeply disappointed with his own account of the event.

'I went over after you two did,' Nestor said, and looked at me as if waiting for another question.

'Did you jump immediately after us?' I asked.

'No. It took me quite a while to get ready,' he said. 'Genaro and the Nagual didn't tell me what to do. That day was a test day for all of us.'

Pablito seemed despondent. He stood up from his chair and paced the room. He sat down again, shaking his head in a gesture of despair.

'Did you actually see us going over the edge?' I asked Nestor.

'I am the Witness,' he said. 'To witness was my path of knowledge; to tell you impeccably what I witness is my task.'

'But what did you really see?' I asked.

'I saw you two holding each other and running towards the edge,' he said. 'And then I saw you both like two kites against the sky. Pablito moved farther out in a straight line and then fell down. You went up a little and then you moved away from the edge a short distance, before falling down.'

'But, did we jump with our bodies?' I asked.

'Well, I don't think there was another way to do it,' he said, and laughed.

'Could it have been an illusion?' I asked.

'What are you trying to say, Maestro?' he asked in a dry tone.

'I want to know what really happened,' I said.

'Did you by any chance black out, like Pablito?' Nestor asked with a glint in his eye.

I tried to explain to him the nature of my quandary about the jump. He could not hold still and interrupted me. Pablito intervened to bring him to order and they became involved in an argument. Pablito squeezed himself out of it by walking half seated around the table, holding on to his chair.

'Nestor doesn't see beyond his nose,' he said to me. 'Benigno is the same. You'll get nothing from them. At least you got my sympathy.'

Pablito cackled, making his shoulders shiver, and hid his face with Benigno's hat.

'As far as I'm concerned, you two jumped,' Nestor said to me in a sudden outburst. 'Genaro and the Nagual had left you with no other choice. That was their art, to corral you and then lead you to the only gate that was open. And so you two went over the edge. That was what I witnessed. Pablito says that he didn't feel a thing; that is questionable. I know that he was perfectly aware of everything, but he chooses to feel and say that he wasn't.'

'I really wasn't aware,' Pablito said to me in an apologetic tone.

'Perhaps,' Nestor said dryly. 'But I was aware myself, and I saw your bodies doing what they had to do, jump.'

Nestor's assertions put me in a strange frame of mind. All along I had been seeking validation for what I had perceived myself. But once I had it, I realized that it made no difference. To know that I had jumped and to be afraid of what I had perceived was one thing; to seek consensual validation was another. I knew then that one had no necessary correlation with the other. I had thought all along that to have someone else corroborate that I had taken that plunge would absolve my intellect of its doubts and fears. I was wrong. I became instead more worried, more involved with the issue.

I began to tell Nestor that although I had come to see the two of them for the specific purpose of having them confirm that I had jumped, I had changed my mind and I really did not want to talk about it any more. Both of them started talking at once, and at that point we fell into a three-way argument. Pablito maintained that he had not been aware, Nestor shouted that Pablito was indulging and I said that I didn't want to hear anything more about the jump.

It was blatantly obvious to me for the first time that none of us had calmness and self-control. None of us was willing to give the other person our undivided attention, the way don Juan and don Genaro did. Since I was incapable of maintaining any order in our exchange of opinions, I immersed myself in my own deliberations. I had always thought that the only flaw that had prevented me from entering fully into don Juan's world was my insistence on rationalizing everything, but the presence of Pablito and Nestor had given me a new insight into myself. Another flaw of mine was my timidity. Once I strayed outside the safe railings of common sense, I could not trust myself and became intimidated by the awesomeness of what unfolded in front of me. Thus, I found it was impossible to believe that I had jumped into an abyss.

Don Juan had insisted that the whole issue of sorcery was perception, and truthful to that, he and don Genaro staged, for our last meeting, an immense, cathartic drama on the flat mountaintop. After they made me voice my thanks in loud clear words to everyone who had ever helped me, I became transfixed with elation. At that point they had caught all my attention and led my body to perceive the only possible act within their frame of references: the jump into the abyss. That jump was the practical accomplishment of my perception, not as an average man but as a sorcerer.

I had been so absorbed in writing down my thoughts I had not noticed that Nestor and Pablito had stopped talking and all three of them were looking at me. I explained to them that there was no way for me to understand what had taken place with that jump.

'There's nothing to understand,' Nestor said. 'Things just

happen and no one can tell how. Ask Benigno if he wants to understand.'

'Do you want to understand?' I asked Benigno as a joke.

'You bet I do!' he exclaimed in a deep bass voice, making everyone laugh.

'You indulge in saying that you want to understand,' Nestor went on. 'Just like Pablito indulges in saying that he doesn't remember anything.'

He looked at Pablito and winked at me. Pablito lowered his head.

Nestor asked me if I had noticed something about Pablito's mood when we were about to take our plunge. I had to admit that I had been in no position to notice anything so subtle as Pablito's mood.

'A warrior must notice everything,' he said. 'That's his trick, and as the Nagual said, there lies his advantage.'

He smiled and made a deliberate gesture of embarrassment, hiding his face with his hat.

'What was it that I missed about Pablito's mood?' I asked him.

'Pablito had already jumped before he went over,' he said. 'He didn't have to do anything. He may as well have sat down on the edge instead of jumping.'

'What do you mean by that?' I asked.

'Pablito was already disintegrating,' he replied. 'That's why he thinks he passed out. Pablito lies. He's hiding something.'

Pablito began to speak to me. He muttered some unintelligible words, then gave up and slumped back in his chair. Nestor also started to say something. I made him stop. I was not sure I had understood him correctly.

'Was Pablito's body disintegrating?' I asked.

He peered at me for a long time without saying a word. He was sitting to my right. He moved quietly to the bench opposite me.

'You must take what I say seriously,' he said. 'There is no way to turn back the wheel of time to what we were before that jump. The Nagual said that it is an honour and a pleasure to be a warrior, and that it is the warrior's fortune to do what he has to do. I have to tell you impeccably what I have witnessed. Pablito was disintegrating. As you two ran towards the edge only you were solid. Pablito was like a cloud. He thinks that he was about to fall on his face, and you think that you held him by the arm to help him make it to the edge. Neither of you is correct, and I wouldn't doubt that it would have been better for both of you if you hadn't picked Pablito up.'

I felt more confused than ever. I truly believed that he was sincere in reporting what he had perceived, but I remembered that I had only held Pablito's arm.

'What would have happened if I hadn't interfered?' I asked.

'I can't answer that,' Nestor replied. 'But I know that you affected each other's luminosity. At the moment you put your arm around him, Pablito became more solid, but you wasted your precious power for nothing.'

'What did you do after we jumped?' I asked Nestor after a long silence.

'Right after you two had disappeared,' he said, 'my nerves were so shattered that I couldn't breathe and I too passed out, I don't know for how long. I thought it was only for a moment. When I came to my senses again, I looked around for Genaro and Nagual; they were gone. I ran back and forth on the top of that mountain, calling them until my voice was hoarse. Then I knew I was alone. I walked to the edge of the cliff and tried to look for the sign that the earth gives when a warrior is not going to return, but I had already missed it. I knew then that Genaro and the Nagual were gone forever. I had not realized until then that they had turned to me after they had said good-bye to you two, and as you were running to the edge they waved their hands and said good-bye to me.

'Finding myself alone at that time of day, on that deserted spot, was more than I could bear. In one sweep I had lost all the friends I had in the world. I sat down and wept. And as I got more and more scared I began to scream as loud as I could. I called Genaro's name at the top of my voice. By then it was pitch-black. I could no longer distinguish any landmarks. I knew that as a warrior I had no business indulging in my grief.

In order to calm myself down I began to howl like a coyote, the way the Nagual had taught me. After howling for a while I felt so much better that I forgot my sadness. I forgot that the world existed. The more I howled the easier it was to feel the warmth and protection of the earth.

'Hours must have passed. Suddenly I felt a blow inside of me, behind my throat, and the sound of a bell in my ears. I remembered what the Nagual had told Eligio and Benigno before they jumped. He said that the feeling in the throat came just before one was ready to change speed, and that the sound of the bell was the vehicle that one could use to accomplish anything that one needed. I wanted to be a coyote then. I looked at my arms, which were on the ground in front of me. They had changed shape and looked like a coyote's. I saw the coyote's fur on my arms and chest. I was a coyote! That made me so happy that I cried like a coyote must cry. I felt my coyote teeth and my long and pointed muzzle and tongue. Somehow, I knew that I had died, but I didn't care. It didn't matter to me to have turned into a coyote, or to be dead, or to be alive. I walked like a coyote, on four legs, to the edge of the precipice and leaped into it. There was nothing else for me to do.

'I felt that I was falling down and my coyote body turned in the air. Then I was myself again twirling in midair. But before I hit the bottom I became so light that I didn't fall any more but floated. The air went through me. I was so light! I believed that my death was finally coming inside me. Something stirred my insides and I disintegrated like dry sand. It was peaceful and perfect where I was. I somehow knew that I was there and yet I wasn't. I was nothing. That's all I can say about it. Then, quite suddenly, the same thing that had made me like dry sand put me together again. I came back to life and I found myself sitting in the hut of an old Mazatec sorcerer. He told me his name was Porfirio. He said that he was glad to see me and began to teach me certain things about plants that Genaro hadn't taught me. He took me with him to where the plants were being made and showed me the mould of plants, especially the marks on the moulds. He said that if I watched for those marks in the plants I could easily tell what they're good for, even if I had never seen those plants before. Then when he knew that I had learned the marks he said good-bye but invited me to come see him again. At that moment I felt a strong pull and I disintegrated, like before. I became a million pieces.

'Then I was pulled again into myself and went back to see Porfirio. He had, after all, invited me. I knew that I could have gone anywhere I wanted but I chose Porfirio's hut because he was kind to me and taught me. I didn't want to risk finding awful things instead. Porfirio took me this time to see the mould of the animals. There I saw my own nagual animal. We knew each other on sight. Porfirio was delighted to see such friendship. I saw Pablito's and your own nagual too, but they didn't want to talk to me. They seemed sad. I didn't insist on talking to them. I didn't know how you had fared in your jump. I knew that I was dead myself, but my nagual said that I wasn't and that you both were also alive. I asked about Eligio, and my nagual said that he was gone forever. I remembered then that when I had witnessed Eligio's and Benigno's jump I had heard the Nagual giving Benigno instructions not to seek bizarre visions or worlds outside his own. The Nagual told him to learn only about his own world, because in doing so he would find the only form of power available to him. The Nagual gave them specific instructions to let their pieces explode as far as they could in order to restore their strength. I did the same myself. I went back and forth from the tonal to the nagual eleven times. Every time, however, I was received by Porfirio who instructed me further. Every time my strength waned I restored it in the nagual until a time when I restored it so much that I found myself back on this earth.'

'Doña Soledad told me that Eligio didn't have to jump into the abyss,' I said.

'He jumped with Benigno,' Nestor said. 'Ask him, he'll tell you in his favourite voice.'

I turned to Benigno and asked him about his jump.

'You bet we jumped together!' he replied in a blasting voice. 'But I never talk about it.'

'What did Soledad say Eligio did?' Nestor asked.

I told them that doña Soledad had said that Eligio was twirled by a wind and left the world while he was working in an open field.

'She's thoroughly confused,' Nestor said. 'Eligio was twirled by the allies. But he didn't want any of them, so they let him go. That has nothing to do with the jump. La Gorda said that you had a bout with allies last night; I don't know what you did, but if you had wanted to catch them or entice them to stay with you, you had to spin with them. Sometimes they come of their own accord to the sorcerer and spin him. Eligio was the best warrior there was so the allies came to him of their own accord. If any of us want the allies, we would have to beg them for years, and even if we did, I doubt that the allies would consider helping us.

'Eligio had to jump like everybody else. I witnessed his jump. He was paired with Benigno. A lot of what happens to us as sorcerers depends on what your partner does. Benigno is a bit off his rocker because his partner didn't come back. Isn't that so, Benigno?'

'You bet it is!' Benigno answered in his favourite voice.

I succumbed at that point to a great curiosity that had plagued me from the first time I had heard Benigno speak. I asked him how he made his booming voice. He turned to face me. He sat up straight and pointed to his mouth as if he wanted me to look fixedly at it.

'I don't know!' he boomed. 'I just open my mouth and this voice comes out of it!'

He contracted the muscles of his forehead, curled up his lips and made a profound booing sound. I then saw that he had tremendous muscles in his temples, which had given his head a different contour. It was not his hairline that was different but the whole upper front part of his head.

'Genaro left him his noises,' Nestor said to me. 'Wait until he farts.'

I had the feeling that Benigno was getting ready to demonstrate his abilities.

'Wait, wait, Benigno,' I said, 'it's not necessary.'

'Oh, shucks!' Benigno exclaimed in a tone of disappointment. 'I had the best one just for you.'

Pablito and Nestor laughed so hard that even Benigno lost his deadpan expression and cackled with them.

'Tell me what else happened to Eligio,' I asked Nestor after they had calmed down again.

'After Eligio and Benigno jumped,' Nestor replied, 'the Nagual made me look quickly over the edge, in order to catch the sign the earth gives when warriors jump into the abyss. If there is something like a little cloud, or a faint gust of wind, the warrior's time on earth is not over yet. The day Eligio and Benigno jumped I felt one puff of air on the side Benigno had jumped and I knew that his time was not up. But Eligio's side was silent.'

'What do you think happened to Eligio? Did he die?'

All three of them stared at me. They were quiet for a moment. Nestor scratched his temples with both hands. Benigno giggled and shook his head. I attempted to explain but Nestor made a gesture with his hands to stop me.

'Are you serious when you ask us questions?' he asked me.

Benigno answered for me. When he was not clowning, his voice was deep and melodious. He said that the Nagual and Genaro had set us up so all of us had pieces of information that the others did not have.

'Well, if that's the case we'll tell you what's what,' Nestor said, smiling as if a great load had been lifted off his shoulders. 'Eligio did not die. Not at all.'

'Where is he now?' I asked.

They looked at one another again. They gave me the feeling that they were struggling to keep from laughing. I told them that all I knew about Eligio was what doña Soledad had told me. She had said that Eligio had gone to the other world to join the Nagual and Genaro. To me that sounded as if the three of them had died.

'Why do you talk like that, Maestro?' Nestor asked with a tone of deep concern. 'Not even Pablito talks like that.'

I thought Pablito was going to protest. He almost stood up, but he seemed to change his mind.

'Yes, that's right,' he said. 'Not even I talk like that.'

'Well, if Eligio didn't die, where is he?' I asked.

'Soledad already told you,' Nestor said softly. 'Eligio went to join the Nagual and Genaro.'

I decided that it was best not to ask any more questions. I did not mean my probes to be aggressive, but they always turned out that way. Besides, I had the feeling that they did not know much more than I did.

Nestor suddenly stood up and began to pace back and forth in front of me. Finally he pulled me away from the table by my armpits. He did not want me to write. He asked me if I had really blacked out like Pablito had at the moment of jumping and did not remember anything. I told him that I had had a number of vivid dreams or visions that I could not explain and that I had come to see them to seek clarification. They wanted to hear about all the visions I had had.

After they had heard my accounts, Nestor said that my visions were of a bizarre order and only the first two were of great importance and of this earth; the rest were visions of alien worlds. He explained that my first vision was of special value because it was an omen proper. He said that sorcerers always took a first event of any series as the blueprint or the map of what was going to develop subsequently.

In that particular vision I had found myself looking at an outlandish world. There was an enormous rock right in front of my eyes, a rock which had been split in two. Through a wide gap in it I could see a boundless phosphorescent plain, a valley of some sort, which was bathed in a greenish-yellow light. On one side of the valley, to the right, and partially covered from my view by the enormous rock, there was an unbelievable domelike structure. It was dark, almost a charcoal grey. If my size was what it is in the world of everyday life, the dome must have been fifty thousand feet high and miles and miles across. Such an enormity dazzled me. I had a sensation of vertigo and plummeted into a state of disintegration.

Once more I rebounded from it and found myself on a very uneven and yet flat surface. It was a shiny, interminable surface just like the plain I had seen before. It went as far as I could see. I soon realized that I could turn my head in any direction I wanted on a horizontal plane, but I could not look at myself. I was able, however, to examine the surroundings by rotating my head from left to right and vice versa. Nevertheless, when I wanted to turn around to look behind me, I could not move my bulk.

The plain extended itself monotonously, equally to my left and to my right. There was nothing else in sight but an endless, whitish glare. I wanted to look at the ground underneath my feet but my eyes could not move down. I lifted my head up to look at the sky; all I saw was another limitless, whitish surface that seemed to be connected to the one I was standing on. I then had a moment of apprehension and felt that something was just about to be revealed to me. But the sudden and devastating jolt of disintegration stopped my revelation. Some force pulled me downward. It was as if the whitish surface had swallowed me.

Nestor said that my vision of a dome was of tremendous importance because that particular shape had been isolated by the Nagual and Genaro as the vision of the place where all of us were supposed to meet them someday.

Benigno spoke to me at that point and said that he had heard Eligio being instructed to find that particular dome. He said that the Nagual and Genaro insisted that Eligio understand their point correctly. They always had believed Eligio to be the best; therefore, they directed him to find that dome and to enter its whitish vaults over and over again.

Pablito said that all three of them were instructed to find that dome if they could, but that none of them had. I said then, in a complaining tone, that neither don Juan nor don Genaro had ever mentioned anything like that to me. I had had no instruction of any sort regarding a dome.

Benigno, who was sitting across the table from me, suddenly stood up and came to my side. He sat to my left and whispered very softly in my ear that perhaps the two old men had instructed me but I did not remember, or that they had not said anything about it so I would not fix my attention on it once I had found it.

'Why was the dome so important?' I asked Nestor.

'Because that's where the Nagual and Genaro are now,' he replied.

'And where's that dome?' I asked.

'Somewhere on this earth,' he said.

I had to explain to them at great length that it was impossible that a structure of that magnitude could exist on our planet. I said that my vision was more like a dream and domes of that height could exist only in fantasies. They laughed and patted me gently as if they were humouring a child.

'You want to know where Eligio is,' Nestor said all of a sudden. 'Well, he is in the white vaults of that dome with the Nagual and Genaro.'

'But that dome was a vision,' I protested.

'Then Eligio is in a vision,' Nestor said. 'Remember what Benigno just said to you. The Nagual and Genaro didn't tell you to find that dome and go back to it over and over. If they had, you wouldn't be here. You'd be like Eligio, in the dome of that vision. So you see, Eligio did not die like a man in the street dies. He simply did not return from his jump.'

His claim was staggering to me. I could not brush aside the memory of the vividness of the visions I had had, but for some strange reason I wanted to argue with him. Nestor, without giving me time to say anything, drove his point a notch further. He reminded me of one of my visions: the next to the last. That particular one had been the most nightmarish of them all. I had found myself being chased by a strange, unseen creature. I knew that it was there but I could not see it, not because it was invisible but because the world I was in was so incredibly unfamiliar that I could not tell what anything was. Whatever the elements of my vision were, they were certainly not from this earth. The emotional distress I experienced upon being lost in such a place was almost more than I could bear. At one moment, the surface where I stood began to shake. I felt that it was caving in under my feet and I grabbed a sort of branch, or an appendage of a thing that reminded me of a tree, which was hanging just above my head on a horizontal plane. The instant I touched it, the thing wrapped around my wrist, as if it had been filled with nerves that sensed everything. I felt that I was being hoisted to a tremendous height. I looked down and saw an incredible animal; I knew it was the unseen creature that had been chasing me. It was coming out of a surface that looked like the ground. I could see its enormous mouth open like a cavern. I heard a chilling, thoroughly unearthly roar, something like a shrill, metallic gasp, and the tentacle that had me caught unravelled and I fell into that cavernous mouth. I saw every detail of that mouth as I was falling into it. Then it closed with me inside. I felt an instantaneous pressure that mashed my body.

'You have already died,' Nestor said. 'That animal ate you. You ventured beyond this world and found horror itself. Our life and our death are no more and no less real than your short life in that place and your death in the mouth of that monster. This life that we are having now is only a long vision. Don't you see?'

Nervous spasms ran through my body.

'I didn't go beyond this world,' he went on, 'but I know what I'm talking about. I don't have tales of horror like you. All I did was to visit Porfirio ten times. If it had been up to me I would've gone there forever, but my eleventh bounce was so powerful that it changed my direction. I felt that I had over-shot Porfirio's hut, and instead of finding myself at his door, I found myself in the city, very close to the place of a friend of mine. I thought it was funny. I knew that I was journeying between the tonal and the nagual. Nobody had said to me that the journeys had to be of any special kind. So I got curious and decided to see my friend. I began to wonder if I really would get to see him. I came to his house and knocked on the door just as I had knocked scores of times. His wife let me in as she had always done and sure enough my friend was home. I told him that I had come to the city on business and he even paid me some money he owed me. I put the money in my pocket. I knew that my friend, and his wife, and the money, and his house, and the city were just like Porfirio's hut, a vision. I knew that a force beyond me was going to disintegrate me any moment. So I sat down to enjoy my friend to the fullest.

We laughed and joked. And I dare say that I was funny and light and charming. I stayed there for a long time, waiting for the jolt; since it didn't come I decided to leave. I said good-bye and thanked him for the money and for his friendship. I walked away. I wanted to see the city before the force took me away. I wandered around all night. I walked all the way to the hills overlooking the city, and at the moment the sun rose a realization struck me like a thunderbolt. I was back in the world and the force that will disintegrate me was at ease and was going to let me stay for a while. I was going to see my homeland and this marvellous earth for a while longer. What a great joy, Maestro! But I couldn't say that I had not enjoyed Porfirio's friendship. Both visions are equal, but I prefer the vision of my form and my earth. It's my indulging perhaps.'

Nestor stopped talking and all of them stared at me. I felt threatened as I had never been before. Some part of me was in awe of what he had said, another wanted to fight with him. I began to argue with him without any sense. My inane mood lasted for a few moments, then I became aware that Benigno was looking at me with a very mean expression. He had fixed his eyes on my chest. I felt that something ominous was suddenly pressing on my heart. I began to perspire as if a heater were right in front of my face. My ears began to buzz.

La Gorda walked up to me at that precise moment. She was a most unexpected sight. I was sure that the Genaros felt the same way. They stopped what they were doing and looked at her. Pablito was the first to recover from his surprise.

'Why do you have to come in like that?' he asked in a pleading tone. 'You were listening from the other room, weren't you?'

She said that she had been in the house only a few minutes and then she stepped out to the kitchen. And the reason she stayed quiet was not so much to listen but to exercise her ability to be inconspicuous.

Her presence had created a strange lull. I wanted to pick up again the flow of Nestor's revelations, but before I could say anything la Gorda said that the little sisters were on their way to the house and would be coming through the door any minute. The Genaros stood up at once as if they had been pulled by the same string. Pablito put his chair on his shoulder.

'Let's go for a hike in the dark, Maestro,' Pablito said to me.

La Gorda said in a most imperative tone that I could not go with them yet because she had not finished telling me everything the Nagual had instructed her to tell me.

Pablito turned to me and winked.

'I've told you,' he said. 'They're bossy, gloomy bitches. I certainly hope you're not like that, Maestro.'

Nestor and Benigno said good night and embraced me. Pablito just walked away carrying his chair like a backpack. They went out through the back.

A few seconds later a horribly loud bang on the front door made la Gorda and me jump to our feet. Pablito walked in again, carrying his chair.

'You thought I wasn't going to say good night, didn't you?' he asked me and left laughing.

5 THE ART OF DREAMING

The next day I was by myself all morning. I worked on my notes. In the afternoon I used my car to help la Gorda and the little sisters transport the furniture from doña Soledad's house to their house.

In the early evening la Gorda and I sat in the dining area alone. We were silent for a while. I was very tired.

La Gorda broke the silence and said that all of them had been too complacent since the Nagual and Genaro had left. Each of them had been absorbed in his or her particular tasks. She said that the Nagual had commanded her to be an impassionate warrior and to follow whatever path her fate selected for her. If Soledad had stolen my power, la Gorda had to flee and try to save the little sisters and then join Benigno and Nestor, the only two Genaros who would have survived. If the little sisters had killed me, she had to join the Genaros because the little sisters would have had no more need to be with her. If I had not survived the attack of the allies and she did, she had to leave that area and be on her own. She told me, with a glint in her eye, that she had been sure that neither one of us would survive, and that that was why she had said good-bye to her sisters, to her house and to the hills.

'The Nagual told me that in case you and I survived the allies,' she went on, 'I have to do anything for you, because that would be my warrior's path. That was why I interfered with what Benigno was doing to you last night. He was pressing on your chest with his eyes. That is his art as a stalker. You *saw* Pablito's hand earlier yesterday; that was also part of the same art.'

'What art is that, Gorda?'

'The art of the stalker. That was the Nagual's predilection and the Genaros are his true children at that. We, on the other hand, are dreamers. Your double is *dreaming*.'

What she was saying was new to me. I wanted her to elucidate her statements. I paused for a moment to read what I had written in order to select the most appropriate question. I told her that I first wanted to find out what she knew about my double and then I wanted to know about the art of stalking.

'The Nagual told me that your double is something that takes a lot of power to come out,' she said. 'He figured that you might have enough energy to get it out of you twice. That's why he set up Soledad and the little sisters either to kill you or to help you.'

La Gorda said that I had had more energy than the Nagual thought, and that my double came out three times. Apparently Rosa's attack had not been a thoughtless action; on the contrary, she had very cleverly calculated that if she injured me, I would have been helpless: the same ploy doña Soledad had tried with her dog. I had given Rosa a chance to strike me when I yelled at her, but she failed to injure me. My double came out and injured her instead. La Gorda said that Lidia had told her that Rosa did not want to wake up when all of us had to rush out of Soledad's house, so Lidia squeezed the hand that had been injured. Rosa did not feel any pain and knew in an instant that I had cured her, which meant to them that I had drained my power. La Gorda affirmed that the little sisters were very clever and had planned to drain me of power; to that effect they had kept on insisting that I cure Soledad. As soon as Rosa realized that I had also cured her, she thought that I had weakened myself beyond repair. All they had to do was to wait for Josefina in order to finish me off.

'The little sisters didn't know that when you cured Rosa and Soledad you also replenished yourself,' la Gorda said, and laughed as if it were a joke. 'That was why you had enough energy to get your double out a third time when the little sisters tried to take your luminosity.'

I told her about the vision I had had of doña Soledad huddled against the wall of her room, and how I had merged that vision with my tactile sense and ended up feeling a viscous substance on her forehead.

'That was true *seeing*,' la Gorda said. 'You *saw* Soledad in her room although she was with me around Genaro's place, and then you *saw* your nagual on her forehead.'

I felt compelled at that point to recount to her the details of my whole experience, especially the realization I had had that I was actually curing doña Soledad and Rosa by touching the viscous substance, which I felt was part of me.

'To *see* that thing on Rosa's hand was also true *seeing*,' she said. 'And you were absolutely right, that substance was yourself. It came out of your body and it was your nagual. By touching it, you pulled it back.'

La Gorda told me then, as though she were unveiling a mystery, that the Nagual had commanded her not to disclose the fact that since all of us had the same luminosity, if my nagual touched one of them, I would not get weakened, as would ordinarily be the case if my nagual touched an average man.

'If your nagual touches us,' she said, giving me a gentle slap on the head, 'your luminosity stays on the surface. You can pick it up again and nothing is lost.'

I told her that the content of her explanation was impossible for me to believe. She shrugged her shoulders as if saying that that was not any of her concern. I asked her then about her usage of the word nagual. I said that don Juan had explained the nagual to me as being the indescribable principle, the source of everything.

'Sure,' she said smiling. 'I know what he meant. The nagual is in everything.'

I pointed out to her, a bit scornfully, that one could also say the opposite, that the tonal is in everything. She carefully explained that there was no opposition, that my statement was correct, the tonal was also in everything. She said that the tonal which is in everything could be easily apprehended by our senses, while the nagual which is in everything manifested itself only to the eye of the sorcerer. She added that we could stumble upon the most outlandish sights of the tonal and be scared of them, or awed by them, or be indifferent to them, because all of us could view those sights. A sight of the nagual, on the other hand, needed the specialized senses of a sorcerer in order to be seen at all. And yet, both the tonal and the nagual were present in everything at all times. It was appropriate, therefore, for a sorcerer to say that 'looking' consisted in viewing the tonal which is in everything, and 'seeing', on the other hand, consisted in viewing the nagual which also is in everything. Accordingly, if a warrior observed the world as a human being, he was looking, but if he observed it as a sorcerer, he was 'seeing', and what he was 'seeing' had to be properly called the nagual.

She then reiterated the reason, which Nestor had given me earlier, for calling don Juan the Nagual and confirmed that I was also the Nagual because of the shape that came out of my head.

I wanted to know why they had called the shape that had come out of my head the double. She said that they had thought they were sharing a private joke with me. They had always called that shape the double, because it was twice the size of the person who had it.

'Nestor told me that that shape was not such a good thing to have,' I said.

'It's neither good nor bad,' she said. 'You have it and that makes you the Nagual. That's all. One of us eight had to be the Nagual and you're the one. It might have been Pablito or me or anyone.'

'Tell me now, what is the art of stalking?' I asked.

'The Nagual was a stalker,' she said, and peered at me. 'You must know that. He taught you to stalk from the beginning.'

It occurred to me that what she was referring to was what don Juan had called the hunter. He had certainly taught me to be a hunter. I told her that don Juan had shown me how to hunt and make traps. Her usage of the term stalker, however, was more accurate.

'A hunter just hunts,' she said. 'A stalker stalks anything, including himself.'

'How does he do that?'

'An impeccable stalker can turn anything into prey. The Nagual told me that we can even stalk our own weaknesses.'

I stopped writing and tried to remember if don Juan had ever presented me with such a novel possibility: to stalk my weaknesses. I could not recall him ever putting it in those terms.

'How can one stalk one's weaknesses, Gorda?'

'The same way you stalk prey. You figure out your routines until you know all the doing of your weaknesses and then you come upon them and pick them up like rabbits inside a cage.'

Don Juan had taught me the same thing about routines, but in the vein of a general principle that hunters must be aware of. Her understanding and application of it, however, were more pragmatic than mine.

Don Juan had said that any habit was, in essence, a 'doing', and that a doing needed all its parts in order to function. If some parts were missing, a doing was disassembled. By doing, he meant any coherent and meaningful series of actions. In other words, a habit needed all its component actions in order to be a live activity.

La Gorda then described how she had stalked her own weakness of eating excessively. She said that the Nagual had suggested she first tackle the biggest part of that habit, which was connected with her laundry work; she ate whatever her customers fed her as she went from house to house delivering her wash. She expected the Nagual to tell her what to do, but he only laughed and made fun of her, saying that as soon as he would mention something for her to do, she would fight not to do it. He said that that was the way human beings are; they love to be told what to do, but they love even more to fight and not do what they are told, and thus they get entangled in hating the one who told them in the first place.

For many years she could not think of anything to do to stalk her weakness. One day, however, she got so sick and tired of being fat that she refused to eat for twenty-three days. That was the initial action that broke her fixation. She then had the idea of stuffing her mouth with a sponge to make her customers believe that she had an infected tooth and could not eat. The subterfuge worked not only with her customers, who stopped giving her food, but with her as well, as she had the feeling of eating as she chewed on the sponge. La Gorda laughed when she told me how she had walked around with a sponge stuffed in her mouth for years until her habit of eating excessively had been broken.

'Was that all you needed to stop your habit?' I asked.

'No. I also had to learn how to eat like a warrior.'

'And how does a warrior eat?'

'A warrior eats quietly, and slowly, and very little at a time. I used to talk while I ate, and I ate very fast, and I ate lots and lots of food at one sitting. The Nagual told me that a warrior eats four mouthfuls of food at one time. A while later he eats another four mouthfuls and so on.

'A warrior also walks miles and miles every day. My eating weakness never let me walk. I broke it by eating four mouthfuls every hour and by walking. Sometimes I walked all day and all night. That was the way I lost the fat on my buttocks.'

She laughed at her own recollection of the nickname don Juan had given her.

'But stalking your weaknesses is not enough to drop them,' she said. 'You can stalk them from now to doomsday and it won't make a bit of difference. That's why the Nagual didn't want to tell me what to do. What a warrior really needs in order to be an impeccable stalker is to have a purpose.'

La Gorda recounted how she had lived from day to day, before she met the Nagual, with nothing to look forward to. She had no hopes, no dreams, no desire for anything. The opportunity to eat, however, was always accessible to her; for some reason that she could not fathom, there had been plenty of food available to her every single day of her life. So much of it, in fact, that at one time she weighed two hundred and thirty-six pounds.

'Eating was the only thing I enjoyed in life,' la Gorda said. 'Besides, I never saw myself as being fat. I thought I was rather pretty and that people liked me as I was. Everyone said that I looked healthy.

'The Nagual told me something very strange. He said that I had an enormous amount of personal power and due to that I had always managed to get food from friends while the relatives in my own house were going hungry.

'Everybody has enough personal power for something. The

trick for me was to pull my personal power away from food to my warrior's purpose.'

'And what is that purpose, Gorda?' I asked half in jest.

'To enter into the other world,' she replied with a grin and pretended to hit me on top of my head with her knuckles, the way don Juan used to do when he thought I was indulging.

There was no more light for me to write. I wanted her to bring a lantern but she complained that she was too tired and had to sleep a bit before the little sisters arrived.

We went into the front room. She gave me a blanket, then wrapped herself in another one and fell asleep instantly. I sat with my back against the wall. The brick surface of the bed was hard even with four straw mats. It was more comfortable to lie down. The moment I did I fell asleep.

I woke up suddenly with an unbearable thirst. I wanted to go to the kitchen to drink some water but I could not orient myself in the darkness. I could feel la Gorda bundled up in her blanket next to me. I shook her two or three times and asked her to help me get some water. She grumbled some unintelligible words. She apparently was so sound asleep that she did not want to wake up. I shook her again and suddenly she woke up; only it was not la Gorda. Whoever I was shaking yelled at me in a gruff, masculine voice to shut up. There was a man there in place of la Gorda! My fright was instantaneous and uncontrollable. I jumped out of bed and ran for the front door. But my sense of orientation was off and I ended up out in the kitchen. I grabbed a lantern and lit it as fast as I could. La Gorda came out of the outhouse in the back at that moment and asked me if there was something wrong. I nervously told her what had happened. She seemed a bit disoriented herself. Her mouth was open and her eyes had lost their usual sheen. She shook her head vigorously and that seemed to restore her alertness. She took the lantern and we walked into the front room.

There was no one in the bed. La Gorda lit three more lanterns. She appeared to be worried. She told me to stay where I was, then she opened the door to their room. I noticed that there was light coming from inside. She closed the door again and said in a matter-of-fact tone not to worry, that it was nothing, and that she was going to make us something to eat. With the speed and efficiency of a short-order cook she made some food. She also made a hot chocolate drink with cornmeal. We sat across from each other and ate in complete silence.

The night was cold. It looked as if it was going to rain. The three kerosene lanterns that she had brought to the dining area cast a yellowish light that was very soothing. She took some boards that were stacked up on the floor, against the wall, and placed them vertically in a deep groove on the transverse supporting beam of the roof. There was a long slit in the floor parallel to the beam that served to hold the boards in place. The result was a portable wall that enclosed the dining area.

'Who was in the bed?' I asked.

'In bed, next to you, was Josefina, who else?' she replied as if savouring her words, and then laughed. 'She's a master at jokes like that. For a moment I thought it was something else, but then I caught the scent that Josefina's body has when she's carrying out one of her pranks.'

'What was she trying to do? Scare me to death?' I asked.

'You're not their favourite, you know,' she replied. 'They don't like to be taken out of the path they're familiar with. They hate the fact that Soledad is leaving. They don't want to understand that we are all leaving this area. It looks like our time is up. I knew that today. As I left the house I felt that those barren hills out there were making me tired. I had never felt that way until today.'

'Where are you going to go?'

'I don't know yet. It looks as if that depends on you. On your power.'

'On me? In what way, Gorda?'

'Let me explain. The day before you arrived the little sisters and I went to the city. I wanted to find you in the city because I had a very strange vision in my *dreaming*. In that vision I was in the city with you. I saw you in my vision as plainly as I see you now. You didn't know who I was but you talked to me. I couldn't make out what you said. I went back to the same vision three times but I was not strong enough in my *dreaming* to find out what you were saying to me. I figured that my vision was telling me that I had to go to the city and trust my power to find you there. I was sure that you were on your way.'

'Did the little sisters know why you took them to the city?' I asked.

'I didn't tell them anything,' she replied. 'I just took them there. We wandered around the streets all morning.'

Her statements put me in a very strange frame of mind. Spasms of nervous excitation ran through my entire body. I had to stand up and walk around for a moment. I sat down again and told her that I had been in the city the same day, and that I had wandered around the marketplace all afternoon looking for don Juan. She stared at me with her mouth open.

'We must have passed each other,' she said and sighed. 'We were in the market and in the park. We sat on the steps of the church most of the afternoon so as not to attract attention to ourselves.'

The hotel where I had stayed was practically next door to the church. I remembered that I had stood for a long time looking at the people on the steps of the church. Something was pulling me to examine them. I had the absurd notion that both don Juan and don Genaro were going to be among those people, sitting like beggars just to surprise me.

'When did you leave the city?' I asked.

'We left around five o'clock and headed for the Nagual's spot in the mountains,' she replied.

I had also had the certainty that don Juan had left at the end of the day. The feelings I had had during that entire episode of looking for don Juan became very clear to me. In light of what she had told me I had to revise my stand. I had conveniently explained away the certainty I had had that don Juan was there in the streets of the city as an irrational expectation, a result of my consistently finding him there in the past. But la Gorda had been in the city actually looking for me and she was the being closest to don Juan in temperament. I had felt all along that his presence was there. La Gorda's statement had merely confirmed something that my body knew beyond the shadow of a doubt.

I noticed a flutter of nervousness in her body when I told her the details of my mood that day.

'What would've happened if you had found me?' I asked.

'Everything would've been changed,' she replied. 'For me to find you would've meant that I had enough power to move forward. That's why I took the little sisters with me. All of us, you, me and the little sisters, would've gone away together that day.'

'Where to, Gorda?'

'Who knows? If I had the power to find you I would've also had the power to know that. It's your turn now. Perhaps you will have enough power now to know where we should go. Do you see what I mean?'

I had an attack of profound sadness at that point. I felt more acutely than ever the despair of my human frailty and temporariness. Don Juan had always maintained that the only deterrent to our despair was the awareness of our death, the key to the sorcerer's scheme of things. His idea was that the awareness of our death was the only thing that could give us the strength to withstand the duress and pain of our lives and our fears of the unknown. But what he could never tell me was how to bring that awareness to the foreground. He had insisted, every time I had asked him, that my volition alone was the deciding factor; in other words, I had to make up my mind to bring that awareness to bear witness to my acts. I thought I had done so. But confronted with la Gorda's determination to find me and go away with me, I realized that if she had found me in the city that day I would never have returned to my home, never again would I have seen those I held dear. I had not been prepared for that. I had braced myself for dying, but not for disappearing for the rest of my life in full awareness, without anger or disappointment, leaving behind the best of my feelings.

I was almost embarrassed to tell la Gorda that I was not a warrior worthy of having the kind of power that must be needed to perform an act of that nature: to leave for good and to know where to go and what to do.

'We are human creatures,' she said. 'Who knows what's waiting for us or what kind of power we may have?'

I told her that my sadness in leaving like that was too great. The changes that sorcerers went through were too drastic and too final. I recounted to her what Pablito had told me about his unbearable sadness at having lost his mother.

'The human form feeds itself on those feelings,' she said dryly. 'I pitied myself and my little children for years. I couldn't understand how the Nagual could be so cruel to ask me to do what I did: to leave my children, to destroy them and to forget them.'

She said that it took her years to understand that the Nagual also had had to choose to leave the human form. He was not being cruel. He simply did not have any more human feelings. To him everything was equal. He had accepted his fate. The problem with Pablito, and myself for that matter, was that neither of us had accepted our fate. La Gorda said, in a scornful way, that Pablito wept when he remembered his mother, his Manuelita, especially when he had to cook his own food. She urged me to remember Pablito's mother as she was: an old, stupid woman who knew nothing else but to be Pablito's servant. She said that the reason all of them thought he was a coward was because he could not be happy that his servant Manuelita had become the witch Soledad, who could kill him like she would step on a bug.

La Gorda stood up dramatically and leaned over the table until her forehead was almost touching mine.

'The Nagual said that Pablito's good fortune was extraordinary,' she said. 'Mother and son fighting for the same thing. If he weren't the coward he is, he would accept his fate and oppose Soledad like a warrior, without fear or hatred. In the end the best would win and take all. If Soledad is the winner, Pablito should be happy with his fate and wish her well. But only a real warrior can feel that kind of happiness.'

'How does doña Soledad feel about all this?'

'She doesn't indulge in her feelings,' la Gorda replied and

sat down again. 'She has accepted her fate more readily than any one of us. Before the Nagual helped her she was worse off than myself. At least I was young; she was an old cow, fat and tired, begging for her death to come. Now death will have to fight to claim her.'

The time element in doña Soledad's transformation was a detail that had puzzled me. I told la Gorda that I remembered having seen doña Soledad no more than two years before and she was the same old lady I had always known. La Gorda said that the last time I had been in Soledad's house, under the impression that it was still Pablito's house, the Nagual had set them up to act as if everything were the same. Doña Soledad greeted me, as she always did, from the kitchen, and I really did not face her. Lidia, Rosa, Pablito and Nestor played their roles to perfection in order to keep me from finding out about their true activities.

'Why would the Nagual go to all that trouble, Gorda?'

'He was saving you for something that's not clear yet. He kept you away from every one of us deliberately. He and Genaro told me never to show my face when you were around.'

'Did they tell Josefina the same thing?'

'Yes. She's crazy and can't help herself. She wanted to play her pranks on you. She used to follow you around and you never knew it. One night when the Nagual had taken you to the mountains, she nearly pushed you down a ravine in the darkness. The Nagual found her in the nick of time. She doesn't do those things out of meanness, but because she enjoys being that way. That's her human form. She'll be that way until she loses it. I've told you that all six of them are a bit off. You must be aware of that so as not to be caught in their webs. If you do get caught, don't get angry. They can't help themselves.'

She was silent for a while. I caught the almost imperceptible sign of a flutter in her body. Her eyes seemed to get out of focus and her mouth dropped as if the muscles of her jaw had given in. I became engrossed in watching her. She shook her head two or three times.

'I've just *seen* something,' she said. 'You're just like the little sisters and the Genaros.'

She began to laugh quietly. I did not say anything. I wanted her to explain herself without my meddling.

'Everybody gets angry with you because it hasn't dawned on them yet that you're no different than they are,' she went on. 'They see you as the Nagual and they don't understand that you indulge in your ways just like they do in theirs.'

She said that Pablito whined and complained and played at being a weakling. Benigno played the shy one, the one who could not even open his eyes. Nestor played to be the wise one, the one who knows everything. Lidia played the tough woman who could crush anyone with a look. Josefina was the crazy one who could not be trusted. Rosa was the bad-tempered girl who ate the mosquitoes that bit her. And I was the fool that came from Los Angeles with a pad of paper and lots of wrong questions. And all of us loved to be the way we were.

'I was once a fat, smelly woman,' she went on after a pause. 'I didn't mind being kicked around like a dog as long as I was not alone. That was my form.

'I will have to tell everybody what I have *seen* about you so they won't feel offended by your acts.'

I did not know what to say; I felt that she was undeniably right. The important issue for me was not so much her accurateness but the fact that I had witnessed her arriving at her unquestionable conclusion.

'How did you *see* all that?' I asked.

'It just came to me,' she replied.

'How did it come to you?'

'I felt the feeling of *seeing* coming to the top of my head, and then I knew what I've just told you.'

I insisted that she describe to me every detail of the feeling of *seeing* that she was alluding to. She complied after a moment's vacillation and gave me an account of the same ticklish sensation I had become so aware of during my confrontations with doña Soledad and the little sisters. La Gorda said that the sensation started on the top of her head and then went down her back and around her waist to her womb. She felt it inside her body as a consuming ticklishness, which turned into the knowledge that I was clinging to my human form, like all the rest, except that my particular way was incomprehensible to them.

'Did you hear a voice telling you all that?' I asked.

'No. I just *saw* everything I've told you about yourself,' she replied.

I wanted to ask her if she had had a vision of me clinging to something, but I desisted. I did not want to indulge in my usual behaviour. Besides, I knew what she meant when she said that she 'saw'. The same thing had happened to me when I was with Rosa and Lidia. I suddenly 'knew' where they lived; I had not had a vision of their house. I simply felt that I knew it.

I asked her if she had also felt a dry sound of a wooden pipe being broken at the base of her neck.

'The Nagual taught all of us how to get the feeling on top of the head,' she said. 'But not everyone of us can do it. The sound behind the throat is even more difficult. None of us has ever felt it yet. It's strange that you have when you're still empty.'

'How does that sound work?' I asked. 'And what is it?'

'You know that better than I do. What more can I tell you?' she replied in a harsh voice.

She seemed to catch herself being impatient. She smiled sheepishly and lowered her head.

'I feel stupid telling you what you already know,' she said. 'Do you ask me questions like that to test if I have really lost my form?'

I told her that I was confused, for I had the feeling that I knew what that sound was and yet it was as if I did not know anything about it, because for me to know something I actually had to be able to verbalize my knowledge. In this case, I did not even know how to begin verbalizing it. The only thing I could do, therefore, was to ask her questions, hoping that her answers would help me.

'I can't help you with that sound,' she said.

I experienced a sudden and tremendous discomfort. I told

her that I was habituated to dealing with don Juan and that I needed him then, more than ever, to explain everything to me.

'Do you miss the Nagual?' she asked.

I said that I did, and that I had not realized how much I missed him until I was back again in his homeland.

'You miss him because you're still clinging to your human form,' she said, and giggled as if she were delighted at my sadness.

'Don't you miss him yourself, Gorda?'

'No. Not me. I'm him. All my luminosity has been changed; how could I miss something that is myself?'

'How is your luminosity different?'

'A human being, or any other living creature, has a pale yellow glow. Animals are more yellow, humans are more white. But a sorcerer is amber, like clear honey in the sunlight. Some women sorceresses are greenish. The Nagual said that those are the most powerful and the most difficult.'

'What colour are you, Gorda?'

'Amber, just like you and all the rest of us. That's what the Nagual and Genaro told me. I've never *seen* myself. But I've *seen* everyone else. All of us are amber. And all of us, with the exception of you, are like a tombstone. Average human beings are like eggs; that's why the Nagual called them luminous eggs. Sorcerers change not only the colour of their luminosity but their shape. We are like tombstones; only we are round at both ends.'

'Am I still shaped like an egg, Gorda?'

'No. You're shaped like a tombstone, except that you have an ugly, dull patch in your middle. As long as you have that patch you won't be able to fly, like sorcerers fly, like I flew last night for you. You won't even be able to drop your human form.'

I became entangled in a passionate argument not so much with her as with myself. I insisted that their stand on how to regain that alleged completeness was simply preposterous. I told her that she could not possibly argue successfully with me that one had to turn one's back to one's own children in order to pursue the vaguest of all possible goals: to enter into the world of the nagual. I was so thoroughly convinced that I was right that I got carried away and shouted angry words at her. She was not in any way flustered by my outburst.

'Not everybody has to do that,' she said. 'Only sorcerers who want to enter into the other world. There are plenty of good sorcerers who *see* and are incomplete. To be complete is only for us Toltecs.

'Take Soledad, for instance. She's the best witch you can find and she's incomplete. She had two children; one of them was a girl. Fortunately for Soledad her daughter died. The Nagual said that the edge of the spirit of a person who dies goes back to the givers, meaning that that edge goes back to the parents. If the givers are dead and the person has children, the edge goes to the child who is complete. And if all the children are complete, that edge goes to the one with power and not necessarily to the best or the most diligent. For example, when Josefina's mother died, the edge went to the craziest of the lot, Josefina. It should have gone to her brother who is a hardworking, responsible man, but Josefina is more powerful than her brother. Soledad's daughter died without leaving any children and Soledad got a boost that closed half her hole. Now, the only hope she has to close it completely is for Pablito to die. And by the same token, Pablito's great hope for a boost is for Soledad to die.'

I told her in very strong terms that what she was saying was disgusting and horrifying to me. She agreed that I was right. She affirmed that at one time she herself had believed that that particular sorcerers' stand was the ugliest thing possible. She looked at me with shining eyes. There was something malicious about her grin.

'The Nagual told me that you understand everything but you don't want to do anything about it,' she said in a soft voice.

I began to argue again. I told her that what the Nagual had said about me had nothing to do with my revulsion for the particular stand that we were discussing. I explained that I liked children, that I had the most profound respect for them, and that I empathized very deeply with their helplessness in the awesome world around them. I could not conceive hurting a child in any sense, not for any reason.

'The Nagual didn't make the rule,' she said. 'The rule is made somewhere out there, and not by a man.'

I defended myself by saying that I was not angry with her or the Nagual but that I was arguing in the abstract, because I could not fathom the value of it all.

'The value is that we need all our edge, all our power, our completeness in order to enter into that other world,' she said. 'I was a religious woman. I could tell you what I used to repeat without knowing what I meant. I wanted my soul to enter the kingdom of heaven. I still want that, except that I'm on a different path. The world of the nagual is the kingdom of heaven.'

I objected to her religious connotation on principle. I had become accustomed by don Juan never to dwell on that subject. She very calmly explained that she saw no difference in terms of life-style between us and true nuns and priests. She pointed out that not only were true nuns and priests complete as a rule, but they did not even weaken themselves with sexual acts.

'The Nagual said that that is the reason they will never be exterminated, no matter who tries to exterminate them,' she said. 'Those who are after them are always empty; they don't have the vigour that true nuns and priests have. I liked the Nagual for saying that. I will always cheer for the nuns and priests. We are alike. We have given up the world and yet we are in the midst of it. Priests and nuns would make great flying sorcerers if someone would tell them that they can do it.'

The memory of my father's and my grandfather's admiration for the Mexican revolution came to my mind. They mostly admired the attempt to exterminate the clergy. My father inherited that admiration from his father and I inherited it from both of them. It was a sort of affiliation that we had. One of the first things that don Juan undermined in my personality was that affiliation.

I once told don Juan, as if I were voicing my own opinion, something I had heard all my life, that the favourite ploy of the Church was to keep us in ignorance. Don Juan had a most serious expression on his face. It was as if my statements had touched a deep fibre in him. I thought immediately of the centuries of exploitation that the Indians had endured.

'Those dirty bastards,' he said. 'They have kept me in ignorance, and you too.'

I caught his irony right away and we both laughed. I had never really examined that stand. I did not believe it but I had nothing else to take its place. I told don Juan about my grandfather and my father and their views on religion as the liberal men they were.

'It doesn't matter what anybody says or does,' he said. 'You must be an impeccable man yourself. The fight is right here in this chest.'

He patted my chest gently.

'If your grandfather and father would be trying to be impeccable warriors,' don Juan went on, 'they wouldn't have time for petty fights. It takes all the time and all the energy we have to conquer the idiocy in us. And that's what matters. The rest is of no importance. Nothing of what your grandfather or father said about the Church gave them well-being. To be an impeccable warrior, on the other hand, will give you vigour and youth and power. So, it is proper for you to choose wisely.'

My choice was the impeccability and simplicity of a warrior's life. Because of that choice I felt that I had to take la Gorda's words in a most serious manner and that was more threatening to me than even don Genaro's acts. He used to frighten me at a most profound level. His actions, although terrifying, were assimilated, however, into the coherent continuum of their teachings. La Gorda's words and actions were a different kind of threat to me, somehow more concrete and real than the other.

La Gorda's body shivered for a moment. A ripple went through it, making her contract the muscles of her shoulders and arms. She grabbed the edge of the table with an awkward rigidity. Then she relaxed until she was again her usual self.

She smiled at me. Her eyes and smile were dazzling. She said in a casual tone that she had just 'seen' my dilemma.

'It's useless to close your eyes and pretend that you don't

want to do anything or that you don't know anything,' she said. 'You can do that with people but not with me. I know now why the Nagual commissioned me to tell you all this. I'm a nobody. You admire great people; the Nagual and Genaro were the greatest of all.'

She stopped and examined me. She seemed to be waiting for my reaction to what she said.

'You fought against what the Nagual and Genaro told you, all the way,' she went on. 'That's why you're behind. And you fought them because they were great. That's your particular way of being. But you can't fight against what I tell you, because you can't look up to me at all. I am your peer; I am in your cycle. You like to fight those who are better than you. It's no challenge to fight my stand. So, those two devils have finally bagged you through me. Poor little Nagual, you've lost the game.'

She came closer to me and whispered in my ear that the Nagual had also said that she should never try to take my writing pad away from me because that would be as dangerous as trying to snatch a bone from a hungry dog's mouth.

She put her arms around me, resting her head on my shoulders, and laughed quietly and softly.

Her 'seeing' had numbed me. I knew that she was absolutely right. She had pegged me to perfection. She hugged me for a long time with her head against mine. The proximity of her body somehow was very soothing. She was just like don Juan at that. She exuded strength and conviction and purpose. She was wrong to say that I could not admire her.

'Let's forget this,' she said suddenly. 'Let's talk about what we have to do tonight.'

'What exactly are we going to do tonight, Gorda?'

'We have our last appointment with power.'

'Is it another dreadful battle with somebody?'

'No. The little sisters are simply going to show you something that will complete your visit here. The Nagual told me that after that you may go away and never return, or that you may choose to stay with us. Either way, what they have to show you is their art. The art of the dreamer.'

'And what is that art?'

'Genaro told me that he tried time and time again to acquaint you with the art of the dreamer. He showed you his other body, his body of *dreaming*; once he even made you be in two places at once, but your emptiness did not let you *see* what he was pointing out to you. It looks as if all his efforts went through the hole in your body.

'Now it seems that it is different. Genaro made the little sisters the dreamers that they are and tonight they will show you Genaro's art. In that respect, the little sisters are the true children of Genaro.'

That reminded me of what Pablito had said earlier, that we were the children of both, and that we were Toltecs. I asked her what he had meant by that.

'The Nagual told me that sorcerers used to be called Toltecs in his benefactor's language,' she replied.

'And what language was that, Gorda?'

'He never told me. But he and Genaro used to speak a language that none of us could understand. And here, between all of us, we understand four Indian languages.'

'Did don Genaro also say that he was a Toltec?'

'His benefactor was the same man, so he also said the same thing.'

From la Gorda's responses I could surmise that she either did not know a great deal on the subject or she did not want to talk to me about it. I confronted her with my conclusions. She confessed that she had never paid much attention to it and wondered why I was putting so much value on it. I practically gave her a lecture on the ethnography of central Mexico.

'A sorcerer is a Toltec when that sorcerer has received the mysteries of stalking and *dreaming*,' she said casually. 'The Nagual and Genaro received those mysteries from their benefactor and then they held them in their bodies. We are doing the same, and because of that we are Toltecs like the Nagual and Genaro.

'The Nagual taught you and me equally to be dispassionate. I am more dispassionate than you because I'm formless. You still have your form and are empty, so you get caught in every snag. One day, however, you'll be complete again and you'll understand then that the Nagual was right. He said that the world of people goes up and down and people go up and down with their world; as sorcerers we have no business following them in their ups and downs.

'The art of sorcerers is to be outside everything and be unnoticeable. And more than anything else, the art of sorcerers is never to waste their power. The Nagual told me that your problem is that you always get caught in idiocies, like what you're doing now. I'm sure that you're going to ask everyone of us about the Toltecs, but you're not going to ask anyone of us about our attention.'

Her laughter was clear and contagious. I admitted to her that she was right. Small issues had always fascinated me. I also told her that I was mystified by her usage of the word attention.

'I've told you already what the Nagual told me about attention,' she said. 'We hold the images of the world with our attention. A male sorcerer is very difficult to train because his attention is always closed, focused on something. A female, on the other hand, is always open because most of the time she is not focusing her attention on anything. Especially during her menstrual period. The Nagual told me and then showed me that during that time I could actually let my attention go from the images of the world. If I don't focus my attention on the world, the world collapses.'

'How is that done, Gorda?'

'It's very simple. When a woman menstruates she cannot focus her attention. That's the crack the Nagual told me about. Instead of fighting to focus, a woman should let go of the images, by gazing fixedly at distant hills, or by gazing at water, like a river, or by gazing at the clouds.

'If you gaze with your eyes open, you get dizzy and the eyes get tired, but if you half-close them and blink a lot and move them from mountain to mountain, or from cloud to cloud, you can look for hours, or days if necessary.

'The Nagual used to make us sit by the door and gaze at

those round hills on the other side of the valley. Sometimes we used to sit there for days until the crack would open.'

I wanted to hear more about it, but she stopped talking and hurriedly sat very close to me. She signalled me with her hand to listen. I heard a faint swishing sound and suddenly Lidia stepped out into the kitchen. I thought that she must have been asleep in their room and the sound of our voices had woken her up.

She had changed the Western clothes she had been wearing the last time I had seen her and had put on a long dress like the Indian women of the area wore. She had a shawl on her shoulders and was barefoot. Her long dress, instead of making her look older and heavier, made her look like a child clad in an older woman's clothes.

She walked up to the table and greeted la Gorda with a formal 'Good evening, Gorda.' She then turned to me and said, 'Good evening, Nagual.'

Her greeting was so unexpected and her tone so serious that I was about to laugh. I caught a warning from la Gorda. She pretended to be scratching the top of her head with the back of her left hand, which was clawed.

I answered Lidia the same way la Gorda had: 'Good evening to you, Lidia.'

She sat down at the end of the table to the right of me. I did not know whether or not to start up a conversation. I was about to say something when la Gorda tapped my leg with her knee, and with a subtle movement of her eyebrows signalled me to listen. I heard again the muffled sound of a long dress as it touched the floor. Josefina stood for a moment at the door before walking towards the table. She greeted Lidia, la Gorda and myself in that order. I could not keep a straight face with her. She was also wearing a long dress, a shawl and no shoes, but in her case the dress was three or four sizes larger and she had put a thick padding into it. Her appearance was thoroughly incongruous; her face was lean and young, but her body looked grotesquely bloated.

She took a bench and placed it at the left end of the table and sat down. All three of them looked extremely serious.

They were sitting with their legs pressed together and their backs very straight.

I heard once more the rustle of a dress and Rosa come out. She was dressed just like the others and was also barefoot. Her greeting was as formal and the order naturally included Josefina. Everyone answered her in the same formal tone. She sat across the table facing me. All of us remained in absolute silence for quite a while.

La Gorda spoke suddenly, and the sound of her voice made everyone else jump. She said, pointing to me, that the Nagual was going to show them his allies and that he was going to use his special call to bring them into the room.

I tried to make a joke and said that the Nagual was not there, so he could not bring any allies. I thought they were going to laugh. La Gorda covered her face and the little sisters glared at me. La Gorda put her hand on my mouth and whispered in my ear that it was absolutely necessary that I refrain from saying idiotic things. She looked right into my eyes and said that I had to call the allies by making the moths' call.

I reluctantly began. But no sooner had I started than the spirit of the occasion took over and I found that in a matter of seconds I had given my maximum concentration to producing the sound. I modulated its outflow and controlled the air being expelled from my lungs in order to produce the longest possible tapping. It sounded very melodious.

I took an enormous gasp of air to start a new series. I stopped immediately. Something outside the house was answering my call. The tapping sounds came from all around the house, even from the roof. The little sisters stood up and huddled like frightened children around la Gorda and myself.

'Please, Nagual, don't bring anything into the house,' Lidia pleaded with me.

Even la Gorda seemed a bit frightened. She gave me a strong command with her hand to stop. I had not intended to keep on producing the sound anyway. The allies, however, either as formless forces or as beings that were prowling outside the door, were not dependent on my tapping sound. I felt again, as I had felt two nights before in don Genaro's house, an unbearable pressure, a heaviness leaning against the entire house. I could sense it in my navel as an itch, a nervousness that soon turned into sheer physical anguish.

The three little sisters were beside themselves with fear, especially Lidia and Josefina. Both of them were whining like wounded dogs. All of them surrounded me and then clung to me. Rosa crawled under the table and pushed her head up between my legs. La Gorda stood behind me as calmly as she could. After a few moments the hysteria and fear of those three girls mounted to enormous proportions. La Gorda leaned over and whispered that I should make the opposite sound, the sound that would disperse them. I had a moment of supreme uncertainty. I really did not know any other sound. But then I had a quick sensation of ticklishness on the top of my head, a shiver in my body, and I remembered out of nowhere a peculiar whistling that don Juan used to perform at night and had endeavoured to teach me. He had presented it to me as a means to keep one's balance while walking so as not to stray away from the trail in the darkness.

I began my whistling and the pressure in my umbilical region ceased. La Gorda smiled and sighed with relief and the little sisters moved away from my side, giggling as if all of it had been merely a joke. I wanted to indulge in some soul-searching deliberations about the abrupt transition from the rather pleasant exchange I was having with la Gorda to that unearthly situation. For an instant I pondered over whether or not the whole thing was a ploy on their part. But I was too weak. I felt I was about to pass out. My ears were buzzing. The tension around my stomach was so intense that I believed I was going to become ill right there. I rested my head on the edge of the table. After a few minutes, however, I was again relaxed enough to sit up straight.

The three girls seemed to have forgotten how frightened they had been. In fact, they were laughing and pushing each other as they each tied their shawls around their hips. La Gorda did not seem nervous nor did she seem relaxed.

Rosa was pushed at one moment by the other two girls and fell off the bench where all three of them were sitting. She landed on her seat. I thought that she was going to get furious but she giggled. I looked at la Gorda for directions. She was sitting with a very straight back. Her eyes were half-closed, fixed on Rosa. The little sisters were laughing very loudly, like nervous schoolgirls. Lidia pushed Josefina and sent her tumbling over the bench to fall next to Rosa on the floor. The instant Josefina was on the floor their laughter stopped. Rosa and Josefina shook their bodies, making an incomprehensible movement with their buttocks; they moved them from side to side as if they were grinding something against the floor. Then they sprang up like two silent jaguars and took Lidia by the arms. All three of them, without making the slightest noise, spun around a couple of times. Rosa and Josefina lifted Lidia by the armpits and carried her as they tiptoed two or three times around the table. Then all three of them collapsed as if they had springs on their knees that had contracted at the same time. Their long dresses puffed up, giving them the appearance of huge balls.

As soon as they were on the floor they became even more quiet. There was no other sound except the soft swishing of their dresses as they rolled and crawled. It was as if I were watching a three-dimensional movie with the sound turned off.

La Gorda, who had been quietly sitting next to me watching them, suddenly stood up and with the agility of an acrobat ran towards the door of their room at the corner of the dining area. Before she reached the door she tumbled on her right side and shoulder just enough to turn over once, then stood up, pulled by the momentum of her rolling, and flung open the door. She performed all her movements with absolute quietness.

The three girls rolled and crawled into the room like giant pill bugs. La Gorda signalled me to come over to where she was; we entered the room and she had me sit on the floor with my back against the frame of the door. She sat to my right with her back also against the frame. She made me interlock my fingers and then placed my hands over my belly button.

I was at first forced to divide my attention between la Gorda, the little sisters and the room. But once la Gorda had arranged my sitting position, my attention was taken up by the room. The three girls were lying in the middle of a large, white, square room with a brick floor. There were four paraffin lanterns, one on each wall, placed on built-in supporting ledges approximately six feet above the ground. The room had no ceiling. The supporting beams of the roof had been darkened and that gave the effect of an enormous room with no top. The two doors were placed on the very corners opposite each other. As I looked at the closed door across from where I was, I noticed that the walls of the room were oriented to follow the cardinal points. The door where we were was at the northwest corner.

Rosa, Lidia and Josefina rolled counterclockwise around the room several times. I strained to hear the swish of their dresses but the silence was absolute. I could only hear la Gorda breathing. The little sisters finally stopped and sat down with their backs against the wall, each under a lantern. Lidia sat at the east wall, Rosa, at the north and Josefina, at the west

La Gorda stood up, closed the door behind us and secured it with an iron bar. She made me slide over a few inches, without changing my position, until I was sitting with my back against the door. Then she silently rolled the length of the room and sat down underneath the lantern on the south wall; her getting into that sitting position seemed to be the cue.

Lidia stood up and began to walk on the tips of her toes along the edges of the room, close to the walls. It was not a walk proper but rather a soundless sliding. As she increased her speed she began to move as if she were gliding, stepping on the angle between the floor and the walls. She would jump over Rosa, Josefina, la Gorda and myself every time she got to where we were sitting. I felt her long dress brushing me every time she went by. The faster she ran, the higher she got on the wall. A moment came when Lidia was actually running silently around the four walls of the room seven or eight feet above the floor. The sight of her, running perpendicular to the walls, was so unearthly that it bordered on the grotesque. Her long gown made the sight even more eerie. Gravity did not seem to have any effect on Lidia, but it did

on her long skirt; it dragged downward. I felt it every time
she passed over my head, sweeping my face like a hanging
drape.

She had captured my attentiveness at a level I could not
imagine. The strain of giving her my undivided attention was
so great that I began to get stomach convulsions; I felt her
running with my stomach. My eyes were getting out of focus.
With the last bit of my remaining concentration, I saw Lidia
walk down on the east wall diagonally and come to a halt in the
middle of the room.

She was panting, out of breath, and drenched in perspiration
like la Gorda had been after her flying display. She could
hardly keep her balance. After a moment she walked to her
place at the east wall and collapsed on the floor like a wet rag.
I thought she had fainted, but then I noticed that she was deliberately breathing through her mouth.

After some minutes of stillness, long enough for Lidia to
recover her strength and sit up straight, Rosa stood up and
ran without making a sound to the centre of the room, turned
on her heels and ran back to where she had been sitting. Her
running allowed her to gain the necessary momentum to make
an outlandish jump. She leaped up in the air, like a basketball
player, along the vertical span of the wall, and her hands went
beyond the height of the wall, which was perhaps ten feet.
I saw her body actually hitting the wall, although there was
no corresponding crashing sound. I expected her to rebound
to the floor with the force of the impact, but she remained
hanging there, attached to the wall like a pendulum. From
where I sat it looked as if she were holding a hook of some
sort in her left hand. She swayed silently in a pendulum-like
motion for a moment and then catapulted herself three or four
feet over to her left by pushing her body away from the wall
with her right arm, at the moment in which her swing was
the widest. She repeated the swaying and catapulting thirty
or forty times. She went around the whole room and then she
went up to the beams of the roof where she dangled precariously,
hanging from an invisible hook.

While she was on the beams I became aware that what I

had thought was a hook in her left hand was actually some quality of that hand that made it possible for her to suspend her weight from it. It was the same hand she had attacked me with two nights before.

Her display ended with her dangling from the beams over the very centre of the room. Suddenly she let go. She fell down from a height of fifteen or sixteen feet. Her long dress flowed upward and gathered around her head. For an instant, before she landed without a sound, she looked like an umbrella turned inside out by the force of the wind; her thin, naked body looked like a stick attached to the dark mass of her dress.

My body felt the impact of her plummeting down, perhaps more than she did herself. She landed in a squat position and remained motionless, trying to catch her breath. I was sprawled out on the floor with painful cramps in my stomach.

La Gorda rolled across the room, took her shawl and tied it around my umbilical region, like a band, looping it around my body two or three times. She rolled back to the south wall like a shadow.

While she had been arranging the shawl around my waist, I had lost sight of Rosa. When I looked up she was again sitting by the north wall. A moment later, Josefina quietly moved to the centre of the room. She paced back and forth with noiseless steps, between where Lidia was sitting and her own spot at the west wall. She faced me all the time. Suddenly, as she approached her spot, she raised her left forearm and placed it right in front of her face, as if she wanted to block me from her view. She hid half of her face for an instant behind her forearm. She lowered it and raised it again, that time hiding her entire face. She repeated the movement of lowering and raising her left forearm countless times, as she paced soundlessly from one side of the room to the other. Every time she raised her forearm a bigger portion of her body disappeared from my view. A moment came when she had hidden her entire body, puffed up with clothes, behind her thin forearm.

It was as if by blocking her view of my body, sitting ten to twelve feet away from her, a thing she could have easily done with the width of her forearm, she also made me block the view of her body, a thing which could not possibly be done with just the width of her forearm.

Once she had hidden her entire body, all I was able to make out was a silhouette of a forearm suspended in midair, bouncing from one side of the room to the other, and at one point I could hardly see the arm itself.

I felt a revulsion, an unbearable nausea. The bouncing forearm depleted me of energy. I slid down on my side, unable to keep my balance. I saw the arm falling to the ground. Josefina was lying on the floor covered with garments, as if her puffed-up clothes had exploded. She lay on her back with her arms spread out.

It took a long time to get back my physical balance. My clothes were soaked in perspiration. I was not the only one affected. All of them were exhausted and drenched in sweat. La Gorda was the most poised, but her control seemed to be on the verge of collapsing. I could hear all of them, including la Gorda, breathing through their mouths.

When I was in full control again everybody sat on her spot. The little sisters were looking at me fixedly. I saw out of the corner of my eye that la Gorda's eyes were half-closed. She suddenly rolled noiselessly to my side and whispered in my ear that I should begin to make my moth call, keeping it up until the allies had rushed into the house and were about to take us.

I had a moment of vacillation. She whispered that there was no way to change directions, and that we had to finish what we had started. After untying her shawl from my waist, she rolled back to her spot and sat down.

I put my left hand to my lips and tried to produce the tapping sound. I found it very difficult at first. My lips were dry and my hands were sweaty, but after an initial clumsiness, a feeling of vigour and well-being came over me. I produced the most flawless tapping noise I had ever done. It reminded me of the tapping noise I had been hearing all along as a response to mine. As soon as I stopped to breathe, I could hear the tapping sound being answered from all directions.

La Gorda signalled me to go on with it. I produced three more series. The last one was utterly mesmeric. I did not need to intake a gulp of air and let it out in small spurts, as I had been doing all along. This time the tapping sound came out of my mouth freely. I did not even have to use the edge of my hand to produce it.

La Gorda suddenly rushed to me, lifted me up bodily by my armpits and pushed me to the middle of the room. Her action disrupted my absolute concentration. I noticed that Lidia was holding on to my right arm, Josefina to my left, and Rosa had backed up against the front of me and was holding me by the waist with her arms extended backward. La Gorda was in back of me. She ordered me to put my arms behind and grab on to her shawl, which she had looped around her neck and shoulders like a harness.

I noticed at that moment that something besides us was there in the room, but I could not tell what it was. The little sisters were shivering. I knew that they were aware of something which I was unable to distinguish. I also knew that la Gorda was going to try to do what she had done in don Genaro's house. All of a sudden, I felt the wind of the eye-door pulling us. I grabbed on to la Gorda's shawl with all my strength while the little sisters grabbed on to me. I felt that we were spinning, tumbling and swaying from side to side like a giant, weightless leaf.

I opened my eyes and saw that we were like a bundle. We were either standing up or we were lying horizontally in the air. I could not tell which because I had no sensorial point of reference. Then, as suddenly as we had been lifted off, we were dropped. I sensed our falling in my midsection. I yelled with pain and my screams were united with those of the little sisters. The insides of my knees hurt. I felt an unbearable jolt on my legs; I thought I must have broken them.

My next impression was that something was getting inside my nose. It was very dark and I was lying on my back. I sat up. I realized then that la Gorda was tickling my nostrils with a twig.

I did not feel exhausted or even mildly tired. I jumped to

my feet and only then was I stricken by the realization that we were not in the house. We were on a hill, a rocky, barren hill. I took a step and nearly fell down. I had stumbled over a body. It was Josefina. She was extremely hot to the touch. She seemed to be feverish. I tried to make her sit up, but she was limp. Rosa was next to her. As a contrast, her body was icy cold. I put one on top of the other and rocked them. That motion brought them back to their senses.

La Gorda had found Lidia and was making her walk. After a few minutes, all of us were standing. We were perhaps half a mile east of the house.

Years before don Juan had produced in me a similar experience but with the aid of a psychotropic plant. He seemingly made me fly and I landed a distance from his house. At the time, I had tried to explain the event in rational terms, but there was no ground for rational explanations and, short of accepting that I had flown, I had to fall back on to the only two avenues left open: I could explain it all by arguing that don Juan had transported me to the distant field while I was still unconscious under the effect of the psychotropic alkaloids of that plant; or by arguing that under the influence of the alkaloids I had believed what don Juan was ordering me to believe, that I was flying.

This time I had no other recourse but to brace myself for accepting, on its face value, that I had flown. I wanted to indulge in doubts and began to wonder about the possibilities of the four girls carrying me to that hill. I laughed loudly, incapable of containing an obscure delight. I was having a relapse of my old malady. My reason, which had been blocked off temporarily, was beginning to take hold of me again. I wanted to defend it. Or perhaps it would be more appropriate to say, in light of the outlandish acts I had witnessed and performed since my arrival, that my reason was defending itself, independently of the more complex whole that seemed to be the 'me' I did not know. I was witnessing, almost in the fashion of an interested observer, how my reason struggled to find suitable rationales, while another, much larger portion of me could not have cared less about explaining anything.

La Gorda made the three girls line up. She then pulled me to her side. All of them folded their arms behind their backs. La Gorda made me do the same. She stretched my arms as far back as they would go and then made me bend them and grab each forearm as tightly as possible as close to the elbows as I could. That created a great muscular pressure at the articulations of my shoulders. She pushed my trunk forward until I was almost stooping. Then she made a peculiar birdcall. That was a signal. Lidia started walking. In the darkness her movements reminded me of an ice skater. She walked swiftly and silently and in a few minutes she disappeared from my view.

La Gorda made two more birdcalls, one after the other, and Rosa and Josefina took off in the same manner Lidia had. La Gorda told me to follow close to her. She made one more birdcall and we both started walking.

I was surprised at the ease with which I walked. My entire balance was centred in my legs. The fact that I had my arms behind my back, instead of hindering my movements, aided me in maintaining a strange equilibrium. But above all what surprised me the most was the quietness of my steps.

When we reached the road we began to walk normally. We passed two men going in the opposite direction. La Gorda greeted them and they answered back. When we arrived at the house we found the little sisters standing by the door, not daring to go in. La Gorda told them that although I could not control the allies I could either call them or tell them to leave, and that the allies would not bother us any longer. The girls believed her, something I myself could not do in that instance.

We went inside. In a very quiet and efficient manner all of them undressed, drenched themselves with cold water and put on a fresh change of clothes. I did the same. I put on the old clothes I used to keep in don Juan's house, which la Gorda brought to me in a box.

All of us were in high spirits. I asked la Gorda to explain to me what we had done.

'We'll talk about that later,' she said a firm tone.

I remembered then that the packages I had for them were still in the car. I thought that while la Gorda was cooking some food for us it would be a good opportunity to distribute them. I went out and got them and brought them into the house. I placed them on the table. Lidia asked me if I had already assigned the gifts as she had suggested. I said that I wanted them to pick one they liked. She declined. She said that no doubt I had something special for Pablito and Nestor and a bunch of trinkets for them, which I would throw on the table with the intention that they fight over them.

'Besides, you didn't bring anything for Benigno,' Lidia said as she came to my side and looked at me with mock seriousness. 'You can't hurt the Genaros' feelings by giving two gifts for three.'

They all laughed. I felt embarrassed. She was absolutely right in everything that she had said.

'You are careless, that's why I've never liked you,' Lidia said to me, changing her smile into a frown. 'You have never greeted me with affection or respect. Every time we saw each other you only pretended to be happy to see me.'

She imitated my obviously contrived effusive greeting, a greeting I must have given her countless times in the past.

'Why didn't you ever ask me what I was doing here?' Lidia asked me.

I stopped writing to consider her point. It had never occurred to me to ask her anything. I told her that I had no excuse. La Gorda interceded and said that the reason that I had never said more than two words to either Lidia or Rosa each time I saw them was because I was accustomed to talking only to women that I was enamoured of, in one way or another. La Gorda added that the Nagual had told them that if I would ask them anything directly they were supposed to answer my questions, but as long as I did not ask, they were not supposed to mention anything.

Rosa said that she did not like me because I was always laughing and trying to be funny. Josefina added that since I had never seen her, she disliked me just for fun, for the hell of it.

'I want you to know that I don't accept you as the Nagual,'

Lidia said to me. 'You're too dumb. You know nothing. I know more than you do. How can I respect you?'

Lidia added that as far as she was concerned I could go back where I came from or go jump in a lake for that matter.

Rosa and Josefina did not say a word. Judging by the serious and mean expressions on their faces, however, they seemed to agree with Lidia.

'How can this man lead us?' Lidia asked la Gorda. 'He's not a true nagual. He's a man. He's going to make us into idiots like himself.'

As she was talking I could see the mean expressions on Rosa's and Josefina's faces getting even harder.

La Gorda intervened and explained to them what she had 'seen' earlier about me. She added that since she had recommended to me not to get entangled in their webs, she was recommending the same thing to them, not to get entangled in mine.

After Lidia's initial display of genuine and well-founded animosity, I was flabbergasted to see how easily she acquiesced to la Gorda's remarks. She smiled at me. She even came and sat next to me.

'You're really like us, eh?' she asked in a tone of bewilderment.

I did not know what to say. I was afraid of blundering.

Lidia was obviously the leader of the little sisters. The moment she smiled at me the other two seemed to be infused instantly with the same mood.

La Gorda told them not to mind my pencil and paper and my asking questions and that in return I would not be flustered when they became involved in doing what they loved the most, to indulge in themselves.

The three of them sat close to me. La Gorda walked over to the table, got the packages and took them out to my car. I asked Lidia to forgive me for my inexcusable blunderings of the past and asked all of them to tell me how they had become don Juan's apprentices. In order to make them feel at ease I gave them an account of how I had met don Juan. Their accounts were the same as what doña Soledad had already told me.

Lidia said that all of them had been free to leave don Juan's world but their choice had been to stay. She, in particular, being the first apprentice, was given an opportunity to go away. After the Nagual and Genaro had cured her, the Nagual had pointed to the door and told her that if she did not go through it then, the door would close her in and would never open again.

'My fate was sealed when that door closed,' Lidia said to me. 'Just like what happened to you. The Nagual told me that after he had put a patch on you, you had a chance to leave but you didn't want to take it.'

I remembered that particular decision more vividly than anything else. I recounted to them how don Juan had tricked me into believing that a sorceress was after him, and then he gave me the choice of either leaving for good or staying to help him wage a war against his attacker. It turned out that his alleged attacker was one of his confederates. By confronting her, on what I thought was don Juan's behalf, I turned her against me and she became what he called my 'worthy opponent'.

I asked Lidia if they had had a worthy opponent themselves.

'We are not as dumb as you are,' she said. 'We never needed anyone to spur us.'

'Pablito is that dumb,' Rosa said. 'Soledad is his opponent. I don't know how worthy she is, though. But as the saying goes, if you can't feed on a capon, feed on an onion.'

They laughed and banged on the table.

I asked them if any of them knew the sorceress don Juan had pitted me against, la Catalina.

They shook their heads negatively.

'I know her,' la Gorda said from the stove. 'She's from the Nagual's cycle, but she looks as if she's thirty.'

'What is a cycle, Gorda?' I asked.

She walked over to the table and put her foot on the bench and rested her chin on her arm and knee.

'Sorcerers like the Nagual and Genaro have two cycles,' she said. 'The first is when they're human, like ourselves. We are in our first cycle. Each of us has been given a task and that task is making us leave the human form. Eligio, the five of us, and the Genaros are of the same cycle.

'The second cycle is when a sorcerer is not human any more, like the Nagual and Genaro. They came to teach us, and after they taught us they left. We are the second cycle to them.

'The Nagual and la Catalina are like you and Lidia. They are in the same positions. She's a scary sorceress, just like Lidia.'

La Gorda went back to the stove. The little sisters seemed nervous.

'That must be the woman who knows power plants,' Lidia said to la Gorda.

La Gorda said that she was the one. I asked them if the Nagual had ever given them power plants.

'No, not to us three,' Lidia replied. 'Power plants are given only to empty people. Like yourself and la Gorda.'

'Did the Nagual give you power plants, Gorda?' I asked loudly.

La Gorda raised two fingers over her head.

'The Nagual gave her his pipe twice,' Lidia said. 'And she went off her rocker both times.'

'What happened, Gorda?' I asked.

'I went off my rocker,' she said as she walked over to the table. 'Power plants were given to us because the Nagual was putting a patch on our bodies. Mine hooked fast, but yours was difficult. The Nagual said that you were crazier than Josefina, and impossible like Lidia, and he had to give you a lot of them.'

La Gorda explained that power plants were used only by sorcerers who had mastered their art. Those plants were such a powerful affair that in order to be properly handled, the most impeccable attention was needed on the part of the sorcerer. It took a lifetime to train one's attention to the degree needed. La Gorda said that complete people do not need power plants, and that neither the little sisters nor the Genaros had ever taken them, but that someday when they had perfected their art as dreamers, they would use them to get a final and total boost, a boost of such magnitude that it would be impossible for us to understand.

'Would you and I take them too?' I asked la Gorda.

'All of us,' she replied. 'The Nagual said that you should understand this point better than any of us.'

I considered the issue for a moment. The effect of psychotropic plants had indeed been terrifying for me. They seemed to reach a vast reservoir in me, and extract from it a total world. The drawback in taking them had been the toll they took on my physical well-being and the impossibility of controlling their effect. The world they plunged me into was unamenable and chaotic. I lacked the control, the power, in don Juan's terms, to make use of such a world. If I would have the control, however, the possibilities would be staggering to the mind.

'I took them, myself,' Josefina said all of a sudden. 'When I was crazy the Nagual gave me his pipe, to cure me or kill me. And it cured me!'

'The Nagual really gave Josefina his smoke,' la Gorda said from the stove and then came over to the table. 'He knew that she was pretending to be crazier than she was. She's always been a bit off, and she's very daring and indulges in herself like no one else. She always wanted to live where nobody would bother her and she could do whatever she wanted. So the Nagual gave her his smoke and took her to live in a world of her liking for fourteen days, until she was so bored with it that she got cured. She cut her indulging. That was her cure.'

La Gorda went back to the stove. The little sisters laughed and patted one another on the back.

I remembered then that at doña Soledad's house Lidia had not only intimated that don Juan had left a package for me but she had actually shown me a bundle that had made me think of the sheath in which don Juan used to keep his pipe. I reminded Lidia·that she had said that they would give me that package when la Gorda was present.

The little sisters looked at one another and then turned to la Gorda. She made a gesture with her head. Josefina stood up and went to the front room. She returned a moment later with the bundle that Lidia had shown me.

I had a pang of anticipation in the pit of my stomach. Josefina carefully placed the bundle on the table in front of me. All of them gathered around. She began to untie it as ceremoniously as Lidia had done the first time. When the package was completely unwrapped, she spilled the contents on the table. They were menstruation rags.

I got flustered for an instant. But the sound of la Gorda's laughter, which was louder than the others', was so pleasing that I had to laugh myself.

'That's Josefina's personal bundle,' la Gorda said. 'It was her brilliant idea to play on your greed for a gift from the Nagual, in order to make you stay.'

'You have to admit that it was a good idea,' Lidia said to me.

She imitated the look of greed I had on my face when she was opening the package and then my look of disappointment when she did not finish.

I told Josefina that her idea had indeed been brilliant, that it had worked as she had anticipated, and that I had wanted that package more than I would care to admit.

'You can have it, if you want it,' Josefina said and made everybody laugh.

La Gorda said that the Nagual had known from the beginning that Josefina was not really ill, and that that was the reason it had been so difficult for him to cure her. People who are actually sick are more pliable. Josefina was too aware of everything and very unruly and he had had to smoke her a great many times.

Don Juan had once said the same thing about me, that he had smoked me. I had always believed that he was referring to having used psychotropic mushrooms to have a view of me.

'How did he smoke you?' I asked Josefina.

She shrugged her shoulders and did not answer.

'The same way he smoked you,' Lidia said. 'He pulled your luminosity and dried it with the smoke from a fire that he had made.'

I was sure that don Juan had never explained such a thing to me. I asked Lidia to tell me what she knew about the subject. She turned to la Gorda.

'Smoke is very important for sorcerers,' la Gorda said. 'Smoke is like fog. Fog is of course better, but it's too hard to handle. It's not as handy as smoke is. So if a sorcerer wants to *see* and know someone who is always hiding, like you and Josefina, who are capricious and difficult, the sorcerer makes a fire and lets the smoke envelop the person. Whatever they're hiding comes out in the smoke.'

La Gorda said that the Nagual used smoke not only to 'see' and know people but also to cure. He gave Josefina smoke baths; he made her stand or sit by the fire in the direction the wind was blowing. The smoke would envelop her and make her choke and cry, but her discomfort was only temporary and of no consequence; the positive effects, on the other hand, were a gradual cleansing of the luminosity.

'The Nagual gave all of us smoke baths,' la Gorda said. 'He gave you even more baths than Josefina. He said that you were unbearable, and you were not even pretending, like she was.'

It all became clear to me. She was right; don Juan had made me sit in front of a fire hundreds of times. The smoke used to irritate my throat and eyes to such a degree that I dreaded to see him begin to gather dry twigs and branches. He said that I had to learn to control my breathing and feel the smoke while I kept my eyes closed; that way I could breathe without choking.

La Gorda said that smoke had helped Josefina to be ethereal and very elusive, and that no doubt it had helped me to cure my madness, whatever it was.

'The Nagual said that smoke takes everything out of you,' la Gorda went on. 'It makes you clear and direct.'

I asked her if she knew how to bring out with the smoke whatever a person was hiding. She said that she could easily do it because of having lost her form, but that the little sisters and the Genaros, although they had seen the Nagual and Genaro do it scores of times, could not yet do it themselves.

I was curious to know why don Juan had never mentioned

the subject to me, in spite of the fact that he had smoked me like dry fish hundreds of times.

'He did,' la Gorda said with her usual conviction. 'The Nagual even taught you fog gazing. He told us that once you smoked a whole place in the mountains and *saw* what was hiding behind the scenery. He said that he was spellbound himself.'

I remembered an exquisite perceptual distortion, a hallucination of sorts, which I had had and thought was the product of a play between a most dense fog and an electrical storm that was occurring at the same time. I narrated to them the episode and added that don Juan had never really directly taught me anything about the fog or the smoke. His procedure had been to build fires or to take me into fog banks.

La Gorda did not say a word. She stood up and went back to the stove. Lidia shook her head and clicked her tongue.

'You sure are dumb,' she said. 'The Nagual taught you everything. How do you think you *saw* what you have just told us about?'

There was an abyss between our understanding of how to teach something. I told them that if I were to teach them something I knew, such as how to drive a car, I would go step by step, making sure that they understood every facet of the whole procedure.

La Gorda returned to the table.

'That's only if the sorcerer is teaching something about the tonal,' she said. 'When the sorcerer is dealing with the nagual, he must give the instruction, which is to show the mystery to the warrior. And that's all he has to do. The warrior who receives the mysteries must claim knowledge as power, by doing what he has been shown.

'The Nagual showed you more mysteries than all of us together. But you're lazy, like Pablito, and prefer to be confused. The tonal and the nagual are two different worlds. In one you talk, in the other you act.'

At the moment she spoke, her words made absolute sense to me. I knew what she was talking about. She went back to the stove, stirred something in a pot and came back again.

'Why are you so dumb?' Lidia bluntly asked me.

'He's empty,' Rosa replied.

They made me stand up and forced themselves to squint as they scanned my body with their eyes. All of them touched my umbilical region.

'But why are you still empty?' Lidia asked.

'You know what to do, don't you?' Rosa added.

'He was crazy,' Josefina said to them. 'He must still be crazy now.'

La Gorda came to my aid and told them that I was still empty for the same reason they still had their form. All of us secretly did not want the world of the Nagual. We were afraid and had second thoughts. In short, none of us was better than Pablito.

They did not say a word. All three of them seemed thoroughly embarrassed.

'Poor little Nagual,' Lidia said to me with a tone of genuine concern. 'You're as scared as we are. I pretend to be tough, Josefina pretends to be crazy, Rosa pretends to be ill-tempered and you pretend to be dumb.'

They laughed, and for the first time since I had arrived they made a gesture of comradeship towards me. They embraced me and put their heads against mine.

La Gorda sat facing me and the little sisters sat around her. I was facing all four of them.

'Now we can talk about what happened tonight,' la Gorda said. 'The Nagual told me that if we survived the last contact with the allies we wouldn't be the same. The allies did something to us tonight. They have hurled us away.'

She gently touched my writing hand.

'Tonight was a special night for you,' she went on. 'Tonight all of us pitched in to help you, including the allies. The Nagual would have liked it. Tonight you *saw* all the way through.'

'I did?' I asked.

'There you go again,' Lidia said, and everybody laughed.

'Tell me about my *seeing*, Gorda,' I insisted. 'You know that I'm dumb. There should be no misunderstandings between us.'

'All right,' she said. 'I see what you mean. Tonight you *saw* the little sisters.'

I said to them that I had also witnessed incredible acts performed by don Juan and don Genaro. I had seen them as plainly as I had seen the little sisters and yet don Juan and don Genaro had always concluded that I had not *seen*. I failed, therefore, to determine in what way could the acts of the little sisters be different.

'You mean you didn't *see* how they were holding on to the lines of the world?' she asked.

'No, I didn't.'

'You didn't see them slipping through the crack between the worlds?'

I narrated to them what I had witnessed. They listened in silence. At the end of my account la Gorda seemed to be on the verge of tears.

'What a pity!' she exclaimed.

She stood up and walked around the table and embraced me. Her eyes were clear and restful. I knew she bore no malice towards me.

'It's our fate that you are plugged up like this,' she said. 'But you're still the Nagual to us. I won't hinder you with ugly thoughts. You can at least be assured of that.'

I knew that she meant it. She was speaking to me from a level that I had witnessed only in don Juan. She had repeatedly explained her mood as the product of having lost her human form; she was indeed a formless warrior. A wave of profound affection for her enveloped me. I was about to weep. It was at the instant that I felt she was a most marvellous warrior that quite an intriguing thing happened to me. The closest way of describing it would be to say that I felt that my ears had suddenly popped. Except that I felt the popping in the middle of my body, right below my navel, more acutely than in my ears. Right after the popping everything became clearer; sounds, sights, odours. Then I felt an intense buzzing, which oddly enough did not interfere with my hearing capacity; the buzzing was loud but did not drown out any other sounds. It was as if I were hearing the buzzing with some part of me other than my ears. A hot flash went through my body. And then I suddenly recalled something I had never seen. It was as though an alien memory had taken possession of me.

I remembered Lidia pulling herself from two horizontal, reddish ropes as she walked on the wall. She was not really walking; she was actually gliding on a thick bundle of lines that she held with her feet. I remembered seeing her panting with her mouth open, from the exertion of pulling the reddish ropes. The reason I could not hold my balance at the end of her display was because I was *seeing* her as a light that went around the room so fast that it made me dizzy; it pulled me from the area around my navel.

I remembered Rosa's actions and Josefina's as well. Rosa had actually brachiated, with her left arm holding on to long, vertical, reddish fibres that looked like vines dropping from the dark roof. With her right arm she was also holding some vertical fibres that seemed to give her stability. She also held on to the same fibres with her toes. Towards the end of her display she was like a phosphorescence on the roof. The lines of her body had been erased.

Josefina was hiding herself behind some lines that seemed to come out of the floor. What she was doing with her raised forearm was moving the lines together to give them the necessary width to conceal her bulk. Her puffed-up clothes were a great prop; they had somehow contracted her luminosity. The clothes were bulky only for the eye that looked. At the end of her display Josefina, like Lidia and Rosa, was just a patch of light. I could switch from one recollection to the other in my mind.

When I told them about my concurrent memories the little sisters looked at me bewildered. La Gorda was the only one who seemed to be following what was happening to me. She laughed with true delight and said that the Nagual was right in saying that I was too lazy to remember what I had 'seen'; therefore, I only bothered with what I had looked at.

Is it possible, I thought to myself, that I am unconsciously selecting what I recall? Or is it la Gorda who is creating all this? If it was true that I had selected my recall at first and then released what I had censored, then it also had to be true that I must have perceived much more of don Juan's and don Genaro's actions, and yet I could only recall a selective part of my total perception of those events.

'It's hard to believe', I said to la Gorda, 'that I can remember now something I didn't remember at all a while ago.'

'The Nagual said that everyone can *see*, and yet we choose not to remember what we *see*,' she said. 'Now I understand how right he was. All of us can *see*; some, more than others.'

I told la Gorda that some part of me knew that I had found then a transcendental key. A missing piece had been handed down to me by all of them. But it was difficult to discern what it was.

She announced that she had just 'seen' that I had practised a good deal of 'dreaming', and that I had developed my attention, and yet I was fooled by my own appearance of not knowing anything.

'I've been trying to tell you about attention,' she proceeded, 'but you know as much as we do about it.'

I assured her that my knowledge was intrinsically different from theirs; theirs was infinitely more spectacular than mine. Anything they might say to me in relation to their practices, therefore, was a bonus to me.

'The Nagual told us to show you that with our attention we can hold the images of a dream in the same way we hold the images of the world,' la Gorda said. 'The art of the dreamer is the art of attention.'

Thoughts came down on me like a landslide. I had to stand up and walk around the kitchen. I sat down again. We remained quiet for a long time. I knew what she had meant when she said that the art of dreamers was the art of attention. I knew then that don Juan had told me and showed me everything he could. I had not been able, however, to realize the premises of his knowledge in my body while he was around. He had said that my reason was the demon that kept me chained, and that I had to vanquish it if I wanted to achieve the realization of his teachings. The issue, therefore, had been how to vanquish my reason. It had never occurred to me to press him for a definition of what he meant by reason. I presumed all along that he meant the capacity for comprehending, inferring or thinking, in an orderly, rational way. From what la Gorda had said, I knew that to him reason meant attention.

Don Juan said that the core of our being was the act of perceiving, and that the magic of our being was the act of awareness. For him perception and awareness were a single, functional, inextricable unit, a unit which had two domains. The first one was the 'attention of the tonal'; that is to say, the capacity of average people to perceive and place their awareness on the ordinary world of everyday life. Don Juan also called this form of attention our 'first ring of power', and described it as our awesome but taken-for-granted ability to impart order to our perception of our daily world.

The second domain was the 'attention of the nagual'; that is to say, the capacity of sorcerers to place their awareness on the nonordinary world. He called this domain of attention the 'second ring of power', or the altogether portentous ability that all of us have, but only sorcerers use, to impart order to the nonordinary world.

La Gorda and the little sisters, in demonstrating to me that the art of dreamers was to hold the images of their dreams with their attention, had brought in the pragmatic aspect of don Juan's scheme. They were the practitioners who had gone beyond the theoretical aspect of his teachings. In order to give me a demonstration of that art, they had to make use of their 'second ring of power', or the 'attention of the nagual'. In order for me to witness their art, I had to do the same. In fact it was evident that I had placed my attention on both domains. Perhaps all of us are continually perceiving in both fashions but choose to isolate one for recollection and discard the other, or perhaps we file it away, as I myself had done. Under certain conditions of stress or acquiescence, the censored memory surfaces and we can then have two distinct memories of one event.

What don Juan had struggled to vanquish, or rather suppress in me, was not my reason as the capacity for rational thought, but my 'attention of the tonal', or my awareness of the world of common sense. His motive for wanting me to do so was explained by la Gorda when she said that the daily world exists because we know how to hold its images; consequently, if one drops the attention needed to maintain those images, the world collapses.

'The Nagual told us that practice is what counts,' la Gorda said suddenly. 'Once you get your attention on the images of your dream, your attention is hooked for good. In the end you can be like Genaro, who could hold the images of any dream.'

'We each have five other dreams,' Lidia said. 'But we showed you the first one because that was the dream the Nagual gave us.'

'Can all of you go into *dreaming* any time you want?' I asked.

'No,' la Gorda replied. '*Dreaming* takes too much power. None of us has that much power. The reason the little sisters had to roll on the floor so many times was that in rolling, the earth was giving them energy. Maybe you could also remember *seeing* them as luminous beings getting energy from the light of the earth. The Nagual said that the best way of getting energy is, of course, to let the sun inside the eyes, especially the left eye.'

I told her that I knew nothing about it, and she described a procedure that don Juan had taught them. As she spoke I remembered that don Juan had also taught the same procedure to me. It consisted in moving my head slowly from side to side as I caught the sunlight with my half-closed left eye. He said that one could not only use the sun but could use any kind of light that could shine on the eyes.

La Gorda said that the Nagual had recommended that they tie their shawls below their waists in order to protect their hipbones when they rolled.

I commented that don Juan had never mentioned rolling to me. She said that only women could roll because they had wombs and energy came directly into their wombs; by rolling around they distributed that energy over the rest of their bodies. In order for a man to be energized he had to be on his back, with his knees bent so that the soles of his feet touched each other. His arms had to be extended laterally, with his forearms raised vertically, and the fingers clawed in an upright position.

'We have been *dreaming* those dreams for years,' Lidia said. 'Those dreams are our best, because our attention is complete. In the other dreams that we have, our attention is still shaky.'

La Gorda said that holding the images of dreams was a Toltec art. After years of consuming practice each one of them was able to perform one act in any dream. Lidia could walk on anything, Rosa could dangle from anything, Josefina could hide behind anything and she herself could fly. But they were only beginners, apprentices of the art. They had complete attention for only one activity. She added that Genaro was the master of 'dreaming' and could turn the tables around and have attention for as many activities as we have in our daily life, and that for him the two domains of attention had the same value.

I felt compelled to ask them my usual question: I had to know their procedures, how they held the images of their dreams.

'You know that as well as we do,' la Gorda said. 'The only thing I can say is that after going to the same dream over and over, we began to feel the lines of the world. They helped us to do what you *saw* us doing.'

Don Juan had said that our 'first ring of power' is engaged very early in our lives and that we live under the impression that that is all there is to us. Our 'second ring of power', the 'attention of the nagual', remains hidden for the immense majority of us, and only at the moment of our death is it revealed to us. There is a pathway to reach it, however, which is available to every one of us, but which only sorcerers take, and that pathway is through 'dreaming'. 'Dreaming' was in essence the transformation of ordinary dreams into affairs involving volition. Dreamers, by engaging their 'attention of the nagual' and focusing it on the items and events of their ordinary dreams, change those dreams into 'dreaming'.

Don Juan said that there were no procedures to arrive at the attention of the nagual. He only gave me pointers. Finding my hands in my dreams was the first pointer; then the exercise of paying attention was elongated to finding objects, looking for specific features, such as buildings, streets and so on. From there the jump was to 'dreaming' about specific places at specific times of the day. The final stage was drawing the 'attention of the nagual' to focus on the total self. Don Juan said that that final stage was usually ushered in by a dream that many of us have had at one time or another, in which one is looking at oneself sleeping in bed. By the time a sorcerer has had such a dream, his attention has been developed to such a degree that instead of waking himself up, as most of us would do in a similar situation, he turns on his heels and engages himself in activity, as if he were acting in the world of everyday life. From that moment on there is a breakage, a division of sorts in the otherwise unified personality. The result of engaging the 'attention of the nagual' and developing it to the height and sophistication of our daily attention of the world was, in don Juan's scheme, the other self, an identical being as oneself, but made in 'dreaming'.

Don Juan had told me that there are no definite standard steps for teaching that double, as there are no definite steps for us to reach our daily awareness. We simply do it by practising. He contended that in the act of engaging our 'attention of the nagual', we would find the steps. He urged me to practise 'dreaming' without letting my fears make it into an encumbering production.

He had done the same with la Gorda and the little sisters, but obviously something in them had made them more receptive to the idea of another level of attention.

'Genaro was in his body of *dreaming* most of the time,' la Gorda said. 'He liked it better. That's why he could do the weirdest things and scare you half to death. Genaro could go in and out of the crack between the worlds like you and I can go in and out a door.'

Don Juan had also talked to me at great length about the crack between the worlds. I had always believed that he was talking in a metaphorical sense about a subtle division between the world that the average man perceives and the world that sorcerers perceive.

La Gorda and the little sisters had shown me that the crack between the worlds was more than a metaphor. It was rather the capacity to change levels of attention. One part of me understood la Gorda perfectly, while another part of me was more frightened than ever.

'You have been asking where the Nagual and Genaro went,' la Gorda said. 'Soledad was very blunt and told you that they went to the other world; Lidia told you they left this area; the Genaros were stupid and scared you. The truth is that the Nagual and Genaro went through that crack.'

For some reason, undefinable to me, her statements plunged me into profound chaos. I had felt all along that they had left for good. I knew that they had not left in an ordinary sense, but I had kept that feeling in the realm of a metaphor. Although I had even voiced it to close friends, I think I never really believed it myself. In the depths of me I had always been a rational man. But la Gorda and the little sisters had turned my obscure metaphors into real possibilities. La Gorda had actually transported us half a mile with the energy of her 'dreaming'.

La Gorda stood up and said that I had understood everything, and that it was time for us to eat. She served us the food that she had cooked. I did not feel like eating. At the end of the meal she stood up and came to my side.

'I think it's time for you to leave,' she said to me.

That seemed to be a cue for the little sisters. They also stood up.

'If you stay beyond this moment, you won't be able to leave any more,' la Gorda went on. 'The Nagual gave you freedom once, but you chose to stay with him. He told me that if we all survive the last contact with the allies I should feed all of you, make you feel good and then say good-bye to all of you. I figure that the little sisters and myself have no place to go, so there is no choice for us. But you are different.'

The little sisters surrounded me and each said good-bye to me.

There was a monstrous irony in that situation. I was free to leave but I had no place to go. There was no choice for me, either. Years before don Juan gave me a chance to back out, I stayed because already then I had no place to go.

'We choose only once,' he had said then. 'We choose either to be warriors or to be ordinary men. A second choice does not exist. Not on this earth.'

6 THE SECOND ATTENTION

'You have to leave later on today,' la Gorda said to me right after breakfast. 'Since you have decided to go with us, you have committed yourself to helping us fulfil our new task. The Nagual left me in charge only until you came. He entrusted me, as you already know, with certain things to tell you. I've told you most of them. But there are still some I couldn't mention to you until you made your choice. Today we will take care of them. Right after that you must leave in order to give us time to get ready. We need a few days to settle everything and to prepare to leave these mountains forever. We have been here a very long time. It's hard to break away. But everything has come to a sudden end. The Nagual warned us of the total change that you would bring, regardless of the outcome of your bouts, but I think no one really believed him.'

'I fail to see why you have to change anything,' I said.

'I've explained it to you already,' she protested. 'We have lost our old purpose. Now we have a new one and that new purpose requires that we become as light as the breeze. The breeze is our new mood. It used to be the hot wind. You have changed our direction.'

'You are talking in circles, Gorda.'

'Yes, but that's because you're empty. I can't make it any clearer. When you return, the Genaros will show you the art of the stalker and right after that all of us will leave. The Nagual said that if you decide to be with us the first thing I should tell you is that you have to remember your bouts with Soledad and the little sisters and examine every single thing that happened to you with them, because everything is an omen of what will happen to you on your path. If you are careful and impeccable, you'll find that those bouts were gifts of power.'

'What's doña Soledad going to do now?'

'She's leaving. The little sisters have already helped her to take her floor apart. That floor aided her to reach her attention of the nagual. The lines had power to do that. Each of them helped her gather a piece of that attention. To be incomplete is no handicap to reaching that attention for some warriors. Soledad was transformed because she got to that attention faster than any of us. She doesn't have to gaze at her floor any more to go into that other world, and now that there is no more need for the floor, she has returned it to the earth where she got it.'

'You are really determined to leave, Gorda, aren't you?'

'All of us are. That's why I'm asking you to go away for a few days to give us time to pull down everything we have.'

'Am I the one who has to find a place for all of you, Gorda?'

'If you were an impeccable warrior you would do just that. But you're not an impeccable warrior, and neither are we. But still we will have to do our best to meet our new challenge.'

I felt an oppressive sense of doom. I have never been one to thrive on responsibilities. I thought that the commitment to guide them was a crushing burden that I could not handle.

'Maybe we don't have to do anything,' I said.

'Yes. That's right,' she said, and laughed. 'Why don't you tell yourself that over and over until you feel safe? The Nagual told you time and time again that the only freedom warriors have is to behave impeccably.'

She told me how the Nagual had insisted that all of them understand that not only was impeccability freedom but it was the only way to scare away the human form.

I narrated to her the way don Juan made me understand what was meant by impeccability. He and I were hiking one day through a very steep ravine when a huge boulder got loose from its matrix on the rock wall and came down with a formidable force and landed on the floor of the canyon, twenty or thirty yards from where we were standing. The size of the boulder made its fall a very impressive event. Don Juan seized the opportunity to create a dramatic lesson. He said that the force that rules our destinies is outside of ourselves and has nothing to do with our acts of volition. Sometimes that force would make us stop walking on our way and bend over to tie our shoelaces, as I had just done. And by making us stop, that force makes us gain a precious moment. If we had kept on walking, that enormous boulder would have most certainly crushed us to death. Some other day, however, in another ravine the same outside deciding force would make us stop again to bend over and tie our shoelaces while another boulder would get loose precisely above where we are standing. By making us stop, that force would have made us lose a precious moment. That time if we had kept on walking, we would have saved ourselves. Don Juan said that in view of my total lack of control over the forces which decide my destiny, my only possible freedom in that ravine consisted in my tying my shoelaces impeccably.

La Gorda seemed to be moved by my account. For an instant she held my face in her hands from across the table.

'Impeccability for me is to tell you, at the right time, what the Nagual told me to tell you,' she said. 'But power has to time perfectly what I have to reveal to you, or it won't have any effect.'

She paused in a dramatic fashion. Her delay was very studied but terribly effective with me.

'What is it?' I asked desperately.

She did not answer. She took me by the arm and led me to the area just outside the front door. She made me sit on the hard-packed ground with my back against a thick pole about one and a half feet high that looked like a tree stump which had been planted in the ground almost against the wall of the house. There was a row of five such poles planted about two feet apart. I had meant to ask la Gorda what their function was. My first impression had been that a former owner of the house had tied animals to them. My conjecture seemed incongruous, however, because the area just outside the front door was a kind of roofed porch.

I told la Gorda my supposition as she sat down next to me to my left, with her back against another pole. She laughed and said that the poles were indeed used for tying animals of sorts, but not by a former owner, and that she had nearly broken her back digging the holes for them.

'What do you use them for?' I asked.

'Let's say that we tie ourselves to them,' she replied. 'And this brings me to the next thing the Nagual asked me to tell you. He said that because you were empty he had to gather your second attention, your attention of the nagual, in a way different from ours. We gathered that attention through *dreaming* and you did it with his power plants. The Nagual said that his power plants gathered the menacing side of your second attention in one clump, and that's the shape that came out of your head. He said that that's what happens to sorcerers when they are given power plants. If they don't die, the power plants spin their second attention into that awful shape that comes out of their heads.

'Now we're coming to what he wanted you to do. He said that you must change directions now and begin gathering your second attention in another way, more like us. You can't keep on the path of knowledge unless you balance your second attention. So far, that attention of yours has been riding on the Nagual's power, but now you are alone. That's what he wanted me to tell you.'

'How do I balance my second attention?'

'You have to do *dreaming* the way we do it. *Dreaming* is the only way to gather the second attention without injuring it, without making it menacing and awesome. Your second attention is fixed on the awful side of the world; ours is on the beauty of it. You have to change sides and come with us. That's what you chose last night when you decided to go with us.'

'Could that shape come out of me at any time?'

'No. The Nagual said that it won't come out again until you're as old as he is. Your nagual has already come out as many times as was needed. The Nagual and Genaro have seen to that. They used to tease it out of you. The Nagual told me that sometimes you were a hair away from dying because your second attention is very indulging. He said that once you even scared him; your nagual attacked him and he had to sing to it to calm it down. But the worst thing happened to you in Mexico City; there he pushed you one day and you went into an office and in that office you went through the crack between the worlds. He intended only to dispel your attention of the tonal; you were worried sick over some stupid thing. But when he shoved you, your whole tonal shrunk and your entire being went through the crack. He had a hellish time finding you. He told me that for a moment he thought you had gone farther than he could reach. But then he *saw* you roaming around aimlessly and he brought you back. He told me that you went through the crack around ten in the morning. So, on that day, ten in the morning became your new time.'

'My new time for what?'

'For everything. If you remain a man you will die around that time. If you become a sorcerer you will leave this world around that time.

'Eligio also went on a different path, a path none of us knew about. We met him just before he left. Eligio was a most marvellous dreamer. He was so good that the Nagual and Genaro used to take him through the crack and he had the power to withstand it, as if it were nothing. He didn't even pant. The Nagual and Genaro gave him a final boost with power plants. He had the control and the power to handle that boost. And that's what sent him to wherever he is.'

'The Genaros told me that Eligio jumped with Benigno. Is that true?'

'Sure. By the time Eligio had to jump, his second attention had already been in that other world. The Nagual said that yours had also been there, but that for you it was a nightmare because you had no control. He said that his power plants had made you lopsided; they had made you cut through your attention of the tonal and had put you directly in the realm of your second attention, but without any mastery over that attention. The Nagual didn't give power plants to Eligio until the very last.'

'Do you think that my second attention has been injured, Gorda?'

'The Nagual never said that. He thought you were dangerously crazy, but that has nothing to do with power plants. He said that both of your attentions are unmanageable. If you could conquer them you'd be a great warrior.'

I wanted her to tell me more on the subject. She put her hand on my writing pad and said that we had a terribly busy day ahead of us and we needed to store energy in order to withstand it. We had, therefore, to energize ourselves with the sunlight. She said that the circumstances required that we take the sunlight with the left eye. She began to move her head slowly from side to side as she glanced directly into the sun through her half-closed eyes.

A moment later Lidia, Rosa and Josefina joined us. Lidia sat to my right, Josefina sat next to her, while Rosa sat next to la Gorda. All of them were resting their backs against the poles. I was in the middle of the row.

It was a clear day. The sun was just above the distant range of mountains. They started moving their heads in perfect synchronization. I joined them and had the feeling that I too had synchronized my motion with theirs. They kept it up for about a minute and then stopped.

All of them wore hats and used the brims to protect their faces from the sunlight when they were not bathing their eyes in it. La Gorda had given me my old hat to wear.

We sat there for about half an hour. In that time we repeated the exercise countless times. I intended to make a mark on my pad for each time but la Gorda very casually pushed my pad out of reach.

Lidia suddenly stood up, mumbling something unintelligible. La Gorda leaned over to me and whispered that the Genaros were coming up the road. I strained to look but there was no one in sight. Rosa and Josefina also stood up and then went with Lidia inside the house.

I told la Gorda that I could not see anyone approaching. She replied that the Genaros had been visible at one point on the road and added that she had dreaded the moment when all of us would have to get together, but that she was confident that I could handle the situation. She advised me to be extra careful with Josefina and Pablito because they had no control over themselves. She said that the most sensible thing for me to do would be to take the Genaros away after an hour or so.

I kept looking at the road. There was no sign of anyone approaching.

'Are you sure they're coming?' I asked.

She said that she had not seen them but that Lidia had. The Genaros had been visible just for Lidia because she had been gazing at the same time she had been bathing her eyes. I was not sure what la Gorda had meant and asked her to explain.

'We are gazers,' she said. 'Just like yourself. We are all the same. There is no need to deny that you're a gazer. The Nagual told us about your great feats of gazing.'

'My great feats of gazing! What are you talking about, Gorda?'

She contracted her mouth and appeared to be on the verge of being irritated by my question; she seemed to catch herself. She smiled and gave me a gentle shove.

At that moment she had a sudden flutter in her body. She stared blankly past me, then she shook her head vigorously. She said that she had just 'seen' that the Genaros were not coming after all; it was too early for them. They were going to wait for a while before they made their appearance. She smiled as if she were delighted with the delay.

'It's too early for us to have them here anyway,' she said. 'And they feel the same way about us.'

'Where are they now?' I asked.

'They must be sitting beside the road somewhere,' she replied. 'Benigno had no doubt gazed at the house as they were walking and saw us sitting here and that's why they have decided to wait. That's perfect. That will give us time.'

'You scare me, Gorda. Time for what?'

'You have to round up your second attention today, just for us four.'

'How can I do that?'

'I don't know. You are very mysterious to us. The Nagual has done scores of things to you with his power plants, but you can't claim that as knowledge. That is what I've been trying to tell you. Only if you have mastery over your second attention can you perform with it; otherwise you'll always stay fixed halfway between the two, as you are now. Everything that has happened to you since you arrived has been directed to force that attention to spin. I've been giving you instructions little by little, just as the Nagual told me to do. Since you took another path, you don't know the things that we know, just like we don't know anything about power plants. Soledad knows a bit more, because the Nagual took her to his homeland. Nestor knows about medicinal plants, but none of us has been taught the way you were. We don't need your knowledge yet. But someday when we are ready you are the one who will know what to do to give us a boost with power plants. I am the only one who knows where the Nagual's pipe is hidden, waiting for that day.

'The Nagual's command is that you have to change your path and go with us. That means that you have to do *dreaming* with us and stalking with the Genaros. You can't afford any longer to be where you are, on the awesome side of your second attention. Another jolt of your nagual coming out of you could kill you. The Nagual told me that human beings are frail creatures composed of many layers of luminosity. When you *see* them, they seem to have fibres, but those fibres are really layers, like an onion. Jolts of any kind separate those layers and can even cause human beings to die.'

She stood up and led me back to the kitchen. We sat down facing each other. Lidia, Rosa and Josefina were busy in the yard. I could not see them but I could hear them talking and laughing.

'The Nagual said that we die because our layers become separated,' la Gorda said. 'Jolts are always separating them but they get together again. Sometimes, though, the jolt is so great that the layers get loose and can't get back together any more.'

'Have you ever *seen* the layers, Gorda?'

'Sure. I *saw* a man dying in the street. The Nagual told me that you also found a man dying, but you didn't *see* his death. The Nagual made me *see* the dying man's layers. They were like the peels of an onion. When human beings are healthy they are like luminous eggs, but if they are injured they begin to peel, like an onion.

'The Nagual told me that your second attention was so strong sometimes that it pushed all the way out. He and Genaro had to hold your layers together; otherwise you would've died. That's why he figured that you might have enough energy to get your nagual out of you twice. He meant that you could hold your layers together by yourself twice. You did it more times than that and now you are finished; you have no more energy to hold your layers together in case of another jolt. The Nagual has entrusted me to take care of everyone; in your case, I have to help you to tighten your layers. The Nagual said that death pushes the layers apart. He explained to me that the centre of our luminosity, which is the attention of the nagual, is always pushing out, and that's what loosens the layers. So it's easy for death to come in between them and push them completely apart. Sorcerers have to do their best to keep their own layers closed. That's why the Nagual taught us *dreaming*. *Dreaming* tightens the layers. When sorcerers learn *dreaming* they tie together their two attentions and there is no more need for that centre to push out.'

'Do you mean that sorcerers do not die?'

'That is right. Sorcerers do not die.'

'Do you mean that none of us is going to die?'

'I didn't mean us. We are nothing. We are freaks, neither here nor there. I meant sorcerers. The Nagual and Genaro are sorcerers. Their two attentions are so tightly together that perhaps they'll never die.'

'Did the Nagual say that, Gorda?'

'Yes. He and Genaro both told me that. Not too long before they left, the Nagual explained to us the power of attention. I never knew about the tonal and the nagual until then.'

La Gorda recounted the way don Juan had instructed them

about that crucial tonal-nagual dichotomy. She said that one day the Nagual had all of them gather together in order to take them for a long hike to a desolate, rocky valley in the mountains. He made a large, heavy bundle with all kinds of items; he even put Pablito's radio in it. He then gave the bundle to Josefina to carry and put a heavy table on Pablito's shoulders and they all started hiking. He made all of them take turns carrying the bundle and the table as they hiked nearly forty miles to that high, desolate place. When they arrived there, the Nagual made Pablito set the table in the very centre of the valley. Then he asked Josefina to arrange the contents of the bundle on the table. When the table was filled, he explained to them the difference between the tonal and the nagual, in the same terms he had explained it to me in a restaurant in Mexico City, except that in their case his example was infinitely more graphic.

He told them that the tonal was the order that we are aware of in our daily world and also the personal order that we carry through life on our shoulders, like they had carried that table and the bundle. The personal tonal of each of us was like the table in that valley, a tiny island filled with the things we are familiar with. The nagual, on the other hand, was the inexplicable source that held that table in place and was like the vastness of that deserted valley.

He told them that sorcerers were obligated to watch their tonals from a distance in order to have a better grasp of what was really around them. He made them walk to a ridge from where they could view the whole area. From there the table was hardly visible. He then made them go back to the table and had them all loom over it in order to show that an average man does not have the grasp that a sorcerer has because an average man is right on top of his table, holding on to every item on it.

He then made each of them, one at a time, casually look at the objects on the table, and tested their recall by taking something and hiding it, to see if they had been attentive. All of them passed the test with flying colours. He pointed out to them that their ability to remember so easily the items on that table was due to the fact that all of them had developed their attention of the tonal, or their attention over the table.

He next asked them to look casually at everything that was on the ground underneath the table, and tested their recall by removing the rocks, twigs or whatever else was there. None of them could remember what they had seen under the table.

The Nagual then swept everything off the top of the table and made each of them, one at a time, lie across it on their stomachs and carefully examine the ground underneath. He explained to them that for a sorcerer the nagual was the area just underneath the table. Since it was unthinkable to tackle the immensity of the nagual, as exemplified by that vast, desolate place, sorcerers took as their domain of activity the area directly below the island of the tonal, as graphically shown by what was underneath that table. That area was the domain of what he called the second attention, or the attention of the nagual, or the attention under the table. That attention was reached only after warriors had swept the top of their tables clean. He said that reaching the second attention made the two attentions into a single unit, and that unit was the totality of oneself.

La Gorda said that his demonstration was so clear to her that she understood at once why the Nagual had made her clean her own life, sweep her island of the tonal, as he had called it. She felt that she had indeed been fortunate in having followed every suggestion that he had put to her. She was still a long way from unifying her two attentions, but her diligence had resulted in an impeccable life, which was, as he had assured her, the only way for her to lose her human form. Losing the human form was the essential requirement for unifying the two attentions.

'The attention under the table is the key to everything sorcerers do,' she went on. 'In order to reach that attention the Nagual and Genaro taught us *dreaming*, and you were taught about power plants. I don't know what they did to you to teach you how to trap your second attention with power plants, but to teach us how to do *dreaming*, the Nagual taught us gazing. He never told us what he was really doing to us. He just taught us to gaze. We never knew that gazing was the way to trap our second attention. We thought gazing was just for fun. That was not so. Dreamers have to be gazers before they can trap their second attention.

'The first thing the Nagual did was to put a dry leaf on the ground and make me look at it for hours. Every day he brought a leaf and put it in front of me. At first I thought that it was the same leaf that he saved from day to day, but then I noticed that leaves are different. The Nagual said that when we realized that, we are not looking any more, but gazing.

'Then he put stacks of dry leaves in front of me. He told me to scramble them with my left hand and feel them as I gazed at them. A dreamer moves the leaves in spirals, gazes at them and then dreams of the designs that the leaves make. The Nagual said that dreamers can consider themselves as having mastered leaf gazing when they dream the designs of the leaves first and then find those same designs the next day in their pile of dry leaves.

'The Nagual said that gazing at leaves fortifies the second attention. If you gaze at a pile of leaves for hours, as he used to make me do, your thoughts get quiet. Without thoughts the attention of the tonal wanes and suddenly your second attention hooks on to the leaves and the leaves become something else. The Nagual called the moment when the second attention hooks onto something stopping the world. And that is correct, the world stops. For this reason there should always be someone around when you gaze. We never know about the quirks of our second attention. Since we have never used it, we have to become familiar with it before we could venture into gazing alone.

'The difficulty in gazing is to learn to quiet down the thoughts. The Nagual said that he preferred to teach us how to do that with a pile of leaves because we could get all the leaves we needed any time we wanted to gaze. But anything else would do the same job.

'Once you can stop the world you are a gazer. And since the only way of stopping the world is by trying, the Nagual made all of us gaze at dry leaves for years and years. I think it's the best way to reach our second attention.

'He combined gazing at dry leaves and looking for our hands in *dreaming*. It took me about a year to find my hands, and four years to stop the world. The Nagual said that once you have trapped your second attention with dry leaves, you do gazing and *dreaming* to enlarge it. And that's all there is to gazing.'

'You make it sound so simple, Gorda.'

'Everything the Toltecs do is very simple. The Nagual said that all we needed to do in order to trap our second attention was to try and try. All of us stopped the world by gazing at dry leaves. You and Eligio were different. You yourself did it with power plants, but I don't know what path the Nagual followed with Eligio. He never wanted to tell me. He told me about you because we have the same task.'

I mentioned that I had written in my notes that I had had the first complete awareness of having stopped the world only a few days before. She laughed.

'You stopped the world before any of us,' she said. 'What do you think you did when you took all those power plants? You've never done it by gazing like we did, that's all.'

'Was the pile of dry leaves the only thing the Nagual made you gaze at?'

'Once dreamers know how to stop the world, they can gaze at other things; and finally when the dreamers lose their form altogether, they can gaze at anything. I do that. I can go into anything. He made us follow a certain order in gazing, though.

'First we gazed at small plants. The Nagual warned us that small plants are very dangerous. Their power is concentrated; they have a very intense light and they feel when dreamers are gazing at them; they immediately move their light and shoot it at the gazer. Dreamers have to choose one kind of plant to gaze at.

'Next we gazed at trees. Dreamers also have a particular kind of tree to gaze at. In this respect you and I are the same; both of us are eucalyptus gazers.'

By the look on my face she must have guessed my next question.

'The Nagual said that with his smoke you could very easily

get your second attention to work,' she went on. 'You focused your attention lots of times on the Nagual's predilection, the crows. He said that once, your second attention focused so perfectly on a crow that it flew away, like a crow flies, to the only eucalyptus tree that was around.'

For years I had dwelled upon that experience. I could not regard it in any other way except as an inconceivably complex hypnotic state, brought about by the psychotropic mushrooms contained in don Juan's smoking mixture in conjunction with his expertise as a manipulator of behaviour. He suggested a perceptual catharsis in me, that of turning into a crow and perceiving the world as a crow. The result was that I perceived the world in a manner that could not have possibly been part of my inventory of past experiences. La Gorda's explanation somehow had simplified everything.

She said that the Nagual next made them gaze at moving, living creatures. He told them that small insects were by far the best subject. Their mobility made them innocuous to the gazer, the opposite of plants which drew their light directly from the earth.

The next step was to gaze at rocks. She said that rocks were very old and powerful and had a specific light which was rather greenish in contrast with the white light of plants and the yellowish light of mobile, living beings. Rocks did not open up easily to gazers, but it was worthwhile for gazers to persist because rocks had special secrets concealed in their core, secrets that could aid sorcerers in their 'dreaming'.

'What are the things that rocks reveal to you?' I asked.

'When I gaze into the very core of a rock,' she said, 'I always catch a whiff of a special scent proper to that rock. When 1 roam around in my *dreaming*, I know where I am because I'm guided by those scents.'

She said that the time of the day was an important factor in tree and rock gazing. In the early morning, trees and rocks were stiff and their light was faint. Around noon was when they were at their best, and gazing at that time was done for borrowing their light and power. In the late afternoon and early evening, trees and rocks were quiet and sad, especially trees. La Gorda said that at that hour trees gave the feeling that they were gazing back at the gazer.

A second series in the order of gazing was to gaze at cyclic phenomena: rain and fog. She said that gazers can focus their second attention on the rain itself and move with it, or focus it on the background and use the rain as a magnifying glass o sorts to reveal hidden features. Places of power or places to be avoided are found by gazing through rain. Places of power are yellowish and places to be avoided are intensely green.

La Gorda said that fog was unquestionably the most mysterious thing on earth for a gazer and that it could be used in the same two ways that rain was used. But it did not easily yield to women, and even after she had lost her human form, it remained unattainable to her. She said that the Nagual once made her 'see' a green mist at the head of a fog bank and told her that was the second attention of a fog gazer who lived in the mountains where she and the Nagual were, and that he was moving with the fog. She added that fog was used to uncover the ghosts of things that were no longer there and that the true feat of fog gazers was to let their second attention go into whatever their gazing was revealing to them.

I told her that once while I was with don Juan I had seen a bridge formed out of a fog bank. I was aghast at the clarity and precise detail of that bridge. To me it was more than real. The scene was so intense and vivid that I had been incapable of forgetting it. Don Juan's comments had been that I would have to cross that bridge someday.

'I know about it,' she said. 'The Nagual told me that someday when you have mastery over your second attention you'll cross that bridge with that attention, the same way you flew like a crow with that attention. He said that if you become a sorcerer, a bridge will form for you out of the fog and you will cross it and disappear from this world forever. Just like he himself has done.'

'Did he disappear like that, over a bridge?'

'Not over a bridge. But you witnessed how he and Genaro stepped into the crack between the worlds in front of your very eyes. Nestor said that only Genaro waved his hand to say good-bye the last time you saw them; the Nagual did not wave because he was opening the crack. The Nagual told me that when the second attention has to be called upon to assemble itself, all that is needed is the motion of opening that door. That's the secret of the Toltec dreamers once they are formless.'

I wanted to ask her about don Juan and don Genaro stepping through that crack. She made me stop with a light touch of her hand on my mouth.

She said that another series was distance and cloud gazing. In both, the effort of gazers was to let their second attention go to the place they were gazing at. Thus, they covered great distances or rode on clouds. In the case of cloud gazing, the Nagual never permitted them to gaze at thunderheads. He told them that they had to be formless before they could attempt that feat, and that they could not only ride on a thunderhead but on a thunderbolt itself.

La Gorda laughed and asked me to guess who would be daring and crazy enough actually to try gazing at thunderheads. I could think of no one else but Josefina. La Gorda said that Josefina tried gazing at thunderheads every time she could when the Nagual was away, until one day a thunderbolt nearly killed her.

'Genaro was a thunderbolt sorcerer,' she went on. 'His first two apprentices, Benigno and Nestor, were singled out for him by his friend the thunder. He said that he was looking for plants in a very remote area where the Indians are very private and don't like visitors of any kind. They had given Genaro permission to be on their land since he spoke their language. Genaro was picking some plants when it began to rain. There were some houses around but the people were unfriendly and he didn't want to bother them; he was about to crawl into a hole when he saw a young man coming down the road riding a bicycle heavily laden with goods. It was Benigno, the man from the town, who dealt with those Indians. His bicycle got stuck in the mud and right there a thunderbolt struck him. Genaro thought that he had been killed. People in the houses had seen what happened and came out. Benigno was more scared than hurt, but his bicycle and all his merchandise were ruined. Genaro stayed with him for a week and cured him.

'Almost the same thing happened to Nestor. He used to buy medicinal plants from Genaro, and one day he followed him into the mountains to see where he picked his plants, so he wouldn't have to pay for them any more. Genaro went very far into the mountains on purpose; he intended to make Nestor get lost. It wasn't raining but there were thunderbolts, and suddenly a thunderbolt struck the ground and ran over the dry ground like a snake. It ran right between Nestor's legs and hit a rock ten yards away.

'Genaro said that the bolt had charred the inside of Nestor's legs. His testicles were swollen and he got very ill. Genaro had to cure him for a week right in those mountains.

'By the time Benigno and Nestor were cured, they were also hooked. Men have to be hooked. Women don't need that. Women go freely into anything. That's their power and at the same time their drawback. Men have to be led and women have to be contained.'

She giggled and said that no doubt she had a lot of maleness in her, for she needed to be led, and that I must have a lot of femaleness in me, for I needed to be contained.

The last series was fire, smoke and shadow gazing. She said that for a gazer, fire is not bright but black, and so is smoke. Shadows, on the other hand, are brilliant and have colour and movement in them.

There were two more things that were kept separate, star and water gazing. Stargazing was done by sorcerers who have lost their human form. She said that she had fared very well at stargazing, but could not handle gazing at water, especially running water, which was used by formless sorcerers to gather their second attention and transport it to any place they needed to go.

'All of us are terrified of water,' she went on. 'A river gathers the second attention and takes it away and there is no way of stopping. The Nagual told me about your feats of water gazing. But he also told me that one time you nearly disintegrated in the water of a shallow river and that you can't even take a bath now.'

Don Juan had made me stare at the water of an irrigation ditch behind his house various times while he had me under the influence of his smoking mixture. I had experienced inconceivable sensations. Once I saw myself all green as if I were covered with algae. After that he recommended that I avoid water.

'Has my second attention been injured by water?' I asked.

'It has,' she replied. 'You are a very indulging man. The Nagual warned you to be cautious, but you went beyond your limits with running water. The Nagual said that you could've used water like no one else, but it wasn't your fate to be moderate.'

She pulled her bench closer to mine.

'That's all there is to gazing,' she said. 'But there are other things I must tell you before you leave.'

'What things, Gorda?'

'First of all, before I say anything, you must round up your second attention for the little sisters and me.'

'I don't think I can do that.'

La Gorda stood up and went into the house. She came back a moment later with a small, thick, round cushion made out of the same natural fibre used in making nets. Without saying a word she led me again to the front porch. She said that she had made that cushion herself for her comfort when she was learning to gaze, because the position of the body was of great importance while one was gazing. One had to sit on the ground on a soft mat of leaves, or on a cushion made out of natural fibres. The back had to be propped against a tree, or a stump, or a flat rock. The body had to be thoroughly relaxed. The eyes were never fixed on the object, in order to avoid tiring them. The gaze consisted in scanning very slowly the object gazed at, going counterclockwise but without moving the head. She added that the Nagual had made them plant those thick poles so they could use them to prop themselves.

She had me sit on her cushion and prop my back against a pole. She told me that she was going to guide me in gazing at a power spot that the Nagual had in the round hills across the valley. She hoped that by gazing at it I would get the necessary energy to round up my second attention.

She sat down very close to me, to my left, and began giving me instructions. Almost in a whisper she told me to keep my eyelids half closed and stare at the place where two enormous round hills converged. There was a narrow, steep water canyon there. She said that that particular gazing consisted of four separate actions. The first one was to use the brim of my hat as a visor to shade off the excessive glare from the sun and allow only a minimal amount of light to come to my eyes; then to half-close my eyelids; the third step was to sustain the opening of my eyelids in order to maintain a uniform flow of light; and the fourth step was to distinguish the water canyon in the background through the mesh of light fibres on my eyelashes.

I could not follow her instructions at first. The sun was high over the horizon and I had to tilt my head back. I tipped my hat until I had blocked off most of the glare with the brim. That seemed to be all that was needed. As soon as I half closed my eyes, a bit of light that appeared as if it were coming from the tip of my hat literally exploded on my eyelashes, which were acting as a filter that created a web of light. I kept my eyelids half closed and played with the web of light for a moment until I could distinguish the dark, vertical outline of the water canyon in the background.

La Gorda told me then to gaze at the middle part of the canyon until I could spot a very dark brown blotch. She said that it was a hole in the canyon which was not there for the eye that looks, but only for the eye that 'sees'. She warned me that I had to exercise my control as soon as I had isolated that blotch, so that it would not pull me towards it. Rather, I was supposed to zoom in on it and gaze into it. She suggested that the moment I found the hole I should press my shoulders on hers to let her know. She slid sideways until she was leaning on me.

I struggled for a moment to keep the four actions coordinated and steady, and suddenly a dark spot was formed in the middle of the canyon. I noticed immediately that I was not seeing it in the way I usually see. The dark spot was rather an impression, a visual distortion of sorts. The moment my control waned it disappeared. It was in my field of perception only if I kept the four actions under control. I remembered then that don Juan had engaged me countless times in a similar activity. He used to hang a small piece of cloth from a low branch of a bush, which was strategically located to be in line with specific geological formations in the mountains in the background, such as water canyons, or slopes. By making me sit about fifty feet away from that piece of cloth, and having me stare through the low branches of the bush where the cloth hung, he used to create a special perceptual effect in me. The piece of cloth, which was always a shade darker than the geological formation I was staring at, seemed to be at first a feature of that formation. The idea was to let my perception play without analysing it. I failed every time because I was thoroughly incapable of suspending judgement, and my mind always entered into some rational speculation about the mechanics of my phantom perception.

This time I felt no need whatsoever for speculations. La Gorda was not an imposing figure that I unconsciously needed to fight, as don Juan had obviously been to me.

The dark blotch in my field of perception became almost black. I leaned on la Gorda's shoulder to let her know. She whispered in my ear that I should struggle to keep my eyelids in the position they were in and breathe calmly from my abdomen. I should not let the blotch pull me, but gradually go into it. The thing to avoid was letting the hole grow and suddenly engulf me. In the event that that happened I had to open my eyes immediately.

I began to breathe as she had prescribed, and thus I could keep my eyelids fixed indefinitely at the appropriate aperture.

I remained in that position for quite some time. Then I noticed that I had begun to breathe normally and that it had not disturbed my perception of the dark blotch. But suddenly the dark blotch began to move, to pulsate, and before I could breathe calmly again, the blackness moved forward and enveloped me. I became frantic and opened my eyes.

La Gorda said that I was doing distance gazing and for that it was necessary to breathe the way she had recommended. She urged me to start all over again. She said that the Nagual used to make them sit for entire days rounding up their second attention by gazing at that spot. He cautioned them repeatedly about the danger of being engulfed because of the jolt the body suffered.

It took me about an hour of gazing to do what she had delineated. To zoom in on the brown spot and gaze into it meant that the brown patch in my field of perception lightened up quite suddenly. As it became clearer I realized that something in me was performing an impossible act. I felt that I was actually advancing towards that spot; thus the impression I was having that it was clearing up. Then I was so near to it that I could distinguish features in it, like rocks and vegetation. I came even closer and could look at a peculiar formation on one rock. It looked like a roughly carved chair. I liked it very much; compared to it the rest of the rocks seemed pale and uninteresting.

I don't know how long I gazed at it. I could focus on every detail of it. I felt that I could lose myself forever in its detail because there was no end to it. But something dispelled my view; another strange image was superimposed on the rock, and then another one, and another yet. I became annoyed with the interference. At the instant I became annoyed I also realized that la Gorda was moving my head from side to side from behind me. In a matter of seconds the concentration of my gazing had been thoroughly dissipated.

La Gorda laughed and said that she understood why I had caused the Nagual such an intense concern. She had seen for herself that I indulged beyond my limits. She sat against the pole next to me and said that she and the little sisters were going to gaze into the Nagual's power place. She then made a piercing birdcall. A moment later the little sisters came out of the house and sat down to gaze with her.

Their gazing mastery was obvious. Their bodies acquired a

strange rigidity. They did not seem to be breathing at all. Their stillness was so contagious that I caught myself half closing my eyes and staring into the hills.

Gazing had been a true revelation to me. In performing it I had corroborated some important issues of don Juan's teachings. La Gorda had delineated the task in a definitely vague manner. 'To zoom in on it' was more a command than a description of a process, and yet it was a description, providing that one essential requirement had been fulfilled; don Juan had called that requirement stopping the internal dialogue. From la Gorda's statements about gazing it was obvious to me that the effect don Juan had been after in making them gaze was to teach them to stop the internal dialogue. La Gorda had expressed it as 'quieting down the thoughts'. Don Juan had taught me to do that very same thing, although he had made me follow the opposite path; instead of teaching me to focus my view, as gazers did, he taught me to open it, to flood my awareness by not focusing my sight on anything. I had to sort of feel with my eyes everything in the 180-degree range in front of me, while I kept my eyes unfocused just above the line of the horizon.

It was very difficult for me to gaze, because it entailed reversing that training. As I tried to gaze, my tendency was to open up. The effort of keeping that tendency in check, however, made me shut off my thoughts. Once I had turned off my internal dialogue, it was not difficult to gaze as la Gorda had prescribed.

Don Juan had asserted time and time again that the essential feature of his sorcery was shutting off the internal dialogue. In terms of the explanation la Gorda had given me about the two realms of attention, stopping the internal dialogue was an operational way of describing the act of disengaging the attention of the tonal.

Don Juan had also said that once we stop our internal dialogue we also stop the world. That was an operational description of the inconceivable process of focusing our second attention. He had said that some part of us is always kept under lock and key because we are afraid of it, and that to our reason, that part of us was like an insane relative that we keep locked in a dungeon. That part was, in la Gorda's terms, our second attention, and when it finally could focus on something the world stopped. Since we, as average men, know only the attention of the tonal, it is not too farfetched to say that once that attention is cancelled, the world indeed has to stop. The focusing of our wild, untrained second attention has to be, perforce, terrifying. Don Juan was right in saying that the only way to keep that insane relative from bursting in on us was by shielding ourselves with our endless internal dialogue.

La Gorda and the little sisters stood up after perhaps thirty minutes of gazing. La Gorda signalled me with her head to follow them. They went to the kitchen. La Gorda pointed to a bench for me to sit on. She said that she was going up the road to meet the Genaros and bring them over. She left through the front door.

The little sisters sat around me. Lidia volunteered to answer anything I wanted to ask her. I asked her to tell me about her gazing into don Juan's power spot, but she did not understand me.

'I'm a distance and shadow gazer,' she said. 'After I became a gazer the Nagual made me start all over again and had me gaze this time at the shadows of leaves and plants and trees and rocks. Now I never look at anything any more; I just look at their shadows. Even if there is no light at all, there are shadows; even at night there are shadows. Because I'm a shadow gazer I'm also a distance gazer. I can gaze at shadows even in the distance.

'The shadows in the early morning don't tell much. The shadows rest at that time. So it's useless to gaze very early in the day. Around six in the morning the shadows wake up, and they are best around five in the afternoon. Then they are fully awake.'

'What do the shadows tell you?'

'Everything I want to know. They tell me things because they have heat, or cold, or because they move, or because they have colours. I don't know yet all the things that colours and heat and cold mean. The Nagual left it up to me to learn.'

'How do you learn?'

'In my *dreaming*. Dreamers must gaze in order to do *dreaming* and then they must look for their dreams in their gazing. For example, the Nagual made me gaze at the shadows of rocks, and then in my *dreaming* I found out that those shadows had light, so I looked for the light in the shadows from then on until I found it. Gazing and *dreaming* go together. It took me a lot of gazing at shadows to get my *dreaming* of shadows going. And then it took me a lot of *dreaming* and gazing to get the two together and really *see* in the shadows what I was seeing in my *dreaming*. See what I mean? Every one of us does the same. Rosa's *dreaming* is about trees because she's a tree gazer and Josefina's is about clouds because she's a cloud gazer. They gaze at trees and clouds until they match their *dreaming*.'

Rosa and Josefina shook their heads in agreement.

'What about la Gorda?' I asked.

'She's a flea gazer,' Rosa said, and all of them laughed.

'La Gorda doesn't like to be bitten by fleas,' Lidia explained. 'She is formless and can gaze at anything, but she used to be a rain gazer.'

'What about Pablito?'

'He gazes at women's crotches,' Rosa answered with a deadpan expression.

They laughed. Rosa slapped me on the back.

'I understand that since he's your partner he's taking after you,' she said.

They banged on the table and shook the benches with their feet as they laughed.

'Pablito is a rock gazer,' Lidia said. 'Nestor is a rain and plant gazer and Benigno is a distance gazer. But don't ask me any more about gazing because I will lose my power if I tell you more.'

'How come la Gorda tells me everything?'

'La Gorda lost her form,' Lidia replied. 'Whenever I lose mine I'll tell you everything too. But by then you won't care to hear it. You care only because you're stupid like us. The day we lose our form we'll all stop being stupid.'

'Why do you ask so many questions when you know all this?' Rosa asked.

'Because he's like us,' Lidia said. 'He's not a true nagual. He's still a man.'

She turned and faced me. For an instant her face was hard and her eyes piercing and cold, but her expression softened as she spoke to me.

'You and Pablito are partners,' she said. 'You really like him, don't you?'

I thought for a moment before I answered. I told her that somehow I trusted him implicitly. For no overt reason at all I had a feeling of kinship with him.

'You like him so much that you fouled him up,' she said in an accusing tone. 'On that mountaintop where you jumped, he was getting to his second attention by himself and you forced him to jump with you.'

'I only held him by the arm,' I said in protest.

'A sorcerer doesn't hold another sorcerer by the arm,' she said. 'Each of us is very capable. You don't need any of us three to help you. Only a sorcerer who *sees* and is formless can help. On that mountaintop where you jumped, you were supposed to go first. Now Pablito is tied to you. I suppose you intended to help us in the same way. God, the more I think about you, the more I despise you.'

Rosa and Josefina mumbled their agreement. Rosa stood up and faced me with rage in her eyes. She demanded to know what I intended to do with them. I said that I intended to leave very soon. My statement seemed to shock them. They all spoke at the same time. Lidia's voice rose above the others. She said that the time to leave had been the night before, and that she had hated it the moment I decided to stay. Josefina began to yell obscenities at me.

I felt a sudden shiver and stood up and yelled at them to be quiet with a voice that was not my own. They looked at me horrified. I tried to look casual, but I had frightened myself as much as I had frightened them.

At that moment la Gorda stepped out to the kitchen as if she had been hiding in the front room waiting for us to start a fight. She said that she had warned all of us not to fall into one another's webs. I had to laugh at the way she scolded us as if we were children. She said that we owed respect to each other, that respect among warriors was a most delicate matter. The little sisters knew how to behave like warriors with each other, so did the Genaros among themselves, but when I would come into either group, or when the two groups got together, all of them ignored their warrior's knowledge and behaved like slobs.

We sat down. La Gorda sat next to me. After a moment's pause Lidia explained that she was afraid I was going to do to them what I had done to Pablito. La Gorda laughed and said that she would never let me help any of them in that manner. I told her that I could not understand what I had done to Pablito that was so wrong. I had not been aware of what I had done, and if Nestor had not told me I would never have known that I had actually picked Pablito up. I even wondered if Nestor had perhaps exaggerated a bit, or that maybe he had made a mistake.

La Gorda said that the Witness would not make a stupid mistake like that, much less exaggerate it, and that the Witness was the most perfect warrior among them.

'Sorcerers don't help one another like you helped Pablito,' she went on. 'You behaved like a man in the street. The Nagual had taught us all to be warriors. He said that a warrior had no compassion for anyone. For him, to have compassion meant that you wished the other person to be like you, to be in your shoes, and you lent a hand just for that purpose. You did that to Pablito. The hardest thing in the world is for a warrior to let others be. When I was fat I worried because Lidia and Josefina did not eat enough. I was afraid that they would get ill and die from not eating. I did my utmost to fatten them and I meant only the best. The impeccability of a warrior is to let them be and to support them in what they are. That means, of course, that you trust them to be impeccable warriors themselves.'

'But what if they are not impeccable warriors?' I said.

'Then it's your duty to be impeccable yourself and not say a word,' she replied. 'The Nagual said that only a sorcerer who *sees* and is formless can afford to help anyone. That's why he helped us and made us what we are. You don't think that you can go around picking people up off the street to help them, do you?'

Don Juan had already put me face to face with the dilemma that I could not help my fellow beings in any way. In fact, to his understanding, every effort to help on our part was an arbitrary act guided by our own self-interest alone.

One day when I was with him in the city, I picked up a snail that was in the middle of the sidewalk and tucked it safely under some vines. I was sure that if I had left it in the middle of the sidewalk, people would sooner or later have stepped on it. I thought that by moving it to a safe place I had saved it.

Don Juan pointed out that my assumption was a careless one, because I had not taken into consideration two important possibilities. One was that the snail might have been escaping a sure death by poison under the leaves of the vine, and the other possibility was that the snail had enough personal power to cross the sidewalk. By interfering I had not saved the snail but only made it lose whatever it had so painfully gained.

I wanted, of course, to put the snail back where I had found it, but he did not let me. He said that it was the snail's fate that an idiot crossed its path and made it lose its momentum. If I left it where I had put it, it might be able again to gather enough power to go wherever it was going.

I thought I had understood his point. Obviously I had only given him a shallow agreement. The hardest thing for me was to let others be.

I told them the story. La Gorda patted my back.

'We're all pretty bad,' she said. 'All five of us are awful people who don't want to understand. I've gotten rid of most of my ugly side, but not all of it yet. We are rather slow, and in comparison to the Genaros we are gloomy and domineering. The Genaros, on the other hand, are all like Genaro; there is very little awfulness in them.'

The little sisters shook their heads in agreement.

'You are the ugliest among us,' Lidia said to me. 'I don't think we're that bad in comparison to you.'

La Gorda giggled and tapped my leg as if telling me to agree with Lidia. I did, and all of them laughed like children.

We remained silent for a long time.

'I'm getting now to the end of what I had to tell you,' la Gorda said all of a sudden.

She made all of us stand up. She said that they were going to show me the Toltec warrior's power stand. Lidia stood by my right side, facing me. She grabbed my hand with her right hand, palm to palm, but without interlocking the fingers. Then she hooked my arm right above the elbow with her left arm and held me tightly against her chest. Josefina did exactly the same thing on my left side. Rosa stood face to face with me and hooked her arms under my armpits and grabbed my shoulders. La Gorda came from behind me and embraced me at my waist, interlocking her fingers over my navel.

All of us were about the same height and they could press their heads against my head. La Gorda spoke very softly behind my left ear, but loud enough for all of us to hear her. She said that we were going to try to put our second attention in the Nagual's power place, without anyone or anything prodding us. This time there was no teacher to aid us or allies to spur us. We were going to go there just by the force of our desire.

I had the invincible urge to ask her what I should do. She said that I should let my second attention focus on what I had gazed at.

She explained that the particular formation which we were in was a Toltec power arrangement. I was at that moment the centre and binding force of the four corners of the world. Lidia was the east, the weapon that the Toltec warrior holds in his right hand; Rosa was the north, the shield harnessed on the front of the warrior; Josefina was the west, the spirit catcher that the warrior holds in his left hand; and la Gorda was the south, the basket which the warrior carries on his back and where he keeps his power objects. She said that the natural position of every warrior was to face the north, since he had to hold the weapon, the east, in his right hand. But the direction that we ourselves had to face was the south, slightly towards the east; therefore, the act of power that the Nagual had left for us to perform was to change directions.

She reminded me that one of the first things that the Nagual had done to us was to turn our eyes to face the southeast. That had been the way he had enticed our second attention to perform the feat which we were going to attempt then. There were two alternatives to that feat. One was for all of us to turn around to face the south, using me as an axis, and in so doing change around the basic value and function of all of them. Lidia would be the west, Josefina the east, Rosa the south and she, the north. The other alternative was for us to change our direction and face the south but without turning around. That was the alternative of power, and it entailed putting on our second face.

I told la Gorda that I did not understand what our second face was. She said that she had been entrusted by the Nagual to try getting the second attention of all of us bundled up together, and that every Toltec warrior had two faces and faced two opposite directions. The second face was the second attention.

La Gorda suddenly released her grip. All the others did the same. She sat down again and motioned me to sit by her. The little sisters remained standing. La Gorda asked me if everything was clear to me. It was, and at the same time it was not. Before I had time to formulate a question, she blurted out that one of the last things the Nagual had entrusted her to tell me was that I had to change my direction by summing up my second attention together with theirs, and put on my power face to see what was behind me.

La Gorda stood up and motioned me to follow her. She led me to the door of their room. She gently pushed me into the room. Once I had crossed the threshold, Lidia, Rosa, Josefina and she joined me, in that order, and then la Gorda closed the door.

The room was very dark. It did not seem to have any windows. La Gorda grabbed me by the arm and placed me in what I thought was the centre of the room. All of them surrounded me. I could not see them at all; I could only feel them flanking me on four sides.

After a while my eyes became accustomed to the darkness. I could see that the room had two windows which had been blocked off by panels. A bit of light came through them and I could distinguish everybody. Then all of them held me the way they had done a few minutes before, and in perfect unison they placed their heads against mine. I could feel their hot breaths all around me. I closed my eyes in order to sum up the image of my gazing. I could not do it. I felt very tired and sleepy. My eyes itched terribly; I wanted to rub them, but Lidia and Josefina held my arms tightly.

We stayed in that position for a very long time. My fatigue was unbearable and finally I slumped. I thought that my knees had given in. I had the feeling that I was going to collapse on the floor and fall asleep right there. But there was no floor. In fact, there was nothing underneath me. My fright upon realizing that was so intense that I was fully awake in an instant; a force greater than my fright, however, pushed me back into that sleepy state again. I abandoned myself. I was floating with them like a balloon. It was as if I had fallen asleep and was dreaming and in that dream I saw a series of disconnected images. We were no longer in the darkness of their room. There was so much light that it blinded me. At times I could see Rosa's face against mine; out of the corner of my eyes I could also see Lidia's and Josefina's. I could feel their foreheads pressed hard against my ears. And then the image would change and I would see instead la Gorda's face against mine. Every time that happened she would put her mouth on mine and breathe. I did not like that at all. Some force in me tried to get loose. I felt terrified. I tried to push all of them away. The harder I tried, the harder they held me. That convinced me that la Gorda had tricked me and had finally led me into a death trap. But contrary to the others la Gorda had been an impeccable player. The thought that she had played an impeccable hand made me feel better. At one point I did not care to struggle any longer. I became curious about the moment of my death, which I believed was imminent, and I let go of myself. I experienced then an unequalled joy, an exuberance that I was sure was the herald of my end, if not my death itself. I pulled Lidia and Josefina even closer to me. At that moment la Gorda was in front of me. I did not mind that she was breathing in my mouth; in fact I was surprised that she stopped then. The instant she did, all of them also stopped pressing their heads on mine. They began to look around and by so doing they also freed my head. I could move it. Lidia, la Gorda and Josefina were so close to me that I could see only through the opening in between their heads. I could not figure out where we were. One thing I was certain of, we were not standing on the ground. We were in the air. Another thing I knew for sure was that we had shifted our order. Lidia was to my left and Josefina, to my right. La Gorda's face was covered with perspiration and so were Lidia's and Josefina's. I could only feel Rosa behind me. I could see her hands coming from my armpits and holding on to my shoulders.

La Gorda was saying something I could not hear. She enunciated her words slowly as if she were giving me time to read her lips, but I got caught up in the details of her mouth. At one instant I felt that the four of them were moving me; they were deliberately rocking me. That forced me to pay attention to la Gorda's silent words. I clearly read her lips this time. She was telling me to turn around. I tried but my head seemed to be fixed. I felt that someone was biting my lips. I watched la Gorda. She was not biting me but she was looking at me as she mouthed her command to turn my head around. As she talked, I also felt that she was actually licking my entire face or biting my lips and cheeks.

La Gorda's face was somehow distorted. It looked big and yellowish. I thought that perhaps since the whole scene was yellowish, her face was reflecting that glow. I could almost hear her ordering me to turn my head around. Finally the annoyance that the biting was causing me made me shake my head. And suddenly the sound of la Gorda's voice became clearly audible. She was in back of me and she was yelling at me to turn my attention around. Rosa was the one who was licking my face. I pushed her away from my face with my forehead. Rosa was weeping. Her face was covered with perspiration. I could hear la Gorda's voice behind me. She said that I had exhausted them by fighting them and that she did not know what to do to catch our original attention. The little sisters were whining.

My thoughts were crystal clear. My rational processes, however, were not deductive. I knew things quickly and directly and there was no doubt of any sort in my mind. For instance, I knew immediately that I had to go back to sleep again, and that that would make us plummet down. But I also knew that I had to let them bring us to their house. I was useless for that. If I could focus my second attention at all, it had to be on a place that don Juan had given me in northern Mexico. I had always been able to picture it in my mind like nothing else in the world. I did not dare to sum up that vision. I knew that we would have ended up there.

I thought that I had to tell la Gorda what I knew, but I could not talk. Yet some part of me knew that she understood. I trusted her implicitly and I fell asleep in a matter of seconds. In my dream I was looking at the kitchen of their house. Pablito, Nestor and Benigno were there. They looked extraordinarily large and they glowed. I could not focus my eyes on them, because a sheet of transparent plastic material was in between them and myself. Then I realized that it was as if I were looking at them through a glass window while somebody was throwing water on the glass. Finally the glass shattered and the water hit me in the face.

Pablito was drenching me with a bucket. Nestor and Benigno were also standing there. La Gorda, the little sisters and I were sprawled on the ground in the yard behind the house. The Genaros were drenching us with buckets of water.

I sprang up. Either the cold water or the extravagant experience I had just been through had invigorated me. La Gorda and the little sisters put on a change of clothes that the Genaros must have laid out in the sun. My clothes had also been neatly laid on the ground. I changed without a word. I was experiencing the peculiar feeling that seems to follow the focusing of the second attention; I could not talk, or rather I could talk but I did not want to. My stomach was upset. La Gorda seemed to sense it and pulled me gently to the area in back of the fence. I became ill. La Gorda and the little sisters were affected the same way.

I returned to the kitchen area and washed my face. The coldness of the water seemed to restore my awareness. Pablito, Nestor and Benigno were sitting around the table. Pablito had brought his chair. He stood up and shook hands with me. Then Nestor and Benigno did the same. La Gorda and the little sisters joined us.

There seemed to be something wrong with me. My ears were buzzing. I felt dizzy. Josefina stood up and grabbed on to Rosa for support. I turned to ask la Gorda what to do. Lidia was falling backward over the bench. I caught her, but her weight pulled me down and I fell over with her.

I must have fainted. I woke up suddenly. I was lying on a straw mat in the front room. Lidia, Rosa and Josefina were sound asleep next to me. I had to crawl over them to stand up. I nudged them but they did not wake up. I walked out to the kitchen. La Gorda was sitting with the Genaros around the table.

'Welcome back,' Pablito said.

He added that la Gorda had woken up a short while before. I felt that I was my old self again. I was hungry. La Gorda gave me a bowl of food. She said that they had already eaten. After eating I felt perfect in every respect except I could not think as I usually do. My thoughts had quieted down tremendously. I did not like that state. I noticed then that it was late afternoon. I had a sudden urge to jog in place facing the sun, the way don Juan used to make me do. I stood up and la Gorda joined me. Apparently she had had the same idea. Moving like that made me perspire. I got winded very quickly and returned to the table. La Gorda followed me. We sat down again. The Genaros were staring at us. La Gorda handed me my writing pad.

'The Nagual here got us lost,' la Gorda said.

The moment she spoke I experienced a most peculiar bursting. My thoughts came back to me in an avalanche. There must have been a change in my expression, for Pablito embraced me and so did Nestor and Benigno.

'The Nagual is going to live!' Pablito said loudly.

La Gorda also seemed delighted. She wiped her forehead in a gesture of relief. She said that I had nearly killed all of them and myself with my terrible tendency to indulge.

'To focus the second attention is no joke,' Nestor said.

'What happened to us, Gorda?' I asked.

'We got lost,' she said. 'You began to indulge in your fear and we got lost in that immensity. We couldn't focus our attention of the tonal any more. But we succeeded in bundling up our second attention with yours and now you have two faces.'

Lidia, Rosa and Josefina stepped out into the kitchen at that moment. They were smiling and seemed as fresh and vigorous as ever. They helped themselves to some food. They sat down and nobody uttered a word while they ate. The moment the last one had finished eating, la Gorda picked up where she had left off.

'Now you're a warrior with two faces,' she went on. 'The Nagual said that all of us have to have two faces to fare well in both attentions. He and Genaro helped us to round up our second attention and turned us around so we could face in two directions, but they didn't help you, because to be a true nagual you have to claim your power all by yourself. You're still a long way from that, but let's say that now you're walking upright instead of crawling, and when you've regained your completeness and have lost your form, you'll be gliding.'

Benigno made a gesture with his hand of a plane in flight and imitated the roar of the engine with his booming voice. The sound was truly deafening.

Everybody laughed. The little sisters seemed to be delighted.

I had not been fully aware until then that it was late afternoon. I said to la Gorda that we must have slept for hours, for we had gone into their room before noon. She said that we had not slept long at all, that most of that time we had been lost in the other world, and that the Genaros had been truly frightened and despondent, because there was nothing they could do to bring us back.

I turned to Nestor and asked him what they had actually

done or seen while we were gone. He stared at me for a moment before answering.

'We brought a lot of water to the yard,' he said, pointing to some empty oil barrels. 'Then all of you staggered into the yard and we poured water on you, that's all.'

'Did we come out of the room?' I asked him.

Benigno laughed loudly. Nestor looked at la Gorda as if asking for permission or advice.

'Did we come out of the room?' la Gorda asked.

'No,' Nestor replied.

La Gorda seemed to be as anxious to know as I was, and that was alarming to me. She even coaxed Nestor to speak.

'You came from nowhere,' Nestor said. 'I should also say that it was frightening. All of you were like fog. Pablito saw you first. You may have been in the yard for a long time, but we didn't know where to look for you. Then Pablito yelled and all of us saw you. We have never seen anything like that.'

'What did we look like?' I asked.

The Genaros looked at one another. There was an unbearably long silence. The little sisters were staring at Nestor with their mouths open.

'You were like pieces of fog caught in a web,' Nestor said. 'When we poured water on you, you became solid again.'

I wanted him to keep on talking but la Gorda said that there was very little time left, for I had to leave at the end of the day and she still had things to tell me. The Genaros stood up and shook hands with the little sisters and la Gorda. They embraced me and told me that they only needed a few days in order to get ready to move away. Pablito put his chair upside down on his back. Josefina ran to the area around the stove, picked up a bundle they had brought from doña Soledad's house and placed it between the legs of Pablito's chair, which made an ideal carrying device.

'Since you're going home you might as well take this,' she said. 'It belongs to you anyway.'

Pablito shrugged his shoulders and shifted his chair in order to balance the load.

Nestor signalled Benigno to take the bundle but Pablito would not let him.

'It's all right,' he said. 'I might as well be a jackass as long as I'm carrying this damn chair.'

'Why do you carry it, Pablito?' I asked.

'I have to store my power,' he replied. 'I can't go around sitting on just anything. Who knows what kind of a creep sat there before me?'

He cackled and made the bundle wiggle by shaking his shoulders.

After the Genaros left, la Gorda explained to me that Pablito began his crazy involvement with his chair to tease Lidia. He did not want to sit where she had sat, but he had gotten carried away, and since he loved to indulge he would not sit anywhere else except on his chair.

'He's capable of carrying it through life,' la Gorda said to me with great certainty. 'He's almost as bad as you. He's your partner; you'll carry your writing pad through life and he'll carry his chair. What's the difference? Both of you indulge more than the rest of us.'

The little sisters surrounded me and laughed, patting me on the back.

'It's very hard to get into our second attention,' la Gorda went on, 'and to manage it when you indulge as you do is even harder. The Nagual said that you should know how difficult that managing is better than any of us. With his power plants, you learned to go very far into that other world. That's why you pulled us so hard today that we nearly died. We wanted to gather our second attention on the Nagual's spot, and you plunged us into something we didn't know. We are not ready for it, but neither are you. You can't help yourself, though; the power plants made you that way. The Nagual was right: all of us have to help you contain your second attention, and you have to help all of us to push ours. Your second attention can go very far, but it has no control; ours can go only a little bit, but we have absolute control over it.'

La Gorda and the little sisters, one by one, told me how

frightening the experience of being lost in the other world had been.

'The Nagual told me,' la Gorda went on, 'that when he was gathering your second attention with his smoke, you focused it on a gnat, and then the little gnat became the guardian of the other world for you.'

I told her that that was true. At her request I narrated to them the experience don Juan had made me undergo. With the aid of his smoking mixture I had perceived a gnat as a hundred-foot-high, horrifying monster that moved with incredible speed and agility. The ugliness of that creature was nauseating, and yet there was an awesome magnificence to it.

I also had had no way to accommodate that experience in my rational scheme of things. The only support for my intellect was my deep-seated certainty that one of the effects of the psychotropic smoking mixture was to induce me to hallucinate the size of the gnat.

I presented to them, especially to la Gorda, my rational, causal explanation of what had taken place. They laughed.

'There are no hallucinations,' la Gorda said in a firm tone. 'If anybody suddenly sees something different, something that was not there before, it is because that person's second attention has been gathered and that person is focusing it on something. Now, whatever is gathering that person's attention might be anything, maybe it's liquor, or maybe it's madness, or maybe it's the Nagual's smoking mixture.

'You *saw* a gnat and it became the guardian of the other world for you. And do you know what that other world is? That other world is the world of our second attention. The Nagual thought that perhaps your second attention was strong enough to pass the guardian and go into that world. But it wasn't. If it had been, you might have gone into that world and never returned. The Nagual told me that he was prepared to follow you. But the guardian didn't let you pass and nearly killed you. The Nagual had to stop making you focus your second attention with his power plants because you could only focus on the awesomeness of things. He had you do *dreaming* instead, so you could gather it in another way. But he was sure your *dreaming* would also be awesome. There was nothing he could do about it. You were following him in his own footsteps and he had an awesome, fearsome side.'

They remained silent. It was as if all of them had been engulfed by their memories.

La Gorda said that the Nagual had once pointed out to me a very special red insect, in the mountains of his homeland. She asked me if I remembered it.

I did remember it. Years before don Juan had taken me to an area unknown to me, in the mountains of northern Mexico. With extreme care he showed me some round insects, the size of a ladybug. Their backs were brilliantly red. I wanted to get down on the ground and examine them, but he would not let me. He told me that I should watch them, without staring, until I had memorized their shape, because I was supposed to remember them always. He then explained some intricate details of their behaviour, making it sound like a metaphor. He was telling me about the arbitrary importance of our most cherished mores. He pointed out some alleged mores of those insects and pitted them against ours. The comparison made the importance of our beliefs look ridiculous.

'Just before he and Genaro left,' la Gorda went on, 'the Nagual took me to that place in the mountains where those little bugs lived. I had already been there once, and so had everyone else. The Nagual made sure that all of us knew those little creatures, although he never let us gaze at them.

'While I was there with him he told me what to do with you and what I should tell you. I've already told you most of what he asked me to, except for this last thing. It has to do with what you've been asking everybody about: Where are the Nagual and Genaro? Now I'll tell you exactly where they are. The Nagual said that you will understand this better than any of us. None of us has ever *seen* the guardian. None of us has ever been in that yellow sulphur world where he lives. You are the only one among us who has. The Nagual said that he followed you into that world when you focused your second attention on the guardian. He intended to go there with you, perhaps forever, if you would've been strong enough to pass.

It was then that he first found out about the world of those little red bugs. He said that their world was the most beautiful and perfect thing one could imagine. So, when it was time for him and Genaro to leave this world, they gathered all their second attention and focused it on that world. Then the Nagual opened the crack, as you yourself witnessed, and they slipped through it into that world, where they are waiting for us to join them someday. The Nagual and Genaro liked beauty. They went there for their sheer enjoyment.'

She looked at me. I had nothing to say. She had been right in saying that power had to time her revelation perfectly if it were going to be effective. I felt an anguish I could not express. It was as if I wanted to weep and yet I was not sad or melancholy. I longed for something inexpressible, but that longing was not mine. Like so many of the feelings and sensations I had had since my arrival, it was alien to me.

Nestor's assertions about Eligio came to my mind. I told la Gorda what he had said, and she asked me to narrate to them the visions of my journey between the tonal and the nagual which I had had upon jumping into the abyss. When I finished they all seemed frightened. La Gorda immediately isolated my vision of the dome.

'The Nagual told us that our second attention would someday focus on that dome,' she said. 'That day we will be all second attention, just like the Nagual and Genaro are, and that day we will join them.'

'Do you mean, Gorda, that we will go as we are?' I asked.

'Yes, we will go as we are. The body is the first attention, the attention of the tonal. When it becomes the second attention, it simply goes into the other world. Jumping into the abyss gathered all your second attention for a while. But Eligio was stronger and his second attention was fixed by that jump. That's what happened to him and he was just like all of us. But there is no way of telling where he is. Even the Nagual himself didn't know. But if he is someplace he is in that dome. Or he is bouncing from vision to vision, perhaps for a whole eternity.

La Gorda said that in my journey between the tonal and the nagual I had corroborated on a grand scale the possibility that our whole being becomes all second attention, and on a much smaller scale when I got all of them lost in the world of that attention, earlier that day, and also when she transported us half a mile in order to flee from the allies. She added that the problem the Nagual had left for us as a challenge was whether or not we would be capable of developing our will, or the power of our second attention to focus indefinitely on anything we wanted.

We were quiet for a while. It seemed that it was time for me to leave, but I could not move. The thought of Eligio's fate had paralysed me. Whether he had made it to the dome of our rendezvous, or whether he had gotten caught in the tremendum, the image of his journey was maddening. It took no effort at all for me to envision it, for I had the experience of my own journey.

The other world, which don Juan had referred to practically since the moment we met, had always been a metaphor, an obscure way of labelling some perceptual distortion, or at best a way of talking about some undefinable state of being. Even though don Juan had made me perceive indescribable features of the world, I could not consider my experiences to be anything beyond a play on my perception, a directed mirage of sorts that he had managed to make me undergo, either by means of psychotropic plants, or by means I could not deduce rationally. Every time that had happened, I had shielded myself with the thought that the unity of the 'me' I knew and was familiar with had been only temporarily displaced. Inevitably, as soon as that unity was restored, the world became again the sanctuary for my inviolable, rational self. The scope that la Gorda had opened with her revelations was terrifying.

She stood up and pulled me up off the bench. She said that I had to leave before the twilight set in. All of them walked with me to my car and we said good-bye.

La Gorda gave me a last command. She told me that on my return I should go directly to the Genaros' house.

'We don't want to see you until you know what to do,' she said with a radiant smile. 'But don't delay too long.'

The little sisters nodded.

'Those mountains are not going to let us stay here much longer,' she said, and with a subtle movement of her chin she pointed to the ominous, eroded hills across the valley.

I asked her one more question. I wanted to know if she had any idea where the Nagual and Genaro would go after we had completed our rendezvous. She looked up at the sky, raised her arms and made an indescribable gesture with them to point out that there was no limit to that vastness.

ARKANA – NEW-AGE BOOKS FOR MIND, BODY AND SPIRIT

A selection of titles

With over 200 titles currently in print, Arkana is the leading name in quality new-age books for mind, body and spirit. Arkana encompasses the spirituality of both East and West, ancient and new, in fiction and non-fiction. A vast range of interests is covered, including Psychology and Transformation, Health, Science and Mysticism, Women's Spirituality and Astrology.

If you would like a catalogue of Arkana books, please write to:

Arkana Marketing Department
Penguin Books Ltd
27 Wright's Lane
London W8 5TZ

ARKANA – NEW-AGE BOOKS FOR MIND, BODY AND SPIRIT

By the same author

The Teachings of Don Juan: A Yaqui Way of Knowledge

In 1960 Carlos Castaneda first met don Juan, a Yaqui Indian feared and shunned by the ordinary folk of the American South West because of his unnatural powers. During the next five years don Juan's arcane knowledge led him into a world of beauty and terror, ruled by concepts far beyond those of western civilization.

A Separate Reality

A Separate Reality is funny, frightening and enriching, a rare glimpse into an alien philosophy.

'A book that soars through the mind like a comet, rare, burning and beautiful' – Theodore Roszak in *New Society*

Tales of Power

'If Castaneda really witnessed the events he describes, this is a fact of extraordinary importance for mankind' – *New Statesman*

Journey to Ixtlan

Journey to Ixtlan ends the unique record of the author's initiation into the mysteries of sorcery – of becoming a 'man of knowledge' – under the guidance of one of the most remarkable personalities to emerge from anthropological investigation, don Juan the Yaqui Indian, whom he met in north-western Mexico.

and The Eagle's Gift